This monograph breaks ground—moving the reader beyond the "popular" narrative of the civil rights movement, which has largely been top-down, male-centered, and regionally focused, and infusing a multi-genre literary lens to interpret one of the most important historical events of the past.

—Thomas L. Bynum, Cleveland State University, author of
NAACP Youth and the Fight for Freedom, 1936–1965

Too often, we've reduced the phase of the African American Freedom Movement associated with "Civil Rights" to a reassuring bedtime story starring Martin Luther King. Appearing at a moment when the need is clear, *Living Legacies* tells a set of better, truer stories. A major contribution to the New Civil Rights History.

—Craig Werner, University of Wisconsin-Madison, author of
A Change is Gonna Come: Music, Race & the Soul of America

LIVING LEGACIES

In this timely and dynamic collection of essays, Laura Dubek brings together a diverse group of scholars to explore the literary response to the most significant social movement of the twentieth century. Covering a wide range of genres and offering provocative readings of both familiar and lesser known texts, *Living Legacies* demonstrates how literature can be used not only to challenge the master narrative of the civil rights movement but also to inform and inspire the next generation of freedom fighters.

Laura Dubek is a Professor of English at Middle Tennessee State University.

LIVING LEGACIES

Literary Responses to the
Civil Rights Movement

Edited by Laura Dubek

NEW YORK AND LONDON

First published 2018
by Routledge
711 Third Avenue, New York, NY 10017

and by Routledge
2 Park Square, Milton Park, Abingdon, Oxon OX14 4RN

Routledge is an imprint of the Taylor & Francis Group, an informa business

© 2018 Taylor & Francis

The right of Laura Dubek to be identified as the author of the editorial material, and of the authors for their individual chapters, has been asserted in accordance with sections 77 and 78 of the Copyright, Designs and Patents Act 1988.

All rights reserved. No part of this book may be reprinted or reproduced or utilized in any form or by any electronic, mechanical, or other means, now known or hereafter invented, including photocopying and recording, or in any information storage or retrieval system, without permission in writing from the publishers.

Trademark notice: Product or corporate names may be trademarks or registered trademarks, and are used only for identification and explanation without intent to infringe.

Library of Congress Cataloging-in-Publication Data
A catalog record for this book has been requested

ISBN: 978-1-138-09397-3 (hbk)
ISBN: 978-1-138-09400-0 (pbk)
ISBN: 978-1-315-10631-1 (ebk)

Typeset in Bembo
by codeMantra

This book is dedicated to Megan and Jessica,
who are just beginning to experience the joy of learning
and the power of stories

CONTENTS

List of Figures   *xi*
Acknowledgments   *xii*
Notes on Contributors   *xiv*

Introduction: "[D]e understandin' to go 'long wid it": Storytelling and (the) Civil Rights Movement   1
Laura Dubek

1 From Alabama to Tahrir Square: *Martin Luther King and The Montgomery Story* Comic as Civil Rights Narrative   17
J. Michael Lyons

2 Inviting Compassion and Caring through Testimony: Participants in the Civil Rights Movement Speak for Themselves   32
Myra Zarnowski

3 "Tomorrow's Great Meeting Place": Collective Autobiographies of the Civil Rights Movement   40
Elizabeth Rodrigues

4 "God Decreed It So": The Rhetoric of Destiny in 1963   54
Corrine E. Hinton and Tonya M. Scott Hill

5 Back to Birmingham: Three Poets Remember the Sixteenth Street Church Bombing   69
StarShield Lortie and Laura Dubek

6 "Pass It On!": Legacy and the Freedom Struggle in Toni Morrison's *Song of Solomon*   80
Laura Dubek

7 "Living Proof of Something So Terrible": Pearl Cleage's *Bourbon at the Border* and the Politics of Civil Rights History and Memory 95
Julius B. Fleming, Jr.

8 "A Living Theater" for Human Rights: Jill Freedman's *Old News* and Visual Legacies of the 1968 Poor People's Campaign 109
Katharina Fackler

9 "Gettin' Ready to Ride into History": Spike Lee's *Get on the Bus* and Sites of Memory 129
Jesse Williams, Jr.

10 "My Childhood Is Ruined!": Harper Lee and Racial Innocence 145
Katherine Henninger

Appendix of Additional Teaching Sources 165
Matthew Spencer

Index 169

FIGURES

I.1 Julian Bond and Laura Dubek in Kelly Ingram Park. Birmingham was the final stop on the University of Virginia Travel & Learn bus tour, Civil Rights South: In the Footsteps of the Movement. March 2008 — 3
1.1 Since 1957, *The Montgomery Story* has appeared in many translations, encouraging freedom movements around the globe. The Spanish version is on display at the National Museum of African American History and Culture in Washington, DC — 18
1.2 Civil rights activists and sympathizers faced intimidation, threats, and sometimes violent retribution in addition to daily humiliations and indignities. Challenging white power took tremendous courage — 23
5.1 "Four Spirits" in Kelly Ingram Park, with the Sixteenth Street Baptist Church in the background. Sculptor Elizabeth MacQueen recognized Addie Mae's sister Sarah with a small medallion on the side of the bench. The sculpture's title comes from Sena Jeter Naslund's 2001 novel of the same name. Photo courtesy of Chuck Offenburger — 71
8.1 Cover photograph of *Old News: Resurrection City*. Photo courtesy of Jill Freedman — 114
8.2 Untitled. *Old News: Resurrection City* 9. Photo courtesy of Jill Freedman — 116
8.3 "Might vs. Right." *Old News: Resurrection City* 14. Photo courtesy of Jill Freedman — 117
8.4 "Busted During Demonstration." *Old News: Resurrection City* 55. Photo courtesy of Jill Freedman — 118
8.5 "To us all. We are all we have." *Old News: Resurrection City*. Photo courtesy of Jill Freedman — 120
8.6 Untitled. *Old News: Resurrection City* 17. Photo courtesy of Jill Freedman — 123
8.7 "Hands Like a Shawl." *Old News: Resurrection City* 32. Photo courtesy of Jill Freedman — 124
9.1 The destination of the riders in *Get on the Bus* is the seat and symbol of (white) power in the US, and the Lincoln Memorial is perhaps the most potent site of memory for the black freedom struggle — 134

ACKNOWLEDGMENTS

I am most grateful to the contributors to this volume, most of whom I have never met but whose work proves that we are kindred spirits. Five of the authors have been with me from the very beginning, having answered the initial call for papers posted in 2014, well before I knew that what I actually had was both a collection of scholarly essays *and* a blueprint for a seminar in civil rights literature. For your patience as the project evolved and for your faith that I would take it over the finish line, thank you, Katharina Fackler, Tonya M. Scott Hill, Corrine E. Hinton, Elizabeth Rodrigues, and especially Jesse Williams, Jr., who sat beside me in Starbucks when I posted that call for papers and who has been encouraging my work on this project ever since.

I am fortunate to have colleagues who show interest in my research while keeping me from taking myself too seriously. Many thanks to Bob Holtzclaw for gifting me a CD of civil rights movement music: when I heard Solomon Burke singing "I Wish I Knew," I knew I had an original idea for an article on Morrison's *Song of Solomon*, which then inspired this book. Thanks to Will Brantley for always saying yes to brunch and for knowing all the answers to my questions about publishing and to Jill Hague for encouraging me over weekly dinners with half-price bottles of Cabernet. I am particularly grateful to Alfred Lutz for embodying the true spirit of collegiality by consistently supporting my intellectual endeavors; leaving clippings about all things related to civil rights studies in my mailbox; and providing thoughtful comments on my writing, including a draft of the introduction to this volume.

This book would have been much harder without support from Middle Tennessee State University, which included professional development grants that made possible travel on two civil rights bus tours with Julian Bond. When the second grant application hit a snag, Tom Strawman, my department chair, and John McDaniel, the Dean of the College of Liberal Arts, marched over to the administration building to set things right, and when the Provost's office refused to budge, Dean McDaniel funded the trip from his own budget. I wish he could see what came from his investment in me. I also received two Faculty Research and Creative Activity grants, one for my work on Morrison's novel, which appeared in *Southern Quarterly* in 2015 and reappears here, and the other to shepherd this book to completion. Finally, thanks to Kevin Donovan and the graduate studies in English program for funding a summer research assistant: Matthew Spencer did the tedious work of converting essays to comply with publishing guidelines and also compiled the appendix.

Many years ago, in the spring semester before I received my B.A. in English from the University of Nebraska-Omaha, I took a course in women's literature that challenged everything

I had been taught about literary studies. Missy Dehn Kubitschek taught that class, and on one of my essays, she scribbled, "You have a career as a literary critic in front of you, if you want it." At the time, I didn't know what a literary critic did exactly, but her belief in my abilities, as well as her emotional support during a difficult period in my life, became the wind at my back, moving me through graduate school at the University of Iowa and into a tenure-track job. For her mentorship, which included introducing me to Zora Neale Hurston, and for many years of friendship, I will be forever grateful.

CONTRIBUTORS

Laura Dubek is a Professor of English at Middle Tennessee State University where she teaches courses in writing and African American literature. Her literary criticism has appeared in *African American Review, Journal of American Culture, Journal of Popular Film & Television, MELUS, Mississippi Quarterly, Southern Literary Journal, Southern Quarterly,* and *Women's Studies: An Interdisciplinary Journal.* In 2009 and 2011, Dubek traveled with Julian Bond on civil rights bus tours through the South. Her conversations with Bond about the role of writers in the civil rights movement inspired this collection of essays.

Katharina Fackler is an Assistant Professor in the Department of American Studies at the University of Graz, Austria. Her teaching and research interests focus on the aesthetics and affects of visual representation, poverty and class, African American protest, Cold War culture, and sensory history. Her essay on iconic photographs of Rosa Parks appeared in a special issue of *Souls* (2016) on African American representation and the politics of respectability. Fackler is currently working on her first monograph, which explores the role of photography in the so-called rediscovery of poverty in the 1960s.

Julius B. Fleming, Jr. is an Assistant Professor of English at the University of Maryland College Park and an Associate Editor of *Callaloo: A Journal of African Diaspora Arts and Letters.* His teaching and research interests include performance studies, visual culture, sound studies, and medicine—especially when they insect with race, gender, and sexuality. Fleming's work has appeared in *American Literary History, Text and Performance Quarterly, James Baldwin Review,* and *Southern Quarterly.* A Carter G. Woodson Postdoctoral Fellow at the University of Virginia (2016–2018), Fleming is currently completing his first book manuscript, tentatively entitled *Black Patience: Radical Performance in the Civil Rights Movement.*

Katherine Henninger is an Associate Professor of American Literature at Louisiana State University in Baton Rouge where she specializes in southern literature, visual culture, childhood studies, and women's and gender studies. She is the author of *Ordering the Façade: Photography and Contemporary Southern Women's Writing* (2007) and numerous articles on photography, film, gender and sexuality, postcolonial theory, and southern literature and culture. She has been an active participant in the Baton Rouge Dialogue on Race and other efforts to address institutional racism. She is currently at work on two monographs: *The Mandingo*

Effect: U.S. Slavery and Sexuality on Film, 1968–2016 and *Made Strangely Beautiful: Southern Childhood in U.S. Literature and Film*. Her work on Harper Lee, race, and nation forms part of the *Southern Childhood* project and is funded by a Fellowship from the National Endowment for the Humanities.

Tonya M. Scott Hill is the Director of TRIO Student Support Services and the immediate past Developmental Education Coordinator at Texas A&M University-Texarkana. Her research and teaching interests include African American Literature and Culture; Discourse Studies; course, program, and curriculum progression, and assessment in Developmental Education; writing program and writing center administration, grant writing; instructional technology; student engagement and success; and equity and inclusivity in education.

Corrine E. Hinton is an Assistant Professor of English and Writing Program Administrator at Texas A&M University-Texarkana where she teaches undergraduate and graduate courses in composition, rhetoric, the teaching of writing, technical writing, literature, and qualitative research methods. Her research interests include first-year composition, veterans studies, social justice rhetorics, Discourse Studies, writing center administration, writing program administration, and historical and contemporary trends in the teaching of writing and English Language Arts. She serves as Assistant Editor of the *Journal of Veterans Studies*.

StarShield Lortie is an award-winning poet whose work has appeared in *Collage* and *The Nashville Arts Magazine*. She is currently a Lecturer at Middle Tennessee State University where she teaches general education courses in writing and literature. Her creative MA thesis, "The Heart of the Matter: Poems Inspired by Civil Rights Movement Photography," led to her work on poetry about the bombing of the Sixteenth Street Church in Birmingham.

J. Michael Lyons is an Assistant Professor in the Department of Communication Studies at Saint Joseph's University. His research and teaching focus on media and social justice. He has published articles on the use of "small" media—comic books, newsletters, movement newspapers—in civil rights struggles both in the US and abroad. A media producer, Lyons is currently working on The Redemption Project, which aims to produce alternative narratives of incarcerated men and women in an effort to "disrupt" the mass media narratives of incarceration and crime that have helped shape crime policy in the US.

Elizabeth Rodrigues is a Humanities and Digital Scholarship Librarian at Grinnell College where she specializes in multiethnic US literatures, life writing, and critical digital studies. After completing her doctoral studies at the University of Michigan, she was a Council for Library and Information Resources Postdoctoral Fellow at Temple University. Her work on life writing has appeared in *Biography* and is forthcoming in *a/b: Autobiography Studies*. She is currently at work on a book manuscript, *Data-Driven Modernism*, which argues that data, as an epistemological concept and representational form, pinpoint an underexplored intersection between modernist aesthetics and theories of race, ethnicity, and nation in the early twentieth-century US.

Matthew Spencer is a PhD candidate at Middle Tennessee State University. His research and teaching interests include twentieth-century American literature, Anglophone literature, and critical theory. He is currently working on his dissertation, "Reimagined Communities: Unwriting the Nation in Contemporary Global Literature and Culture," which examines imaginative reactions to resurgent nationalism.

Jesse Williams, Jr. is a Lecturer in the English Department at Middle Tennessee State University where he teaches courses in writing, African American literature, and US film and popular culture. His work on Spike Lee's WWII film *Miracle at St. Anna* was featured on the cover of *Journal of Popular Film and Television* in 2015. His work on the Native American literary tradition and Alejandro Iñárritu's *The Revenant* is forthcoming in *Literature/Film Quarterly*. Williams is currently working on a series of essays that puts Lee in conversation with nineteenth-century American literature.

Myra Zarnowski is a Professor in the Department of Elementary and Early Childhood at Queens College, CUNY, where she teaches courses in literacy and social studies. She is the author of *Making Sense of History: Using High-Quality Literature and Hands-On Experience to Build Content Knowledge* (Scholastic 2006) and *History Makers* (Heinemann 2003), two books that deal with teaching history using nonfiction literature. She has served on the Orbis Pictus Award Committee that selects outstanding nonfiction for children as well as the committee that prepares the yearly list of Notable Children's Trade Books in Social Studies.

INTRODUCTION

"[D]e understandin' to go 'long wid it": Storytelling and (the) Civil Rights Movement

Laura Dubek

At the beginning of Zora Neale Hurston's *Their Eyes Were Watching God* (1937), Janie returns to Eatonville "full of that oldest human longing—self-revelation."[1] She has been away for more than a year, and when her best friend Phoeby arrives at her door with a plate of mulatto rice, Janie welcomes the opportunity to tell her story. At first, the weary traveler gives Phoeby an abbreviated version, explaining that she is back because Tea Cake, the much younger man with whom she left Eatonville, is "gone." An eager but confused Phoeby confesses that "[i]t's hard for me to understand what you mean, de way you tell it." Janie then settles in to tell a much longer story because "'tain't no use in me telling you somethin' unless Ah give you de understandin' to go 'long wid it."[2] Almost two hundred pages later, Janie brings her story to an end, and an astonished Phoeby declares, "Lawd!...Ah done growed ten feet higher from jus' listenin' tuh you, Janie. Ah ain't satisfied wid mahself no mo'."[3] Phoeby's dissatisfaction signals a change in her critical consciousness that then prompts action: from now on, she will insist that her husband Sam take her along when he goes fishing, perhaps as a way to make her marriage more of a partnership, modeled after Janie and Tea Cake's egalitarian relationship. But that's not all Phoeby will do. She will also share Janie's story with the porch-dwellers, Eatonville residents, who, in the opening pages of the novel, are as anxious as Phoeby to know what happened to Janie. "You can tell 'em what Ah say if you wants to," Janie tells Phoeby. "Dat's just de same as me 'cause mah tongue is in mah friend's mouf."[4] An exemplar of the power of storytelling to move an audience, Phoeby will now carry the word(s) to her community.

Literary critics have recognized the importance of *Their Eyes Were Watching God*'s frame story and of Phoeby's role as listener. In a paradigm-shifting essay published in 1983 during a renaissance of Hurston studies, Missy Dehn Kubitschek proposed that the novel's ending suggested the possibility of group ascent, "with Janie and a whole group of Phoebys growing 'ten feet tall,' traveling in company 'tuh de horizon and back,' ever constructing and renewing both individual and community."[5] Kubitschek's argument pushed against charges of Hurston's supposed apolitical posture, charges that carried over to her most beloved fictional character and that originated with Richard Wright. In his review of *Their Eyes* for *New Masses*, Wright dismissed it as "carr[ying] no theme, no message, no thought."[6] His (mis)reading of Hurston's novel betrays a bias toward particular models of leadership as well as strategies for prompting political and social change. While the novel clearly demonstrates the feminist adage that the personal is political, it also insists that the political must begin with the person(al) and in this case, with one black woman talking to another black woman. Words may indeed be used as weapons, as

Wright argues in *Black Boy* (1945), but words are effective only in so far as they move people. Janie puts it this way: "talkin' don't amount tuh uh hill uh beans when yuh can't do nothin' else."[7] The something else a person must do is act—that's the understanding that Janie's story gives Phoeby. While we do not know whether Phoeby's actions will go beyond her relationship with Sam, the novel leaves us with the possibility of critical consciousness-raising, prompted by storytelling, leading to mass mobilization—"a whole group of Phoebys…traveling in company" and (re)building the beloved community.[8]

The model of black female leadership presented in *Their Eyes* describes, in many ways, the grassroots organizing that distinguishes the political activism of Ella Jo Baker. While literary critics and folklorists claim Hurston (1891–1960), historians, particularly of social movements, claim Baker (1903–1986). During their lifetimes and for at least two decades after their deaths, the considerable contributions of both women to their respective fields were largely overshadowed by men—Hurston by Wright and a particular brand of "protest fiction" and Baker by Martin Luther King, Jr. and a particular view of (black) leadership and effective political process. Although no evidence exists that Hurston and Baker ever crossed paths in any meaningful way, they chose the same sparring partners (most notably, W. E. B. DuBois); flouted gender norms; traveled extensively out of a deep commitment to their work; and, most importantly, shared a perspective about process and purpose that valued the "Negro farthest down." Reading these two women alongside one another should prompt more attention not only to Hurston's political essays, in an effort to understand her supposed "conservative turn" in the 1950s, but also to the rhetorical strategies of Baker's public speeches. Thinking of Hurston and Baker as contemporaries, and within the specific context of the civil rights movement, should also challenge us to cross traditional disciplinary borders and consider the role of the artist in crafting historical memory and creating and sustaining (new) movements for social change.

In 2008, I rode a bus through Georgia and Alabama, traveling in company with Julian Bond, history professor and veteran of the civil rights movement, and an eager group of teachers, activists, and citizens participating in a University of Virginia Travel & Learn program. In my professional development grant application for Civil Rights South: In the Footsteps of the Movement, I quoted Hurston's *Their Eyes*, arguing that "[i]t's uh known fact…you got tuh *go* there tuh *know* there."[9] The Dean of the College of Liberal Arts, a Shakespeare scholar, smiled at the literary reference but wanted me to be more specific—what exactly would be the outcome of this bus tour? I responded by suggesting an honors interdisciplinary seminar in civil rights literature. Two years later, I traveled with Bond again, this second tour beginning in Memphis, Tennessee and stopping in Little Rock, Arkansas; Greenwood and Clarksville, Mississippi; and New Orleans, Louisiana. During both trips, I talked with Bond about the intersection of our two disciplines and the role of the artist in movements for social change. His contention that creative writers do not get nearly enough attention in discussions of the civil rights movement became the catalyst for this book. *Living Legacies: Literary Responses to the Civil Rights Movement* seeks both to bring attention to literature about the civil rights movement and to suggest a special topics course—a literary equivalent to the kind of history courses that Bond himself taught at the University of Virginia up until his death in 2015 (Figure I.1).

Established in 1990 by (creative writer) Marita Golden and (cultural historian) Clyde McElvene, the Wright/Hurston Foundation exists at the intersection of literary aesthetics, history, and political activism. Self-described as a "literary education institution," the foundation sponsors workshops to support black writers; it also presents annual Legacy Awards in fiction, debut fiction, nonfiction, and poetry as well as three Merit Awards.[10] In 2017, the Board of Trustees honored Congressman and civil rights icon John Lewis (Bond's colleague in SNCC, the Student Nonviolent Coordinating Committee) with the Ella Baker Merit Award, which recognizes writers for creative work that promotes social justice. The foundation's press release

FIGURE I.1 Julian Bond and Laura Dubek in Kelly Ingram Park. Birmingham was the final stop on the University of Virginia Travel & Learn bus tour, Civil Rights South: In the Footsteps of the Movement. March 2008.

mentions three of Lewis's memoirs: *Walking with the Wind: A Memoir of the Movement* (1998); *Across That Bridge: Life Lessons and a Vision for Change* (2012); and *March: Book Three* (2016), his National Book Award-winning graphic memoir. Like *Their Eyes*, the *March* trilogy underscores the role of storytelling in a participatory democracy with a frame story that sets up a storytelling situation and a final call to action. Dedicated to "the past and future children of the movement," *March: Book One* begins on January 20, 2009. Two young boys and their mother arrive at Congressman Lewis's Capitol Hill office on their way to the inauguration of the first African American president. Lewis, "full of that oldest human longing," welcomes the visitors and, over the course of three books, tells his personal story. As the wide-eyed boys listen, they learn not just what the civil rights icon did (his actions) but why he chose to act (his adherence to the philosophy of nonviolence), with whom he acted (SNCC), and how segregationists (groups of white citizens as well as political leaders, such as Alabama Governor George Wallace) responded to demands that the US "be true to what you said on paper."[11] The boys thus get more than a timeline of historical events: they get "de understandin' to go 'long wid it."

Lewis's trilogy joins a tradition of civil rights literature that has been garnering more attention in the last ten years for its potential to challenge and enrich our understanding of a social movement too often summed up in four words: bus, bridge, Martin, and march.[12] By linking individual reflection and critical consciousness to movement and mass mobilization, Lewis and his collaborators hope to nurture the next generation of freedom fighters.[13] The final pages of *March: Book Three* make clear the role of storytelling in that process. The morning after the inauguration, Lewis shows up early for work and tells his aide, Andrew Aydin, that he has been "thinking about that comic book idea." Aydin is surprised: "You're serious?!" "Yeah, I'm serious. We have to tell the story," Lewis says. "We'll have to find a great artist – someone who can make the words SING."[14] As the two men enter the office, the phone rings: "RRRIIIIINNNGG." Just below the second ring, the illustrator, Nate Powell, put his initials, along with the dates that encompass his collaboration with Lewis and Aydin on the *March* trilogy: 2009–2016. The facing page is blank, so the memoir seems to come to its end with the idea that Lewis's work continues into and beyond the Obama presidency. But when readers turn this last page, they find, in the lower right-hand corner, one image—a cell phone. This phone is also ringing, its screen lit up with an "Incoming Call." The last image of a cell phone in *March: Book Three* appeared on the page before the Congressman's talk with his aide. Heavily shaded to indicate night as well as a dark, tragic past, this page shows Lewis returning home after the 2009 inauguration festivities to find twenty-eight messages on his cell phone. He pushes a button and hears the voice of Senator Ted Kennedy:

> I was thinking of you. I was thinking of you and Martin. I was thinking about the years of work, the bloodshed ... the people who didn't live to see this day. I was thinking about Jack and Bobby....[15]

Sitting on the edge of his bed, his head bowed, shoulders hunched, Lewis covers his face with his left hand, while his right hand holds the phone to his ear. While many Americans may have been celebrating Obama's inauguration as a sign of a supposed post-racial present and hoped-for future, veterans of the civil rights movement, such as Kennedy and Lewis, carried the weight and pain of history that day. This history of "years of work" and "bloodshed" is the story that Lewis insists must be told—the story of the ancestors, marching from Selma to Montgomery for voting rights, depicted in a faded, ghost-like pencil drawing opposite the acknowledgments page in the final installment of *March*.

With that final image of a cell phone, *March: Book Three* comes full circle (as did *Their Eyes*), underscoring the necessity for forward movement. Just as the title of Lewis's book stands for both a thing and an action, the civil rights movement refers to a particular series of historical events as well as a process of (personal) discovery and (societal) change. This kind of movement must continue, no matter who occupies the White House, controls Congress, or exercises power at the state and local levels. In his award-winning graphic memoir, Lewis issues a compelling call for action with faith that those of us listening to his story will declare ourselves dissatisfied and respond by actively working toward equality and justice, not just in our own lives but for all.

The New Civil Rights Studies

Living Legacies responds to the call for scholarship that makes civil rights harder, a call made by Jacquelyn Dowd Hall in "The Long Civil Rights Movement and the Political Uses of the Past."

Published in the *Journal of American History* in 2005, Hall's oft-quoted essay is a revision of remarks delivered in her presidential address to the Organization of American Historians in 2004, fifty years after *Brown v. Board* and the beginning of what scholars consider the classical phase of the civil rights movement.[16] Hall's essay references hundreds of books and articles while calling on historians to make the struggle for civil rights even *harder*: "Harder to celebrate as a natural progression of American values. Harder to cast as a satisfying morality tale. Most of all, harder to simplify, appropriate, and contain."[17] The simplified version of the story—also referred to as the consensus, dominant, or master narrative—limits the civil rights struggle to 1954–1965 (*Brown v. Board* to the Civil Rights Voting Act), mythologizes King as a one-dimensional figure with a dream, restricts movement activities to the South, ignores diversity in ideological perspectives, and focuses primarily, if not exclusively, on racial (identity-based) politics. A more accurate, and thus more useful, narrative of the civil rights movement would contextualize its classical period within a much broader time frame, restoring its radical agenda by focusing on the economic roots of (racial) oppression that remain *the* challenge of a participatory democracy.[18]

Hall argues that the work of narrating a long civil rights movement is important because "remembrance is always a form of forgetting," and the simplified version of this historical period leaves us vulnerable to policies that assume an even playing field, even as deep structural inequities remain.[19] In a 2013 review essay of eight books on women in the civil rights and black freedom movements for the *Journal of Feminist Studies in Religion*, Charon Hribar puts it this way: "Dominant narratives of the CRM made the movement and its leaders into symbols of a civil religion of American exceptionalism and reinforced ignorance regarding why inequalities persist in our society."[20] The 2013 Supreme Court ruling that removes a key provision of the 1965 Voting Rights Act illustrates Hall and Hribar's concern. Written by Chief Justice John Roberts, the decision in *Shelby County v. Holder* justifies relaxing federal oversight of voting laws in states such as Alabama on the grounds that "our country has changed."[21] Roberts's argument flies in the face of recent judicial findings of deliberate racial gerrymandering in states such as North Carolina and Texas as well as persistent efforts to suppress minority voting through voter ID laws.

The resistance to the simplified version of the civil rights movement is thus understood to be an urgent political matter, one that affects the lives of Americans living now. Participating in the resistance, Hall argues, means engaging in a sustained rhetorical battle between narratives "spun by the new conservatives…that avoid uncomfortable questions about the relationship between cumulative white advantage and present social ills" and "countervailing stories that could make themselves heard and could even, under the right circumstances, prevail."[22] Countervailing stories prompt a different, more complex understanding of the past by eschewing "formulaic mantras." In both her remarks to the Organization of American Historians and the article in the *Journal of American History* that followed, Hall urges scholars in her discipline to compose such stories:

> To tell our stories both truly and effectively we need modes of writing and speaking that emphasize individual agency, the *sine qua non* of narrative, while also dramatizing the hidden history of policies and institutions—the publicly sanctioned choices that continually shape and reshape the social landscape and yet are often invisible to citizens trained in not seeing and in thinking exclusively in ahistorical, personal terms. Only such novel forms of storytelling can convey what it means to have lived through an undefeated but unfinished revolution, a world-defining social movement that has experienced both reversals and victories and whose victories are now, once again, being partially reversed. Both the victories and the reversals call us to action as citizens and as historians with powerful stories to tell. Both are part of a long and ongoing civil rights movement. Both can help us imagine—for our own times—a new way of life, a continuing revolution.[23]

Those "novel forms of storytelling" that "convey what it means to have lived through an undefeated but unfinished revolution" can be found in the rich tradition of civil rights literature, in creative works like Lewis's *March* that "emphasize individual agency...while also dramatizing the hidden history of policies and institutions."

Historians responded to Hall's call by renewing their efforts to make civil rights harder although, as Christopher Metress points out, largely without any consideration of how the civil rights movement gets remembered through literature. In "Making Civil Rights Harder: Literature, Memory, and the Black Freedom Struggle" (2008), Metress responds directly to Hall, arguing for more attention to literary texts as "verbal artifacts of historical memory."[24] To make his case, Metress juxtaposes King's memoir *Why We Can't Wait* (1964), typically claimed by historians, and Anthony Grooms's novel *Bombingham* (2001), a work of historical fiction that might appear on the reading list for a course in African American literature. In *Why We Can't Wait*, a cherished figure in US history tells the story of Birmingham, advancing his argument that "justice too long delayed is justice denied" while promoting precisely the kind of triumphant narrative of civil rights struggle and American progress Hall warns against.[25] In *Bombingham*, on the other hand, Grooms fictionalizes the events of 1963 in a way that challenges King's redemption story, complicating the consensus narrative in precisely the way Hall calls for. Metress's reading of *Bombingham* focuses on the protagonist's loss of hope: Walter Burke *had* a dream, but after a devastating childhood in Birmingham, he concludes that "[t]o hope will only set you up for disappointment."[26] Reading these texts together strengthens the argument that waging an effective and sustained rhetorical battle against the consensus narrative requires taking advantage of a much wider range of texts and artifacts. Including novels, poems, and plays in discussions of the civil rights movement will, Metress insists, further the historian's goal of giving the movement "a deeper and more expansive legacy," thereby "keep[ing] alive the movement's power to speak effectively to the unresolved challenges of our times."[27]

Grooms's novel contains within it a compelling argument for the power of storytelling in relation to (the) civil rights movement. By framing *Bombingham* with a US soldier's struggles with letter-writing, Grooms underscores the necessity of storytelling as well as the dangers of "formulaic mantras." As Metress points out, two promises haunt Walter throughout the novel. Significantly, both promises relate to historical (civil rights) myth-making. In Chapter 1, set in Vietnam, Walter witnesses his buddy Haywood's gruesome death as their regiment takes incoming fire, a death that obligates him to write a letter to Haywood's parents. Walter understands the expectations for such a letter and just cannot do it—just as he could not talk about what had happened in Birmingham in 1963 despite Haywood's persistent prompting and obvious eagerness to hear the story. "It's not as cool as you think," Walter tells him. "But that's all I've heard," Haywood says. "I mean, it's supposed to be the Magic City, and it's the cradle of the movement. That's all I ever heard about it. What a beautiful place it was and how we won our rights there."[28] Walter repeatedly dodges and demurs, even mocking his friend's explanation for why this story is so important. "It changed things," Haywood declares; to which Walter replies, "It changed the fucking world, didn't it?"[29] Exasperated, he finally resorts to lying, telling Haywood that he never met King and never marched. Walter's refusal to perpetuate myths about Birmingham, to present the so-called Magic City as King did in *Why We Can't Wait*, is his way of protecting Haywood: "The way you think. It'll get you hurt," Walter warns.[30] But the novel makes clear that the way Walter thinks *also* hurts. Feeling "dead already," Walter has carried the pain of his childhood in Birmingham to Vietnam, where, in the opening scene of the novel, he shoots a papa-san running across a rice paddy without a second thought.[31]

By refusing to perpetuate myths about Birmingham—a place Walter associates with his mother's death from inoperable brain cancer, his father's excessive drinking and public humiliation while attempting to secure the release of his little sister from a make-shift detention center, and his best friend Lamar's murder while riding on the handlebars of Walter's bicycle[32]—the veteran essentially accepts that for blacks, the US is now, as it has always been, a battlefield littered with the dead and near-dead bodies of black men, women, and children. Chapter 1 ends with Walter waiting for the enemy to make a move, declaring himself "ready to move away from [Haywood], but the mud cradled my body, and I was afraid to move."[33] In one of many parallels, direct and indirect, between Vietnam and Birmingham, Grooms juxtaposes US imperialism and domestic racism, underscoring the fact that blacks continue to face an enemy in the country of their birth. Walter's (black) body is in danger in Birmingham, "the cradle of the movement," just as it is in Vietnam, where the mud cradles his body. In both war zones, movement is risky and potentially deadly. Dedicating his novel "to the children of 'Bombingham,' wherever that might be," Grooms draws attention to the devastating effects of living under constant threat of violence, a traumatic experience that to varying degrees affects all blacks in the US, no matter where (or when) they live, making them "afraid to move." This sort of "understandin' to go 'long wid it"—the persistent and sometimes paralyzing fear that results from experiencing trauma—is sorely lacking in discussions of civil rights activity and coalition building that focus primarily on challenging racist and discriminatory policies.

By consistently returning to the present, where Walter makes multiple attempts to write Mr. and Mrs. Jackson about Haywood's death, Grooms situates his contemporary novel within the slave narrative tradition, a tradition that privileges literacy as "the pathway from slavery to freedom."[34] Walter knows the formula for such a letter, the primary purpose of which is to give comfort by ignoring uncomfortable truths:

> *Dear Mr. and Mrs. Jackson, I was with your beloved Haywood at the end, and I can assure you that it came quickly and without any pain. In his last breath he whispered about you, about home, about home sweet home.*[35]

Walter's dilemma is profound and constitutes the crisis at the core of this civil rights novel. To confront the truth about Haywood's death, which is to say the deaths of "many thousands gone," from the Middle Passage to the streets of Birmingham, is to live with unbearable pain and to risk losing hope. But choosing instead to believe in myths means living a lie—the same lie about US exceptionalism that got Haywood's head blown off. Walter's freedom depends on his ability to speak and tell the truth, to counter "all [Haywood] ever heard" about Birmingham, which is to say his country, his "*home sweet home.*"

Grooms's novel does not end with a reaffirmation of the US commitment to the difficult and sometimes deadly work of forming a more perfect union. Instead, it ends with personal struggle and the idea of (civil rights) movement as a physical and psychic process requiring considerable strength and intense introspection. In the final pages of the novel, Walter imagines various versions of a letter to the Jacksons only to conclude, "I will never write this letter. It's a letter that can't be written."[36] His thoughts then immediately drift to his mother's funeral, memories mixed with the "dreamscape" of Vietnam. In the last paragraph, Walter focuses on an image of his father, seated in the pew during the funeral service, struggling to stand up after Walter's sister has gone limp in his arms: "*Father was still trying to stand up; it seemed an interminable process.*"[37] When Haywood is shot down in Da Nang, Walter knows that if he rises up, he will most likely be killed. Standing up would be suicide, so he stays down and survives. As a (civil rights battle) survivor and witness, Walter carries the weight of all the deaths, the humiliations and daily indignities, the deep and bitter dissatisfaction with a country that refuses to acknowledge the blood at its root and the emptiness of its promise for equality and justice for all. What might make carrying that weight a bit easier is compassion:

> *What we learn from suffering, from grief, is what every other person is learning. It's human compassion, like no other. I forgot about compassion. When Haywood asked me to tell him about Birmingham, I should have told him about compassion.*[38]

With a new understanding that "*the world is a tumultuous place and every soul in it suffers*,"[39] Walter can now write the letter, the beginning of which constitutes the last line of the novel: "*Dear Mr. and Mrs. Jackson, I was trying to stand up beside him.*"[40] The letter that "can't be written" is thus the one that must be written (and read), over and over again, on behalf of every black American languishing in "a Birmingham jail" and yearning to be free.

In their introduction to *Emmett Till in Literary Memory and Imagination* (2008), co-editors Metress and Harriet Pollack frame their collection of essays in terms of the "special power" of literature to contribute to "our recovery from cultural trauma."[41] Although Metress does not make this particular point in his response to Jacquelyn Dowd Hall, by focusing on literature's affective power, he and Pollack strengthen the argument for crossing traditional disciplinary borders in order to make civil rights harder and, perhaps, (the) civil rights *movement* easier. In *Eyes on the Prize*, the award-winning documentary series narrated by Julian Bond, Bernice Johnson Reagon describes the mass meetings in Albany, Georgia that brought together the foot soldiers of the movement:

> There was more singing than there was talking. And so, most of the work that was done in terms of taking care of movement business had to do with nurturing the people who had come and there would be two or three people who would talk, but basically songs was the bed of everything.[42]

Recognizing the connection between cultural trauma and civil rights activism helps us understand not only that Hall's rhetorical battle must be fought on multiple fronts but also that it must begin by bearing witness and mustering the strength to stand up with and for others. A member of the Grammy Award-winning Sweet Honey in the Rock, Reagon believes fiercely in the power of song to strengthen both the singer and the listener, but she adds that

> it is not a hearing experience. Your ears are not enough. Your eyes are not enough. Your body is not enough and you can't block it. The only way you survive the singing is to open up and let go and be moved by the singing to another space. So the singing really is just used to just move people.[43]

On that January morning following Obama's inauguration in 2009, when Lewis surprises his aide by bringing up the idea of a comic book, he insists that the words must *sing*. A living witness and civil rights battle survivor, Lewis wants to do more than inform his audience: he wants to *move* them.

Civil rights literature sings America in order to move its readers to stand up for freedom and justice. In the last ten years, literary scholars have begun to define this tradition by producing anthologies, editing special issues of academic journals, and publishing articles and book-length studies—a growing body of scholarship that participates in what Julie Armstrong calls "the new civil rights studies" in her introduction to *The Cambridge Companion to American Civil Rights Literature* (2015), itself a ground-breaking publication that "survey[s] significant traditions, genres, themes, and critical approaches."[44] What literary scholars have brought to this field of study is an insistence that literary texts challenge the consensus narrative of the civil rights movement in ways that open up possibilities for continued (personal and political) change. Implicit in this argument is the responsibility of literary critics to address this void not only in their scholarship but also in their classrooms. Indeed, Armstrong frames the essays in the *Cambridge Companion* by privileging the transformative power inherent in the interaction between a reader and a text. Well before Armstrong began work surveying the critical landscape of civil rights literature, she was one of four editors of *Teaching the Civil Rights Movement: Freedom's Bittersweet Song* (2002). The result of a 1998 NEH seminar (that included sessions with Bond), *Teaching* includes sample syllabi and resources for educators who want to tell the story of the civil rights movement. While none of the essays imagine a special topics course in literature, several of the contributors (the majority of whom are historians) include literary texts— Anne Moody's memoir *Coming of Age in Mississippi* is mentioned most often—in their required reading lists. By suggesting a sequence of texts that could be covered in a fifteen-week semester, and by including discussion questions and ideas for research and writing projects after each chapter as well as an appendix of media resources, *Living Legacies* fills a gap in *Teaching the American Civil Rights Movement* while also contributing to the burgeoning field of civil rights literary studies.

Living Legacies enters a marketplace in the midst of a renaissance of cultural work related to the civil rights movement. While this renaissance began in 2004, with the fiftieth anniversary of *Brown v. Board*, recent tragic events in US cities from Ferguson (2014) to Charlottesville (2017) have focused more than just the scholarly community's attention on civil rights history, widening the audience for civil rights movement literature. The literary event of 2015 occurred with the arrival of Ta-Nehisi Coates's *Between the World and Me*, subsequent winner of the National Book Award for nonfiction, on the same day as the wildly anticipated *Go Set a Watchman*, Harper Lee's supposed sequel to *To Kill a Mockingbird*, a Pulitzer Prize-winning novel (and 1962 award-winning film) that looms large in the US popular imagination. While Coates's work invited comparisons to James Baldwin's *The Fire Next Time* (1963), Lee's novel sparked intense debate, in mainstream newspapers and magazines, over the status of Atticus Finch as America's exemplar of white anti-racist attitudes and behaviors. In 2016, a new anthology of essays, *The Fire This Time: A New Generation Speaks about Race*, hit bookstores along with the final installment of Lewis's *March*, but the literary event of that year having to do with civil rights has to be the opening of the spectacular Museum of African American History and Culture in Washington, DC. This addition to the Smithsonian participates in Armstrong's "new civil rights studies" by exhibiting the "long civil rights movement" envisioned by Jacquelyn Dowd Hall. Indeed, a special screening of WGN's TV series *Underground* (2016–2017), followed by a discussion with cast members and co-creator Misha Green, took place during the museum's opening ceremonies in late September, with Green describing the underground railroad as "the first integrated civil rights movement."[45] Lonnie G. Bunch III, the founding director, defines the museum's mission this way: "to build a living monument to people whose experiences and contributions have so often been left out of our national story through ignorance, neglect, and even overt efforts to suppress accounts of African American struggles and triumphs."[46]

What Metress and Pollack call the "special power" of literary texts as artifacts of historical memory can be seen and heard and felt throughout this "living monument." In his remarks at the dedication, Obama began by quoting and then repeating a line from "Sonny's Blues," Baldwin's short story about two brothers, one a teacher, the other a jazz musician: "For while the tale of how we suffer, and how we are delighted, and how we may triumph is never new, it always must be heard." After giving thanks and connecting the sacrifices of "the Civil War vets" to those of "the Civil Rights foot soldiers," including Lewis, whom he called "one of my heroes," Obama focused on the consequences of the choices we make about what to commemorate:

> The best history helps us recognize the mistakes that we've made, and the dark corners of the human spirit that we need to guard against. And yes, a clear-eyed view of history can make us uncomfortable. It will shake us out of familiar narratives.

The "richer and fuller story of who we are" that the museum tells, Obama argued, "needs to be told now more than ever": "And so this museum provides context for the debates of our times, it illuminates them, and gives us some sense of how they evolved, and perhaps keeps them in proportion." A student of history, particularly of the civil rights movement, as well as an avid reader of literature, Obama echoed Langston Hughes in his assertion that "I, too, am America." He may as well have honored Hurston, Hughes's lifelong friend and sometime collaborator: after all, what the museum offers, and the reason I consider its opening to be the literary event of 2016 as well as a stunning example of the new civil rights studies, is "de understandin' to go 'long wid it." Interest in the museum has greatly exceeded expectations, with people, young and old, coming from around the globe for this understanding. They stand in long lines, every day, holding their time-stamped ticket in anticipation of traveling, in company, "tuh de horizon and back."

Special Topics in US History: Civil Rights Movement Literature

The contributors to *Living Legacies* come from a variety of academic disciplines and critical perspectives, including visual media and performance studies, composition and rhetoric, communication studies, early childhood education, women's and gender studies, and southern, US ethnic, and African American literary studies. The texts under discussion represent multiple genres: comic books, nonfiction (essay, speech, biography, memoir), fiction, poetry, drama, photography, and film.[47] Some texts, such as Wallace's inaugural address and Lee's *To Kill a Mockingbird*, appeared during the classical phase of the civil rights movement. Michael Harper's poem "American History," Jill Freedman's photobook *Old News: Resurrection City*, and Toni Morrison's *Song of Solomon* are among the texts published in the ten-year period after King's assassination. Other works appeared more recently, including the children's book *Claudette Colvin: Twice toward Justice* (2009) and the collection of women's autobiographical writing, *Hands on the Freedom Plow: Personal Accounts by Women in SNCC* (2010). While each of the ten chapters stands on its own as a significant contribution to civil rights literary studies, the volume coheres as a multi-vocal response to the call to make civil rights harder by both complicating and contextualizing the classical period of the movement.

In Chapter 1, "From Alabama to Tahrir Square," J. Michael Lyons offers the first extended analysis of a text Lewis calls the Bible of the civil rights movement. While historians have documented the role of the press and broadcast media during the movement's classical phase, Lyons turns his attention to a less studied form of media—the comic book. Lyons draws on archival materials from the Fellowship of Reconciliation, a pacifist Christian organization established in 1915, as well as Aydin's MA thesis (Aydin collaborated with Lewis on *March*) to present *Martin Luther King and the Montgomery Story* as a rhetorical document with a clear catalyst, audience, and purpose. Lyons shows that despite its specific intent, this sixteen-page comic has had tremendous staying power, influencing social movements around the globe, most notably in South Africa; in 2011, *The Montgomery Story* showed up in Cairo's Tahrir Square, circulating among a mix of source material as Egyptians and others followed movement activities in real time via Facebook and Twitter. Lewis's *March: Book One* pays tribute to the 1957 comic with a cut-out showing its role in providing him and other students in Nashville an education as well as a sense of purpose they were not getting in their college classrooms. By constructing an origin story for both King and the movement, *The Montgomery Story* comic did more, however, than successfully recruit college students such as Lewis and Diane Nash: it promoted a simplified version of a complex, multi-faceted social movement with various factions, competing ideologies, and an incredibly large cast of characters.

The next two chapters exemplify efforts to expand civil rights studies by making visible actors who, in the top-down male-centered narrative, remain in King's shadow and also by connecting movement activities in the classical period with collective action that came after. In "Inviting Compassion and Caring Through Testimony," Myra Zarnowski challenges the consensus narrative that casts King in the leading role with readings of two children's books published in 2009—*Claudette Colvin* and *Marching for Freedom: Walk Together, Children, and Don't You Grow Weary*. Zarnowski argues that both texts "support children's development of historical memory by helping them to care about the past and have compassion for those who lived before them." In "Tomorrow's Great Meeting Place," Elizabeth Rodrigues also focuses on the power of first-person testimony, reading two anthologies of women's autobiographical writing—*Deep in Our Hearts: Nine White Women in the Freedom Movement* (2000) and *Hands on the Freedom Plow* (2010). Rodrigues demonstrates how each collection

> re-imagines the narrative form of the civil rights movement through its exchange of the third-person, biographical 'he'/'she' narrative as a hero-driven movement, for first-person 'I' and 'we' narratives that insist on the contingencies, conflicts, and continuing trajectories of activism that interracial organizing of the 1960s seeded.

The next three chapters focus on the political maelstrom enveloping the country in 1963. That year in US history witnessed the inauguration (and "segregation forever" speech) of Wallace as the Governor of Alabama on January 14 and the assassination of President John F. Kennedy in Dallas on November 22. Those two events bookend a cycle of protest and backlash that includes Wallace's infamous stand in the schoolhouse door, the historic and much-celebrated March on Washington for Jobs and Freedom (and King's "I Have a Dream" speech), and the publication of Baldwin's *The Fire Next Time*, which landed him on the cover of *Time*. In "God Decreed It So," Corrine E. Hinton and Tonya M. Scott Hill read selected nonfiction by Wallace, Kennedy, King, and Baldwin, examining how these men use *destiny* as a rhetorical device in their essays and speeches. They argue that each writer/speaker

> advances his own ideas by purposefully blending and blurring religious, historical, and national characterizations of destiny, thereby intentionally wielding these rhetorical manipulations both as demonstrations of their own power and as provocations for readers and listeners to reaffirm, advance, and capitalize on the destiny promised to them.

Their examination of Kennedy's final, undelivered remarks is especially useful in our current historical moment: Hinton and Hill draw attention to this refrain from the Cold War president's note cards:

> America's leadership must be guided by the lights of learning and reason—or else those who confuse rhetoric with reality and the plausible with the possible will gain the popular ascendency with their seemingly swift and simple solutions to every world problem.

If the 1955 lynching of fifteen-year-old Emmett Till in Mississippi haunts literary memory and imagination, so too does the 1963 bombing of the Sixteenth Street Church in Birmingham that killed four black girls. While the bombing has a place in the narrative of the civil rights movement, what happened on that day (and why) receives much less (if any) attention in the larger story we tell ourselves about our country. In "Back to Birmingham," StarShield Lortie and Laura Dubek focus on how three poets use the bombing as a site of memory (and mourning) to both critique and move a country to confront its violent past and present. Harper's "American History" and Hughes's "Birmingham Sunday" both cast the four little girls as "young warriors and innocent casualties of a war against oppression stretching back centuries and occurring around the globe." In contrast, Alice Walker's "Winking at a Funeral" does not historicize the event so much as "affirm the experiences and feelings of the young survivors." Referencing a wide range of other literary works on the church bombing—music, young adult fiction, television drama, documentary, sculpture, plays, and nonfiction—Lortie and Dubek's chapter suggests a book-length study of literary responses to this single tragic and traumatic event.

In Morrison's *Song of Solomon*, the Birmingham bombing prompts action on the part of a black male vigilante group calling themselves The Seven Days. In "Pass it On!", Dubek explores how Morrison not only extends the chronology of civil rights history to include African slaves, such as the protagonist's great-grandfather Solomon, but also validates a range of ideological perspectives regarding effective responses to the condition of living black in white America. Arguably the most autobiographical of her novels, *Song of Solomon* begins on Morrison's date of birth (February 18, 1931) and ends in 1963, the year Nina Simone identifies as pivotal for civil rights activists like herself who felt compelled to choose between two ways forward—integration and nonviolent resistance (King) or separation and black nationalism (Malcolm X). Taking inspiration from the gospel singer Solomon Burke, Morrison sings her own freedom song in this civil rights novel, rejecting either/or thinking and urging her audience "to open up and let go and be moved by the singing to another space," a space where the listener can connect with the sustaining power of the ancestors. When Obama gave Morrison the Presidential Medal of Freedom in 2012, the author of *Dreams from My Father: A Story of Race and Inheritance* singled out *Song of Solomon* as a book that taught him "how to be and how to think."[48]

In "Living Proof of Something So Terrible," Julius B. Fleming, Jr. discusses collective memory and bodily trauma in *Bourbon at the Border*. Pearl Cleage's two-act play takes its audience back to Mississippi in 1964, presenting a "dramatized microhistory of Freedom Summer." May and Charlie Thompson, a married couple living in mid-1990s Detroit, each carry the weight and pain of their experiences with racial violence while working to register voters during Freedom Summer, three decades earlier. Cleage's dramatization of the "transhistorical life" of racial injustice describes the real-life experiences of Sarah Collins Rudolph, the fifth (and often forgotten) girl in that Birmingham church basement. The sole living witness to the explosion, Rudolph broke decades of silence in 2015 to say, "It's still in me." The dynamite lit by the Klan on that Sunday morning in 1963 took Rudolph's right eye; every time she looks in the mirror, she is reminded of the loss, and when she puts on make-up, "it hurts." A half-century later, Rudolph still reacts to loud noises and rushing water, which "always take me back."[49] In *Bourbon at the Border*, May recalls suffering sexual assault, while police officers forced Charlie to watch, wife and husband both carrying the physical and psychological trauma of that event into the rest of their lives. Citing the work of Jonathan Holloway, Fleming posits that black bodies are key sites of "archival memory," arguing that

> through the transmission of May's traumatic memories, Cleage utilizes drama to reinterpret and rewrite histories of the modern civil rights movement, not only by engaging rape, but also by acknowledging the centrality of black women's experiences to histories and memories of the movement.

The next two chapters focus on different forms of visual art—photography and film—while taking viewers back to the National Mall in Washington, DC, the most potent symbol of US (white) power as well as a site of memory for an enduring tradition of (civil rights) protest. In "'A Living Theater' for Human Rights," Katharina Fackler analyzes the visual rhetoric of Freedman's *Old News: Resurrection City*, a photobook of the 1968 Poor People's Campaign, arguing that the photographs challenge the "riot iconography" of popular depictions of protest(ers). Fackler shows how *Old News* expands the visual legacy of the civil rights movement in ways that perform the crucial work of intersectionality—integrating issues of poverty, race, and global economic justice to remind us that the struggle did not end with the Voting Rights Act or King's death.

Largely forgotten in histories of the civil rights movement, the Southern Christian Leadership Conference's staged protest of poverty in 1968 has recently been revived by North Carolina's Reverend William Barber. Known locally for his Moral Mondays, in May 2017, Barber announced his intention to lead a new Poor People's Campaign, which he calls a "national moral revival."[50] Freedman calls the 1968 PPC the "Original Occupy Movement," and in email correspondence with Fackler, she insisted on the importance of young people seeing her photographs, seven of which accompany Fackler's chapter.

Jill Freedman and Spike Lee share the perspective that students can never be taught enough history. In "Gettin' Ready to Ride Into History," Jesse Williams, Jr. explores Lee's pedagogical impulse in *Get on the Bus*, a film that features the fictional pilgrimage of black men from Los Angeles to Washington, DC for the 1995 Million Man March. Reading the film in the context of the OJ Simpson verdict, Williams argues that *Bus* extends the parameters of civil rights history, its opening sequence depicting the Middle Passage and its ending a critique of mass incarceration as a means of controlling black male bodies. While *Bus* (often mistaken for documentary film) may seem an unlikely choice to represent civil rights movement film, Williams persuasively argues that it is essentially a film *about* civil rights movement cinema. Lee fashions the chartered bus, appropriately named the Spotted Owl, into the chronotope of a slave ship while revising and restaging various sites of memory from the classical period of the civil rights movement: Los Angeles, Dallas, Memphis, Little Rock, the freedom rides, lunch counter sit-ins, and the steps of the Lincoln Memorial. With one of the characters documenting the trip with a hand-held camera and Lee underscoring the *intra*racial diversity of the male riders, Williams shows how *Bus* functions as "protest against the US motion picture industry for its tendency to construct and (re)affirm monolithic mythologies about black folk and black life," prompting new understandings of Hollywood as a powerful and pernicious site of civil rights memory. Only one of two Spike Lee Joints whose title is a command, *Get on the Bus* urges viewers to get on board, to ride into history or, as Morrison suggests in *Song of Solomon*, to continually turn *back* in order to move forward.

The volume ends with a chapter on Lee's *Go Set a Watchman*, the title of which is also a command, from the Old Testament's Book of Isaiah: "For thus hath the Lord said unto me, Go, set a watchman, let him declare what he seeth."[51] In "My Childhood is Ruined!", Katherine Henninger seeks to understand the intense negative reaction of many readers to *Watchman*, the novel that by all accounts Lee wanted her late 1950s audience to wrestle with. Henninger reads *Watchman* in the context of the much beloved *To Kill a Mockingbird*, a novel that Ibram X. Kendi calls "the 'Uncle Tom's Cabin' of the civil rights movement."[52] Henninger makes this connection, too, calling *Mockingbird* "a clear heir to the *Uncle Tom's Cabin* childhood-industrial complex" while presenting a provocative argument for viewing the critically-acclaimed novel as "a dramatic curtailment" and "complete betrayal" of Lee's original project—"a white female coming of age story where maturity is utterly contingent on recognizing and confronting whiteness as the source of racial injustice—not just individual whites but *whiteness* itself." Henninger's bold examination of white racial anxiety and (national) identity formation in *Watchman* provides a fitting final chapter to a collection that seeks to prompt the kind of dissatisfaction with self that led Phoeby, in Hurston's *Their Eyes*, to declare that a change is gonna come. While Phoeby's change is a modest one, acknowledging whiteness as a social (and narrative) construction with devastating force and effect would be a major step for any white American who wants to address the cause, not just the symptoms, of the (dis)ease afflicting the nation.

On January 11, 2017, during his farewell address in Chicago's McCormick Park, Obama dropped a literary reference that left some listeners confused. It was not the first time he quoted Atticus Finch, but it was the first time he did so since Atticus had been outed in *Watchman* as a staunch segregationist and member of Maycomb, Alabama's White Citizens Council. Some observers believe that Obama referenced *Mockingbird*'s, not *Watchman*'s Atticus when he urged his audience to heed the advice the fictional father gives to his children: "you never really understand a person until you consider things from his point of view…until you climb into his skin and walk around in it."[53] In characteristic fashion, the hope and change candidate who won two presidential elections in a deeply divided country argued that as we become increasingly diverse, we must take seriously the perspective of the white worker displaced by and fearful of globalization, just as we must consider the perspective of a black person struggling with the legacies of slavery and Jim Crow. Such understanding would presumably lead to productive dialogue across all kinds of difference. But what if Obama was referencing both novels?

Consider another Atticus quote from *Mockingbird*, one that does not get repeated as often and that appears to explain the white lawyer's passionate defense of Tom Robinson, the black man falsely accused of raping a white woman: "simply because we were licked a hundred years before we started is no reason for us not to try to win."[54] Given what we now know about Lee's original intent and given that for her audience in 1960, "a hundred years before we started" would have been the dawn of the Civil War, what Atticus seems to be saying (and what *Watchman* confirms) is that the battle for white southern sovereignty, *not* Tom Robinson's rights, must continue.

And so it has, from Reconstruction to Jim Crow to mass incarceration, *Shelby v. Holder*, battles over Confederate monuments, and the election of a man Ta-Nehisi Coates calls "The First White President."[55] As both an exemplar of and a firm believer in the power of storytelling, Obama stood up, for the last time as president, and tried his best to move his audience. The fact that his strategy included referencing a literary character that embodies "the dark corners of the human spirit we need to guard against" simply underscores the fierce urgency of the historical moment. A white savior in *Mockingbird* and a Klan sympathizer and performer of "racial innocence" in *Watchman*, Atticus *is* (white) America. And there is no hope of change if we do not have the courage to confront that truth. Perhaps I am giving Obama too much credit, but I suspect the politician with a penchant for quoting James Baldwin knew that—that's "the understandin' to go 'long wid it" that the first black president offered his listeners nine days before he transferred power to his successor. Whether and how we choose to respond to that understanding is up to us.

Notes

1 Zora Neale Hurston, *Their Eyes Were Watching God* (New York: HarperCollins, 2000), 8.
2 Ibid., 9.
3 Ibid., 226.
4 Ibid., 7.
5 Missy Dehn Kubitschek, "'Tuh de horizon and Back': The Female Quest in *Their Eyes Were Watching God*," *Black American Literature Forum* 17.3 (1983), 114.
6 Richard Wright, "Between Laughter and Tears," *New Masses*, October 5, 1937.
7 Hurston, *Their Eyes*, 226.
8 "Beloved community" is an idea originating with Josiah Royce (1855–1916), a philosopher-theologian and the founder of the Fellowship of Reconciliation. Martin Luther King, Jr., a member of the FOR, popularized the term, using it in many of his speeches. The King Philosophy presents the beloved community as "a realistic, achievable goal that could be attained by a critical mass of people committed to and trained in the philosophy and methods of nonviolence" (*thekingcenter.org*). The FOR, with King's support and assistance, funded the comic book *Martin Luther King and the Montgomery Bus Boycott*, a publication intended to spread the word of nonviolence and thus expand the beloved community. J. Michael Lyons discusses this comic book in Chapter 1 of this volume.

9. Hurston, *Their Eyes*, 226.
10. Hurston/Wright Foundation: A World of Black Writers, *hurstonwright.org* (2017).
11. Martin Luther King, Jr., "I See the Promised Land," *I Have a Dream: Writings and Speeches That Changed the World*, ed. James M. Washington (San Francisco: HarperCollins, 1986), 197.
12. Before MSNBC canceled her show in 2016, Melissa Harris-Perry, a history professor and former student of Maya Angelou, often focused her viewers' attention on civil rights matters as well as the untold stories of the civil rights movement. On February 9, 2014, she framed a segment on a new documentary, *The Spies of Mississippi*, by lamenting the fact that the movement is too often reduced to four words: bus, boycott, Martin, and march.
13. Anecdotal evidence suggests that Lewis is achieving his goal. My colleague Jason Vance's eleven-year-old son Henry read the entire *March* trilogy, heard Lewis speak at MLK Magnet School in Nashville on November 19, 2016, and delivered a speech on John Lewis for a competition at Beta Convention a few days later. The convention theme was "community service." On Saturday, January 21, 2017, as the Vance family was preparing to participate in the Women's March on Nashville, Henry told his father, "I'm ready to be arrested at the march." And when Jason explained that it wasn't that kind of march, Henry said, "Still, I'm okay with it because it's good trouble."
14. John Lewis, Andrew Aydin, and Nate Powell, *March: Book Three* (Marietta, GA: Top Shelf, 2016), 246.
15. Ibid., 245.
16. Certainly, significant scholarship on the civil rights movement predates 2004, but the fiftieth anniversary of *Brown v. Board* marks the beginning of a concerted effort to remember the civil rights movement. Part of the reason may be because the generation of mid-century civil rights activists is passing on. For his oral history project at the University of Virginia, Julian Bond began every interview by asking his guest what they remember about the Supreme Court's decision declaring segregation in schools unconstitutional. Another part of the reason is, as Julie Armstrong notes in her introduction to *Cambridge Companion to Civil Rights Literature*, that "anniversaries stand as reminders that the fight for civil rights in this country remains a series of gains and losses extending beyond one short period of 'movement' during the mid-twentieth century" (3). This reminder, which constitutes the core of Jacquelyn Dowd Hall's argument in 2004, generated a great deal of scholarship, with nearly every contributor in this volume responding directly to Hall's essay.
17. Jacquelyn Dowd Hall, "The Long Civil Rights Movement and the Political Uses of the Past," *Journal of American History* 91.4 (March 2005), 1235.
18. David Levering Lewis, author of *W.E.B. Du Bois: The Fight for Equality and the American Century, 1919–1963* (2017), responds to a question about what Du Bois would consider the problems to be now by calling attention to economic injustice: "in the end, the truth embraced by Du Bois was not so much that the problem of the 20th century was the color-line, but that it was much more a matter of the cash-line."
19. Hall, "The Long Civil Rights Movement," 1233.
20. Charon Hribar, "Radical Women in the Struggle: A Review of Recent Literature on the Civil Rights and Black Freedom Movements," *Journal of Feminist Studies in Religion* 29.2 (2013), 115. One of the books Hribar reviews is *Hands on the Freedom Plow*, a collection of women's autobiography Elizabeth Rodrigues discusses in Chapter 3 of this volume.
21. Adam Liptak, "Supreme Court Invalidates Key Part of Voting Rights Act," *The New York Times*, June 25, 2013.
22. Hall, "The Long Civil Rights Movement," 1262.
23. Ibid., 1263.
24. Christopher Metress, "Making Civil Rights Harder: Literature, Memory, and the Black Freedom Struggle," *Southern Literary Journal* 40.2 (Spring 2008), 148.
25. Martin Luther King, Jr., "Letter from Birmingham Jail," *I Have a Dream: Writings and Speeches that Changed the World*, ed. James M. Washington (San Francisco: HarperCollins, 1986), 88.
26. Anthony Grooms, *Bombingham* (New York: Ballantine, 2001), 299.
27. Metress, "Making Civil Rights Harder," 148.
28. Grooms, *Bombingham*, 28.
29. Ibid., 11.
30. Ibid.
31. Ibid., 6.
32. Thirteen-year-old Virgil Ware, while riding on the handlebars of his brother's bicycle, was shot and killed by Larry Sims, a white Eagle Scout, the afternoon of the church bombing. Virgil and his brother James, like Walter and Lamar in *Bombingham*, shared a paper route.
33. Grooms, *Bombingham*, 12.
34. Frederick Douglass, *Narrative of the Life of Frederick Douglass, an American Slave*, 2nd edition. Ed. William L. Andrews and William S. McFeely (New York: Norton, 2017), 31.

35 Grooms, *Bombingham*, 7.
36 Ibid., 301.
37 Ibid., 304.
38 Ibid., 302.
39 Ibid.
40 Ibid., 304.
41 Christopher Metress and Harriet Pollack, eds., *Emmett Till in Literary Memory and Imagination* (Baton Rouge: Louisiana State University Press, 2008), 41. The essays included in this volume originated as papers at a 2004 conference, "Unsettling Memories: Culture and Trauma in the Deep South."
42 *Eyes on the Prize: No Easy Walk 1961–1963*, PBS (1987).
43 Ibid.
44 Anthologies include Margaret Whitt, *Short Stories of the Civil Rights Movement* (Athens: University of Georgia Press, 2006); Julie Armstrong and Amy Schmidt, *The Civil Rights Reader: American Literature from Jim Crow to Reconstruction* (Athens: University of Georgia Press, 2009); and Jeffrey Lamar Coleman, *Words of Protest, Words of Freedom: Poetry of the American Civil Rights Movement* (Durham: Duke University Press, 2012). *South Atlantic Quarterly* (Durham: Duke University Press, 2013) and *Southern Quarterly* (Hattiesburg: University of Southern Mississippi, 2014) both published special issues on the civil rights movement. In the notes to her introduction to the *Cambridge Companion*, Armstrong describes the scholarship on the new civil rights studies as "extensive," though that seems to include all work, no matter the discipline, that complicates and contextualizes the classical phase of the movement. The number of articles and book-length studies focused on literary responses to the movement, though clearly growing in number, is still relatively small.
45 Julia Felsenthal, "The Cocreators of *Underground* on Bringing Slave Stories to the Small Screen," *Vogue*, March 9, 2016.
46 "An Interview with Founding Director Lonnie G. Bunch III," *Charter Member News*, National Museum of African American History and Culture Newsletter 2.2 (Summer 2016), 5–6.
47 Notably absent is a chapter on civil rights music, although two of the chapters, on *Song of Solomon* and *Get on the Bus*, incorporate music into their analyses as well as their discussion questions and research projects.
48 Barack Obama, "Remarks by the President at the Medal of Freedom Ceremony," *obamawhitehouse.archives.gov*, May 29, 2012.
49 "A Conversation with Sarah Collins Rudolph," Conversations from Penn State, *wpsu.psu.edu*, February 6, 2015.
50 Dani McClain, "The Rev. William Barber is Bringing MLK's Poor People's Campaign Back to Life," *The Nation*, May 19, 2017.
51 Isa 21:6.
52 Ibram X. Kendi, "Rights, Wrongs and Roots: A Decade-by-Decade History of Race and Racism in America, in 24 Chapters," *The New York Times Book Review*, February 26, 2017.
53 Barack Obama, "Remarks by the President in Farewell Address," *obamawhitehouse.archives.gov*, January 10, 2017.
54 Harper Lee, *To Kill a Mockingbird* (New York: Grand Central, 1960), 39.
55 Ta-Nehisi Coates, "The First White President," *The Atlantic*, October 2017. Coates's essay generated a great deal of critical response.

1

FROM ALABAMA TO TAHRIR SQUARE

Martin Luther King and The Montgomery Story Comic as Civil Rights Narrative

J. Michael Lyons

On February 4, 1960, four African American college students walked into a Woolworth's store in downtown Greensboro, North Carolina, prepared to protest. Like many stores across the American South, the lunch counter at the Greensboro Woolworth's was segregated. Blacks were prohibited from sitting in the "whites only" section, a manifestation of Jim Crow laws in the South (and as far west as Kansas and Oklahoma) that proliferated after the 1896 separate-but-equal ruling in *Plessy v. Ferguson*. Despite contemporaneous news reports that this and other sit-ins had been spontaneous acts, the Greensboro Four had, in fact, been prepared.[1] The young men planned to sit at the counter and when refused service and asked to leave, remain seated in an act of nonviolent protest. Contrary to some popular and scholarly reports of this best known of the sit-ins during the classical phase of the civil rights movement, these men were very familiar with the techniques of nonviolent protest. They had heard about the bus boycott four years earlier in Montgomery, Alabama, led by a charismatic preacher named Dr. Martin Luther King, Jr., and at least one of them had read a comic book published in late 1957 that told the story of the Montgomery boycott and the nonviolent approach King endorsed.[2] *Martin Luther King and The Montgomery Story*, a sixteen-page, four-color comic book, connected Montgomery, Alabama to India's struggle for national independence less than ten years earlier; it also encouraged further movement by explaining the underlying philosophy of nonviolent protest and including a step-by-step guide on how to start a campaign using "The Montgomery Method." That method would manifest fifty-three years later in Cairo's Tahrir Square. In 2011, Egyptians and others could follow (the) movement in real time via Facebook and Twitter; included in the circulating mix of information was the same comic book, translated into Arabic, that had been read during the early years of the US civil rights movement. *The Montgomery Story* had also been circulated in apartheid South Africa, Latin America, and even Vietnam, its various translations a testament to the popularity of a narrative told in the simple but effective form of a comic book.[3]

Archives, anecdotal accounts, and the comic book itself provide a triangulated and rich history of how civil rights movement actors created and shared narratives in a way that propelled (the) movement forward. *The Montgomery Story* appears only briefly in popular histories and memoirs of the civil rights movement. Much of the evidence of its reception is thus anecdotal. The comic book is mentioned in one popular documentary history of the movement, *Eyes on the Prize*, the script of which implies that it was a factor in the decision of the Greensboro Four to sit at that Woolworth's lunch counter. The book that accompanies the film series includes a sidebar on the comic book.[4] This chapter provides the first extensive scholarly examination of

The Montgomery Story and archival documents associated with it housed at Swarthmore College's Peace Collection as part of the records of the Fellowship of Reconciliation (FOR), a pacifist Christian organization that helped King and others spread the message of nonviolent protest and civil disobedience throughout the South in the late 1950s and early 1960s (Figure 1.1).

The first instance of *The Montgomery Story* affecting the civil rights movement can be traced to sit-ins that precede Greensboro, though the comic was most likely misidentified. In the spring of 1958, led by the Wichita Youth Council of the National Association for the Advancement of Colored People (NAACP), activists began training for sit-ins by enacting social dramas in a church basement. In one organizer's account, they used a comic book that, although not mentioned by name, was *The Montgomery Story*. Similarly, in Oklahoma City, there is anecdotal

FIGURE 1.1 Since 1957, *The Montgomery Story* has appeared in many translations, encouraging freedom movements around the globe. The Spanish version is on display at the National Museum of African American History and Culture in Washington, DC.

evidence that the NAACP's Youth Council used the comic book as it prepared to launch sit-ins at five businesses. This first documented use of the comic in the context of protest is a telling illustration of its distribution over subsequent years. While scant evidence exists to tell us about the reception of the comic book in rural areas or among less-educated people, the book was clearly popular among educated activists, particularly college students in the South.[5] Georgia Congressman John Lewis, a college student and activist in Nashville when the book was published, has provided much of what we know about its reception. *The Montgomery Story* affected Lewis so much that from 2009 to 2016, he collaborated with Andrew Aydin and Nate Powell on the *March* trilogy, an award-winning memoir in comic book form that chronicles Lewis's participation in the civil rights movement.[6]

Historians have helped us understand the role of the press and broadcast media during the classical phase of the civil rights movement (1954–1965), but little has been written about the role of other forms of mass media and their impact on the diffusion of protest tactics or the philosophical foundations that helped guide them.[7] *The Montgomery Story* offers insight into the narratives and stories designed to buttress, and in many cases counter, characterizations of civil rights actors and aims published in press reports.[8] In this chapter, I describe the production; distribution; and, to a lesser extent, reception of *The Montgomery Story* and provide insight into the construction of narrative by historical actors themselves as they devised a print publication—complete with plot and characters—that appealed to a young generation of civil rights activists both in the US, particularly among black college students in the South, and abroad, including those fighting apartheid in South Africa.

The Montgomery Story is an exemplar of a movement narrative that uses a mass media form—the comic book—to tell a story efficiently, with a blend of strategic details and omissions. Through the frugal use of words and images, comic book writers and artists can quickly guide readers through complex social issues and emotions, what comic book artist and scholar Scott McCloud calls "amplification through simplification."[9] Other texts on the Montgomery boycott were available to disseminate to prospective activists, including broadcast reports, press articles, pamphlets, and even films, but *The Montgomery Story* in particular was embraced, remembered, and reprinted in the US and abroad. Why? A simple answer might be that the comic book, designed to diffuse a church-centered, nonviolent protest of Jim Crow laws, was a provocative piece of propaganda. A close examination of both the book's contents and associated archives, however, yields a more nuanced explanation. I will argue that *The Montgomery Story*, as a civil rights narrative, functioned in three important and related ways. First, it provided civil rights organizers, including King, with a movement narrative that allowed activists to talk about their work using a common vocabulary and with a common set of iconic moments and characters. Second, it provided an origin story for the modern movement and also for King himself. And third, the comic book's production and distribution illustrate its value as a nodal text, a work that served as a junction and contained a shared vision that represented the social justice aspirations of many different organizations and individuals.

"The Die Has Been Cast": FOR and the Civil Rights Movement

The New York-based FOR began in 1915 as a Christian pacifist organization that promoted nonviolent methods for resolving conflicts. Embracing nonviolence regardless of religious affiliation, FOR opposed US entry into World War I; supported Gandhi's efforts in India; and, in 1947, helped establish the Congress of Racial Equality (CORE). In 1955, FOR sent Glenn Smiley, a white Southern minister, to offer organizing and educational assistance to civic and spiritual leaders interested in nonviolent protest of Jim Crow laws in the South. Smiley had attended some rallies in Montgomery soon after the bus boycott started in December 1955, and in late February, he met King, who had recently finished his doctoral degree at Boston University and accepted the pastor position at Montgomery's Dexter Avenue Baptist Church. In a letter to his friend, Methodist leader Heil Bollinger in Nashville, Smiley sensed the importance of the struggle in Montgomery and described his first meeting with King:

> The die has been cast, [sic] there is a crisis of terrifying intensity and I believe God has called Martin Luther King to lead a great movement here in the South. But why does God lay such a burden on one so young, so inexperienced, so good? King can be a Negro Gandhi, or he can be made into an unfortunate demagogue destined to swing from a lynch mob's tree....Of his own free will, he has sought counsel from some of us. May he burst, like a fruit out of season, into the type of leader required this hour.[10]

Soon after that first meeting with King, Smiley appeared on the schedule of speakers for FOR-sponsored nonviolent workshops intended to teach the nonviolent tactics employed in Montgomery as well as Orangeburg, South Carolina and Tallahassee, Florida. King and his close friend and associate Ralph Abernathy were also on the schedule.[11]

Back in Nyack, New York, FOR's executive secretary, Columbia University-educated journalist and life-long pacifist Alfred Hassler, conceived of publishing a comic book as a way to get the story of the Montgomery boycott to "masses of people who cannot be reached by various other forms of pamphleteering." Six months into the boycott, in May 1956, Hassler wrote to the Fund for the Republic, a non-profit that supported civil rights activities, stating that he was convinced of the "efficacy of the comic book" as a popular medium that would accurately distill the essence of boycott. In a brief outline of his ideas for the book, Hassler wrote that Montgomery's story would be "simply but movingly told" to convey in "human terms with a Christian orientation" the importance of events there and "the importance of dealing with the whole struggle in nonviolent, Christian, potentially reconciling terms rather than with violence and bitterness." Hassler also described a section that would include King telling Gandhi's story, which FOR officials saw as an important precursor to events in the South, and a final section that emphasized the "key ingredients," in narrative form, of a "successful campaign of this sort."[12] Hassler later reinforced this point to Benton Resnik, the comic book's author. Blacklisted by the Committee on Evaluation of Comic Books, Resnik had submitted a draft copy of the script for Hassler to review.[13] In his review, he wrote that the script was "too heavy and literary for our purposes." The primary purpose of the comic, Hassler continued in a letter to Resnik, "is getting to people who have relatively little education."[14]

Hassler worked tirelessly to make the comic a reality. He requested a $10,000 grant from the Fund for the Republic to contract with associates of renowned comic book artist Al Capp and produce 250,000 copies of the book. The potential funders liked the idea, but they wanted some evidence that FOR could distribute the book widely and that it would be received enthusiastically among potential activists and others. Archival evidence shows that Hassler began writing letters asking for letters of interest back from a far-reaching network of churches, unions, spiritual organizations, and universities—institutions that became the backbone of the civil rights movement. Through the summer and fall of 1956, Hassler assembled letters of support and pre-orders of an estimated 50,000 copies of the book.[15] In November 1956, as he waited for the letters to arrive, he sketched out a more detailed outline. He put King center stage, with a large illustrated portrait of the preacher on the cover. Hassler also wanted to include a story to "show what it feels like to be an individual Negro in the South, with the constant sense of humiliation and indignity to which Negros are subjected." Importantly, he wrote, the story should be "done in a way that would carry kind of an identification without arousing bitterness."[16] Convinced that Gandhi should figure prominently in the story of Montgomery, Hassler also outlined a section entitled "A Nation Wins Its Freedom by Using The Montgomery Method" to show that "nonviolence used in the context of love is not something brand new but that it has a history and record of success." Finally, the book would conclude with a two-page section showing how the method worked, step-by-step.[17]

By August 1957, Hassler had received enough positive feedback and commitments to buy and distribute the comic book that the Fund for the Republic cut a $5,000 check to FOR, less than Hassler had requested but enough to get production started. Within two days of getting the go-ahead, Hassler sent a telegram to King telling him the news and asking if he would proofread the script before it goes to print.[18] It is still unclear who illustrated the book.[19] Hassler worked closely with Resnik, who represented the New York-based Graphic Information Service owned by well-known comic artist Elliot Caplin (Al Capp's brother). Caplin had started Toby Press, which reprinted a number of Capp's comic strips, including *Li'l Abner*, and although this press published its final comic in 1955, it had the same address as the Graphic Information Service letterhead on which Resnik corresponded with Hassler.[20]

"Something Ought to Be Done": Civil Disobedience and Courage

King is the hero of *The Montgomery Story*. Relatively unknown outside of activist circles at that time, he (like any comic book hero) needed an origin story explaining where he came from, the philosophy guiding his actions, and his role in the Montgomery bus boycott. Illustrators, writers, and historians use the phrase *origin story* to refer to the narrative of a character's earlier life, including any special powers the character may have and "why he does what he does."[21] Given the limited space of *The Montgomery Story* comic, King's origin story would have to be succinct, stressing only the key points that would serve the movement narrative that the book was trying to tell.

King is introduced on the second page of the book, his connection to nonviolence made clear. The first of seven panels that constitute his introduction contains a simple scroll with text (all bolding is from the original) that reads,

> In Montgomery, Alabama, 50,000 Negroes found a new way to work for freedom **without violence and without hating**. Because they did, they put new hope in all men who seek brotherhood, and who know you don't build it with bullets. No one person made The Montgomery Story, but one man's name stood out among the hundreds who worked so hard and unselfishly. That man was 29-year-old Martin Luther King Jr., minister of the Dexter Avenue Baptist Church and president of the Montgomery Improvement Association.[22]

The ensuing panels sketch King's early story. He is shown sitting beside his mother in church, reading from the Bible; the accompanying text identifies the Bible as "the basic book in the King house." Another panel explains that King's father, also a minister, taught young Martin about the power of *Love*. "Love thy neighbor as thyself," the elder King tells his son.[23] These opening panels establish the strong Christian foundation of the movement King led and came to represent. In correspondence to potential distributors and supporters, Hassler consistently emphasized the "Christian orientation" of the book. The emphasis on King's Christian upbringing helped strengthen and propel a narrative that the protest tactics to come were not radical but rather grounded in Scripture.

King's origin story also includes his work across racial lines, such cross-racial coalition building emerging as a crucial component of the comic book's plot. One panel depicts King's time at Morehouse College in Atlanta: he is sitting and talking among a group of students, half of them white. The text describes the scene as a meeting of the city's Intercollegiate Christian Council. "Some of **us** don't like discrimination either, Martin," a white female college student says.[24] From Morehouse, the story takes the reader to the campus of Crozer Seminary, where Martin, "one of six negroes among nearly 100 students," was elected president of the student body. The opening section of King's origin story closes with two small panels that tell the reader that he went on to earn a PhD from Boston University, where he met and married Coretta Scott. Martin then decides to return to the South, telling his wife that "It's **here** that God wants me to be."[25]

King's early story introduces two key themes that run throughout the narrative. First, his philosophy of nonviolence was founded on biblical and, most importantly, *Christian* principles, a point that will be stressed later in the book when Gandhi appears. Second, King's early success was tied to interracial dialogue, which reinforced a rhetorical strategy stressing Christian universalism that would accompany demands for civil rights. *The Montgomery Story* thus gives (the) civil rights movement a foundation built on morality and democratic principles.

The comic book's next section provides a narrative for the discontent in Montgomery, including vignettes that show the impact of Jim Crow laws on individual residents. The main character is a black man, Jones, who in the section's opening panel is staring into a bureau drawer at a pistol: "I'm a peaceful man – But I have a gun. For a long time I thought I might have to use it some day. Now I don't know," the text reads.[26] A nonviolent approach to confronting Jim Crow laws and discrimination in the South was never inevitable, not even among African American church and civic leaders. The possibility of armed resistance is illustrated in letters between Hassler and well-known civil rights activist Will Campbell, a white Southern preacher who was invited by King to help start the Southern Christian Leadership Conference (SCLC) in 1957. Campbell wrote approvingly of the proposed comic book in July 1957: "So many people still feel that the only way to fight is with the same weapon as the aggressor."[27] Matthew McCollum, the pastor of the Trinity Methodist Church in Orangeburg, South Carolina, where boycotts began in 1955 against businesses that opposed school desegregation following *Brown v. Board*, wrote to FOR with similar concerns:

> I could see no other way to combat the evil of racism except by violence. The situation in our city hovered on the edge of violence, and if it had gone over that edge the whole South might well have gone with it.[28]

Many African Americans, including King himself, owned guns, so the illustration of Jones contemplating the use of his weapon would not have been at all shocking for many of the readers the comic book originally targeted. A key purpose of the comic book was to acknowledge that armed confrontation was an option for those frustrated by Jim Crow and other forms of violence and discrimination but that exercising that option would be counter-productive in the long run.[29] *The Montgomery Story* sought to convince people to incorporate nonviolent principles and actions into their everyday lives. Another key goal of the book was to dispel the notion among many blacks that nonviolence was passive or naïve. One panel in this section shows Jones, who becomes the narrator for the Montgomery boycott, washing a car. A white man, presumably the car's owner, scowls at him and barks, "Snap it up boy. I want that car in a hurry." Jones laments this part of his life in the South: "I love Montgomery, but I've hated it too. A Negro anywhere in the Deep South has a hard time. **Jim Crow** sits might heavy on a man's spirit."[30] Readers are then introduced to Jones's family—his wife and baby boy. Panels continue to flesh out Jones's growing commitment to nonviolence as he talks about how he and his son used to play next to the bureau with the loaded gun and how he wonders if he would have the "courage" to use the

From Alabama to Tahrir Square   23

weapon to defend his family: "Lately I've started to wonder if that would really be courage at all," Jones says.[31]

While these panels help strengthen the idea that nonviolent protest is a courageous act, countering the idea among many doubters that it was passive, they also make visible Jones's vulnerability: he has much at stake—the welfare of his family—if he gets involved in the protests. Many blacks were reluctant to join in acts of civil disobedience out of fear of reprisals, which could include the loss of employment and the ostracizing of family members, particularly among the less educated. The turning point for Jones comes in the next series of panels, which illustrate the arrest of Rosa Parks after she refuses to give up her seat on a bus to a white man. Up late ruminating over Parks's arrest, Jones tells his wife, "Something ought to be done. Rosa is a good woman and not a troublemaker."[32] Origin stories are effective because they often provide instructive vignettes drawn from specific moments that serve to reify abstract ideas that a narrator or narrative device (such as a comic book) is trying to establish as part of a larger story. *The Montgomery Story* uses Parks's story to form a larger narrative of action and to simplify the larger philosophical framework of a movement that was obviously far more complicated (Figure 1.2).

From the coffee shops where Jones and other Montgomery residents organized the boycott, the reader is taken to the streets of the city, where the logistics of the boycott, such as the establishment of an alternative transportation system using taxis and station wagons, unfold in a series of panels. These panels also depict the founding of the Montgomery Improvement Association (MIA) and the introduction of King to the wider Montgomery community. Pictured in a preacher's robe, King speaks in a church so full that loudspeakers are set up for the

FIGURE 1.2   Civil rights activists and sympathizers faced intimidation, threats, and sometimes violent retribution in addition to daily humiliations and indignities. Challenging white power took tremendous courage.

crowds outside. King says, "This is a **nonviolent** protest against injustice. Our chief weapons are moral and spiritual forces. We depend on love! Love and goodwill toward **all** men must be at the forefront of our movement if it is to be successful."[33] An important moment of crisis in the section about the boycott takes the reader inside a church where King speaks on January 30, 1956. Over a series of panels, he is informed that his house has been bombed. King rushes to the scene and finds an angry crowd gathered outside. King calms the crowd and repeats his ideas about peace and nonviolence, ideas instructive to Jones: "If a man can see his home bombed and not fight back—except with love—then there is hope for all of us."[34] The explosion at King's house, which would have been treated as a discrete news event by media outlets, is in the comic book made to represent the movement as a whole and is emplotted into the much larger narrative about King and the philosophical scaffolding of the movement. Also, like any good movement narrative, the comic book attempts to elicit an emotional response to perceived injustice and then to "modulate and channel" it into civil disobedience.[35]

In subsequent panels, as the Supreme Court considers segregation on Montgomery's buses, readers are introduced to Abernathy, who helps organize and act out scenarios that (freedom) riders of desegregated buses might face. These are important instructional vignettes that would become an integral tactic to diffuse the methods of nonviolent civil disobedience at workshops and teach-ins around the South. The panels show Abernathy as the driver of a fictitious bus, sitting in the first in a row of chairs. "Riders" are taught to clasp their hands in front of them if they are verbally or physically abused by the driver or other passengers. These "social dramas" were not new, but many activists would first learn about them in the pages of *The Montgomery Story*. Another panel shows a young black man boarding the bus on December 21, 1956, *after* the Supreme Court ruling, and being verbally abused by a white man in a business suit. A thought bubble above the young man's head reinforces his understanding of the emerging philosophy of nonviolence: "Once I would have gotten sore about that .... And shouted dirty words back – and maybe hit back!"[36] This section also includes a panel that helps to reinforce the philosophy from a white man's perspective. As news photographers approach the man who spouted the verbal abuse, presumably after having witnessed the incident with the young man, he smiles at them as they ask questions: "Hey! You're smiling! I thought you were mad at these people." He replies, "I am! But it's pretty hard to **stay** mad when they don't fight back."[37]

The story of the Montgomery bus boycott concludes with a series of panels that depict the escalation of violence in Montgomery that followed desegregation of the buses, including Ku Klux Klan marches, cross burnings, and church bombings. But it ends with a panel showing Jones standing at a bus stop reiterating why he chose nonviolence to confront discrimination:

> If what happened here is a victory for anyone, it's for all of Montgomery. We respect ourselves more and we know that the idea of love and non-violence is spreading. I've thrown my gun away – it had gotten much too heavy for me ever to lift again.[38]

The first nine pages of the comic tell the story of Montgomery in a memorable and simple form, and, together with the next section on Gandhi's employment of nonviolent civil disobedience, provide an uncluttered origin story for King and the movement he led. Hassler included a section on Gandhi to illustrate the historical precedence for nonviolence but also, and more importantly, to show that it worked. King, the narrator for the two-page section on Gandhi, stands at a pulpit telling his congregation about the massacre at Amritsar, when British troops fired into a crowd of peaceful protesters, killing hundreds; Gandhi's many terms of imprisonment in India for civil disobedience; the protest of the British salt tax and the "salt march," which led to the imprisonment of tens of thousands of Indiana protestors; and Gandhi's campaign to improve the lives of the "untouchables," members of India's lowest caste. Gandhi's section, though crucial, is short so as not to muddle the focus on "Christian love" and the black church as an institution—two key elements of the story of Montgomery and the civil rights movement in general. As King wrote in his memoir of the boycott, published shortly after the comic book, "Christ furnished the spirit and motivation, while Gandhi furnished the method."[39]

That Gandhi-inspired method makes up the last four pages of the comic. King walks the reader through "The Montgomery Method," a "nonviolent Christian action" that can be used "anywhere …. against any kind of evil." King focuses on individual agency and responsibility: "**You** are important. **You** need to change things."[40] He goes on to explain the philosophical underpinnings of the technique—that protesters have to help their enemy "see **you** as a human being." Even when confronted with violence, King continues, you must not strike back. "you must go on **Loving** him." Here, the comic includes a small illustration of a scene from the integration of Central High School in Little Rock, Arkansas in September 1957, a few months before the comic was published, using what may have seemed, at least tactically, an unrelated event to stitch together a larger narrative.[41] The comic closes with a vignette preparing the reader for the possible consequences of this nonviolent protest. King tells the story of Abernathy's fear the first time he went to jail. Abernathy is comforted because, King says, he found God waiting for him in the cell. In the last panel, King speaks directly to the reader:

> That's how it will be with you, too. When the going gets hardest, if you remain true to Christian Love, you'll find God waiting there for you, holding you and supporting you, giving you a victory far beyond what you had hoped.[42]

In a letter dated November 1, 1957, a few weeks before the comic book went to print, King wrote to Hassler that he had "very scrutinizingly" read through the script, adding, "Frankly there is hardly anything I could add or subtract. It is certainly an excellent piece of work." In the same letter, he wrote, "You have done a marvelous job of grasping the underlying truth and philosophy of the movement."[43] With King's approval, the comic went to press. Some 250,000 copies were printed, and Hassler and other members of the FOR staff began contacting a wide range of organizations to find distribution outlets.

"Spread the Word Around": The Bible for (a) Movement

In August 1957, while *The Montgomery Story* was in the final production stages, Hassler wrote to King to ask for a blurb that he could use to promote sales of the book. The cover price was 10 cents, with bulk orders substantially discounted; sales at churches, civic meetings, and on college campuses seem to be the primary way the book reached readers. Hassler wrote to the NAACP's Roy Wilkins to ask if the organization would endorse the comic book and circulate promotional materials to its branches.[44] He wrote to A. Philip Randolph of the Brotherhood of Sleeping Car Porters, a key trade union in the South,[45] and he sent a letter to Russell Lasley of the Chicago-based United Packinghouse Workers of America. Both unions were key supporters of the Montgomery bus boycotts, and Lasley was invited to the founding meeting of the Southern Christian Leadership Council.[46] Along with his letters to potential distribution partners, Hassler included promotional material extoling the potential of the comic book to inform people about the events of the Montgomery boycott and serve as a "signpost, a book of directions for others who would work for freedom and brotherhood." The material also included a blurb from King, which he wrote to Hassler in an undated letter on MIA letterhead, in which King said that he hopes the comic book will be widely distributed "among both Negroes and whites." He continued, "This book will help spread the word around."[47]

Once word began circulating through the network of churches, trade unions, colleges, and movement organization that helped build and sustain (the) civil rights movement, individuals and organizations began writing Hassler, asking how they could get copies of the book. In April 1958, several months after the book was published, an official from the National Conference of Christians and Jews wrote, assuring Hassler that the "splendid" work had been "called to the attention of every one of our 63 regional offices."[48] Some groups used the bulk discount to help raise funds by selling it at the 10-cent cover price at events. The Gary Fair Share Organization, a civil rights group in Gary, Indiana, ordered 5,000 copies to distribute during a talk King gave in April 1958.[49] In Nashville, James Lawson, an FOR official, introduced the eighteen-year-old John Lewis and others to the comic book, carrying it in his luggage to workshops on nonviolent protest. In a 2012 interview, Lawson said that the comic was part of a larger curriculum about the uses of nonviolent protest: "Part of its value was that it gave people a brief story of a very effective non-violent campaign, something they could refer to and memorize and study."[50] Lewis and about twenty students from a number of colleges in the Nashville area met once a week to study the tactics and philosophy of nonviolence. In a 2013 interview about *March*, his graphic memoir, Lewis remembers the impact of the 1957 comic:

> And *The Montgomery Story*, this comic book that sold for 10 cents, became like our Bible. It was our guide. And I think it helped complement what Jim Lawson was teaching. It made it simple, it made it plain and it made it very clear.[51]

The comic book form that amplified through simplifying made *The Montgomery Story* an appealing text for international activist audiences. The bus boycott and the tactics illustrated in the comic appealed to movements in South Africa, Latin America, and later in Vietnam and Egypt. The comic has been translated into Spanish, Vietnamese, Farsi, Arabic, and Italian, and distributed, sometimes clandestinely, among activists.[52] It had particular resonance in South Africa, where the anti-apartheid movement was beginning to build in earnest in the late 1950s and 1960s. FOR received several requests for copies of *The Montgomery Story* from young activists and clergy. One of the country's largest newspapers covering the black community, the Cape Town weekly *The New Age*, requested the right to serialize the comic book.[53] (FOR also gave publication permission to *The Peace News*, a pacifist newspaper published in London, beginning in January 1958, a few months after the comic was released.[54]) A young minister in Johannesburg wrote to FOR in September 1958 requesting several copies:

> I am able to reach scores of our young people with the Message of love; and after reading 'Martin Luther King and The Montgomery Story' I feel all the more challenged to do what I can to apply the suggestions outlined in the closing pages to our local situations, which, as you know, are far from being commendable.[55]

FOR's chapter in South Africa regularly asked for the comic until at least 1966, when it requested 1,000 copies. In a newsletter sent to its readership in March 1966, a promotional message reads, "Chiefly we want to get them [copies of *The Montgomery Story*] to thinking young people of all races who will one day take the lead." By 1967, the comic had been banned and copies of it seized by security police in many parts of South Africa.[56]

The most recent instance of *The Montgomery Story* circulating among freedom fighters occurred in 2011. Dalia Ziada, an Egyptian blogger who in 2009 headed the American Islamic Congress's North African Bureau, discovered the comic book during a conference in 2006. She subsequently spearheaded an effort to produce and distribute an Arab translation, which was released in 2008. Ziada's remarks about the reproduction closely resemble the words of Lewis and others during the classical phase of the civil rights movement: "The main motive was for me to have this book available for young activists in the region." Thousands of copies of the book were distributed in Egypt, Tunisia, Yemen, and Egypt, including in Tahrir Square during the January 2011 uprising.[57]

From Person to Person: Networking a Social Movement

In the late 1950s and early 1960s, members of FOR did not necessarily consider *The Montgomery Story* a success because "semiliterate" blacks did not use the comic book the way many had hoped they would.[58] But the history of journalism and mass communication is filled with instances in which an intended audience ignores a publication or broadcast only for it to be embraced by another audience. In *The Montgomery Story*'s case, that appears to have been young activists both in the American South and abroad.

The comic book's current value includes the insight it provides to historians examining the relationship between various forms of media and social justice movements.[59] Clearly, *The Montgomery Story* served as a narrative device that used the story of the Montgomery bus boycotts—vignettes of key events, people involved, and the methods employed—to create a shared understanding of nonviolent civil disobedience among fledgling activists and citizens who were new to or not yet involved in the movement. The book's publishers intended that shared understanding to include blacks with less education who were less likely to be reached by other means, including traditional mass media or social connections. In their analysis of why sit-ins, which began as *The Montgomery Story* was being released and distributed, occurred in some Southern cities but not others, Kenneth Andrews and Michael Biggs point to several factors, including the development of "activist cadres"; the expansion of historically black colleges (and networks created by students who attended them); and increased reporting on events, including the boycott in Montgomery and the desegregation of Central High School in Little Rock.[60] These methods of diffusion often bypassed less-educated people, and Hassler and others at FOR hoped a comic book would establish an easily understandable context within which people could make sense of (and relate to) the movement.

But anecdotal evidence from both FOR and activists at the time shows that the book was eagerly consumed by college students, who seemed to be drawn to the strength of the simplicity of its didactic narrative, which leads to an important point: the comic book provides a movement narrative for civil rights activists in the late 1950s and early 1960s that includes an origin story marking the Montgomery bus boycott as the *beginning* of a new era of civil rights protest in what has subsequently become known as the "long" struggle for civil rights by blacks in the US. Historian Jacquelyn Dowd Hall argues that the dominance of this classical phase of the movement (a term she borrows from activist Bayard Rustin), which began with the 1954 *Brown v. Board* decision and ended with the passage of the Civil Rights Act in 1964 and the Voting Rights Act in 1965, has minimized the work that came later. King, Hall argues, is "frozen in 1963" in the "I Have a Dream" speech, his opposition to the Vietnam War and his work on behalf of unions in the North subsumed under the weight of this dominant narrative. Likewise, civil rights work that grew out of radicalization in the 1930s is truncated from the "modern" movement as defined by this same narrative.[61] The lack of national news coverage of this earlier work on civil rights and racial discrimination likely contributed to its relegation in the popular narrative of the civil rights movement. In their work on coverage of civil rights, Gene Roberts and Hank Klibanoff outline the paucity of coverage of race and attempts at reform in the late 1930s, noting that "only once between 1935 and 1940, in a story involving A. Philip Randolph, the Negro labor leader, did *The New York Times* run a front-page story mentioning the name of any of the country's leading Negro racial reformists."[62]

The Montgomery Story exemplifies how a publication can truncate and simplify a narrative while also moving it forward through recruitment and education. While the struggle for freedom and civil rights has always included a wide range of strategies, including nonviolent resistance, what happened after *Brown v. Board* seemed to many at the time to be different. *The Montgomery Story* amplified this difference by linking the boycott to King's leadership, the consensus narrative of the civil rights movement thus becoming synonymous with "the King years." In narrative discourse, sociologist Joseph Davis explains that "[p]ast events are selected and configured into a plot, which portrays them as a meaningful sequence and schematic whole with beginning, middle and end."[63] In the plot of the civil rights movement, King is the larger-than-life protagonist who propels the plot forward. But by simplifying complex political and social processes, movement narratives such as *The Montgomery Story* leave gaps in the reader's understanding as well as the historical record. To do justice to the story of Montgomery, to make civil rights harder to simplify (and thus more useful to contemporary social justice movements), means providing the necessary context for reading the comic as a rhetorical document with a particular purpose and audience in mind.

Archival evidence shows that at the time of its publication, *The Montgomery Story* meant to serve as a nodal text to connect the multitude of movement actors (from churches and trade unions to college students and people living in rural areas) through a shared story of the emotional distress of Jim Crow laws, the desire to take some kind of action, and the efficacy of nonviolent protest as an effective means of working for change. Much attention has been paid to movement networks recently, with the increased importance of digital media, the Internet, and "networked social movements" in diffusing movement technique and galvanizing support. The uprising and eventual revolution in Egypt began with a story—the narrative of the brutal murder of a young man, Khaled Said, by Egyptian police. The story spread through online networks, such as Facebook, and led to the fomenting of protest, particularly among young, educated Egyptians.[64]

But social movements have always been "networked" and often coalesce around stories in the form of texts. *The Montgomery Story* provides insight into how movement actors used a text, in this case a comic book, to support movement activities and doctrine. Movement leaders, including King, recognized the importance of "spreading the word around" on the movement's own terms—within a narrative the movement itself crafted. The velocity and global reach of such spreading has increased exponentially, but the paths from person to person are similar to those taken by *The Montgomery Story* over sixty years from Montgomery to Tahrir Square.

Teaching Approaches to *The Montgomery Story* Comic

Discussion Questions

1. Why do you think civil rights organizers decided to use a comic book to tell the story of the Montgomery bus boycott? What made a comic book, which includes a combination of text and images, an effective tool in a grassroots social movement at that time? With the increased use of social media in social movements, do you think a comic book would be effective today in spreading messages of nonviolent protest? Why?
2. *The Montgomery Story* is called a "movement narrative" in this chapter. What does that mean? How is it different from a mass media narrative of the Montgomery bus boycott in, for example, a newspaper or magazine?
3. One of the main themes of *The Montgomery Story* is Dr. King's adherence to Christian principles. What are these principles, and why do you think the authors of the comic book put so much emphasis on them?

4 A valid critique of *The Montgomery Story* is that it presents a simplified version of the Montgomery bus boycott, mythologizes King as the movement's leader, and defines protest too narrowly—in terms of *either* violent *or* nonviolent resistance. What are the dangers of oversimplifying the story of the civil rights movement?

Research and Writing Projects

1 Using a newspaper archive, research depictions of the Montgomery bus boycott in the mass media of the time, for example, in *The New York Times* (mainstream) and *Birmingham World* (black local press). Prepare a multimodal presentation in which you compare and contrast how the boycott is framed in these contemporaneous mass media accounts and in the comic book.
2 Using *The Montgomery Story* as a model, write a proposal for a comic that presents an origin story for another social justice campaign. Keep in mind that a comic book or graphic novel needs characters; a plot; and, to be an effective tool in a social movement, a call to action. You can choose to research an earlier era, such as the anti-lynching campaign, or something contemporary, such as Black Lives Matter.
3 *The Montgomery Story* traveled around the globe to influence other social justice campaigns. Focus on one particular location—South Africa, Egypt, or Latin America, for example—and prepare a presentation in which you make connections between the US civil rights movement (catalyst, philosophy/practices, actors, events, effects) and a movement for social change in another part of the world.
4 In recent years, middle-school teachers have started including comics, such as Lewis's *March*, in their curriculums. As both history and art, *March* presents interesting possibilities for teaching young people lessons that cross disciplinary borders. Prepare a lesson plan that includes questions, group activities, and research projects for a fifth-grade Social Studies class reading *March: Book One*.

Notes

1 On the spontaneity of the sit-ins in news reports, see Helen Fuller, "We Are So Very Happy," *The New Republic*, April 25, 1960, 13–16.
2 Several popular and scholarly histories of the sit-ins mention that at least one of the original Greensboro Four read the comic book. See Juan Williams, *Eyes on the Prize: America's Civil Rights Years, 1954–1965* (New York: Penguin, 1987), 124–125; Aldon Morris, *The Origins of the Civil Rights Movement* (New York: The Free Press, 1984), 165–166; and John Lewis, *Walking with the Wind: A Memoir of the Movement* (New York: Simon and Schuster, 1998), 91.
3 Jesse Singal, "Did a Martin Luther King Comic Book Help Inspire the Egyptian Revolution?" *Boston.com*, February 11, 2011.
4 Juan Williams, *Eyes on the Prize: America's Civil Rights Years, 1954–1965* (New York: Penguin, 1987), 124–125.
5 Ronald Walters, "The Great Plains Sit-in Movement, 1958–60," *Great Plains Quarterly* (1996), Paper 1093.
6 John Lewis, Andrew Aydin, and Nate Powell, *March: Book One* (Marietta: Top Shelf Productions, 2013). Laura Dubek discusses the significance of the *March* trilogy in the introduction to this volume.
7 On diffusion, see Kenneth T. Andrews and Michael Biggs, "The Dynamics of Protest Diffusion: Movement Organizations, Social Networks and News Media in the 1960 Sit-ins," *American Sociological Review* 71 (2006), 752–777. On this particular gap in the scholarship on civil rights literature, see Julie Armstrong, *The Cambridge Companion to Civil Rights Literature* (Oxford: Oxford University Press, 2015), 12.
8 See Gene Roberts and Hank Klibanoff, *The Race Beat: The Press, the Civil Rights Struggle and the Awakening of a Nation* (New York: Knopf, 2006). For a study of public relations during the civil rights era (including the use of comics), see Vanessa Murphee, *The Selling of Civil Rights: The Student Nonviolent Coordinating Committee and the Use of Public Relations* (London: Routledge, 2006).

9 Scott McCloud, *Understanding Comics* (New York: William Morrow, 1994), 30.
10 Glenn Smiley to Heil Bolinger, February 29, 1956, The Fellowship of Reconciliation Records (DG 013), Swarthmore College Peace Collection, box 19 (below cited as FORR).
11 Document entitled "Non-Violent Workshops," FORR, box 19.
12 Hassler to Edward Reed, May 2, 1956, FORR, box 19.
13 Resnik had authored several titles that were reviewed by the Committee and deemed "objectionable" as part of the 1950s regulation of comic books under the "Comics Code." For Resnik, see Andrew V.B. Aydin, "The Comic Book That Changed the World" (master's thesis, Georgetown University, 2012), 55. On the "Comics Code," see Amy Kiste Nyberg, *Seal of Approval: The History of the Comics Code* (Oxford: University of Mississippi Press, 1998).
14 Hassler to Benton Resnik, May 4, 1957, FORR, box 19.
15 Ibid.
16 "Proposed Comic Book for Use in South," November 23, 1956, FORR, box 19.
17 Ibid.
18 Hassler to Martin Luther King, Jr., September 24, 1957, FORR, box 19.
19 As part of his study, Andrew Aydin consulted Eddie Campbell, a comic book expert, to examine the art in *The Montgomery Story*. Campbell concluded that because the art in the book was "generic in so many ways," it was difficult to conclude with certainty who drew it. He added that it was very different from Capp's style. Aydin, "The Comic Book That Changed the World," 65.
20 On the connection of Resnik to Toby Press, see Andrew V.B. Aydin, "The Comic Book That Changed the World" (master's thesis, Georgetown University, 2012), 55.
21 J.K. Griffin, "A Brief Glossary of Comic Book Terminology," *Serials Review* 24.1 (1998), 74.
22 *Martin Luther King and The Montgomery Story*, The Fellowship of Reconciliation, 1. Like most comic books, *The Montgomery Story* was clearly a collaborative effort. It is unclear who the author of the text was as archival documents show that Alfred Hassler, Benton Resnik, and even Martin Luther King, Jr. all had input on the script. The artist is unknown, and no credit is given anywhere in the book to the publisher. All bolding is in the original.
23 Ibid.
24 Ibid.
25 Ibid.
26 *The Montgomery Story*, 2.
27 Will Campbell to Hassler, July 17, 1957, FORR, box 19.
28 Matthew McCollum to Hassler, undated, FORR, box 19.
29 On gun ownership among African Americans, see Charles E. Cobb, Jr., *This Nonviolent Stuff'll Get You Killed: How Guns Made the Civil Rights Movement Possible* (New York: Basic Books, 2014); and Nicholas Johnson, *Negroes and the Gun: The Black Tradition of Arms* (New York: Prometheus Books, 2014).
30 *The Montgomery Story*, 2.
31 Ibid.
32 Ibid. King talks about the fear of "economic reprisals" among Montgomery's less educated in Martin Luther King, Jr., *Stride Toward Freedom* (New York: Harper & Row, 1958), 37.
33 *The Montgomery Story*, 4.
34 Ibid., 6.
35 Francesca Polletta, "Plotting Protest," in *Stories of Change*, ed. Joseph E. Davis (Albany: State University of New York Press, 2002), 37. Polletta uses the term "emplotted" to describe the way a plot is crafted in movement narratives. Christopher Metress uses the same term, via Hayden White, to argue for more attention to literary texts in discussions about the civil rights movement in his response to Jacquelyn Dowd Hall, "Making Civil Rights Harder: Literature, Memory, and the Black Freedom Struggle," *Southern Literary Journal* 40.2 (2008), 138–150. See Elizabeth Rodrigues's discussion of emplottedness in the context of collective women's autobiography in Chapter 3 of this volume.
36 *The Montgomery Story*, 8.
37 Ibid.
38 Ibid., 9.
39 *Stride to Freedom*, 85.
40 *The Montgomery Story*, 12.
41 Ibid., 13.
42 Ibid., 16.
43 King to Hassler, November 1, 1957, FORR, box 19.
44 Hassler to Roy Wilkins, August 2, 1957, FORR, box 19.
45 Hassler to A. Philip Randolph, August 23, 1957, FORR, box 19.
46 Hassler to Russell Lasley, August 25, 1957, FORR, box 19.

47 King to Hassler, undated, FORR, box 19. Flyer entitled "The Montgomery Story!" FORR, box 19.
48 Roy McCorkel to Hassler, April 8, 1958, FORR, box 19.
49 Hilbert L. Bradley to Hassler, February 18, 1959, FORR, box 19.
50 Aydin, "The Comic Book That Changed the World," 70.
51 Joseph Hughes, "Congressman John Lewis and Andrew Aydin Talk 'Inspiring the Children of the Movement' with 'March' [Interview]," *Comics Alliance*, September 16, 2013.
52 Copies of the book in these languages are available in the FOR archive at Swarthmore College, FORR, box 19.
53 Brian Percy Bunting to Hassler, June 17, 1958, FORR, box 19.
54 Hassler to Hugh Brock, February 21, 1958, FORR, box 19.
55 Jerome N. Nkosi to FOR, July 27, 1959, FORR, box 19.
56 "South African Fellowship of Reconciliation News Letter," No. 35, March 1966, FORR, box 19.
57 Michael Cavna, "Amid Revolution, Arab Cartoonists Draw Attention to Their Cause," *The Washington Post*, March 7, 2011.
58 The word "semiliterate" is used in a letter written in 1997 by then Director of Communication Richard Deats to describe the intended audience of the comic book. Richard Deats to Paul Gravett, April 30, 1997, FORR, box 19.
59 See Brian Ward, *Radio and the Struggle for Civil Rights in the South* (Gainesville: University Press of Florida, 2004); Kay Mills, *Changing Channels: The Civil Rights Case that Transformed Television* (Jackson: University of Mississippi Press, 2004); Sasha Torres, *Black, White and in Color: Television and Black Civil Rights* (Princeton: Princeton University Press, 2003); and Brian Ward, ed., *Media, Culture, and the Modern African American Freedom Struggle* (Gainesville: University of Florida Press, 2001).
60 Andrews and Biggs, "The Dynamics of Protest Diffusion: Movement Organizations, Social Networks and News Media in the 1960 Sit-Ins," 770.
61 Jacquelyn Dowd Hall, "The Long Civil Rights Movement and the Political Uses of the Past," *Journal of American History* 91.4 (March 2005), 1234. On Rustin, see Bayard Rustin, *Down the Line: The Collected Writings of Bayard Rustin* (Chicago: Quadrangle Books, 1971), 111. See also Charles W. Eagles, "Toward New Histories of the Civil Rights Era," *Journal of Southern History*, 66 (November 2000): 815–848.
62 Gene Roberts and Hank Klibanoff, *The Race Beat: The Press, The Civil Rights Struggle, and the Awakening of a Nation* (New York: Alfred A. Knopf, 2006), 11.
63 Joseph E. Davis, ed., "Introduction," in *Stories of Change* (Albany: State University of New York Press, 2002), 11.
64 See Manuel Castells, *Networks of Outrage and Hope: Social Movements in the Internet Age* (Malden: Polity Press, 2012); Wael Ghonim, *Revolution 2.0: The Power of the People is Greater than the People in Power: A Memoir* (New York: Houghton, Mifflin, Harcourt, 2012); and Barry Wellman and Lee Rainie, *Networked* (Cambridge, MA: MIT Press, 2012).

2

INVITING COMPASSION AND CARING THROUGH TESTIMONY

Participants in the Civil Rights Movement Speak for Themselves

Myra Zarnowski

Years ago, when I was working with a fourth-grade class studying the civil rights movement, a nine-year-old black girl said to me, "It's so hard to believe that all this really happened. My white friends are so nice to me." Her comment speaks to an enduring challenge in childhood education: how do we help young readers connect with difficult stories from the past, stories that involve racism, violence, hatred, and denial of freedom and equality? More to the point, how can literature support children's development of historical memory, helping them care about the past and develop compassion for those who lived before them?

Historical Literature that Includes Testimonial Accounts

Literature that openly deals with painful and complex social issues is considered "risky historical text."[1] Such literature allows children to "explore difficult social and cultural issues in our society."[2] While in the past, Holocaust literature, "the literature of atrocity,"[3] largely defined risky text, scholars have called for a broader view to include "under-represented histories and repressed sites of violence and suffering."[4] This broader view of risky historical text includes "books about African American life [which are] historical and often traumatic in emphasis, so pervasive is the legacy of slavery, Reconstruction, and the fight for civil rights."[5]

This chapter looks at two recently published risky historical texts—civil rights narratives that invite compassion and caring through the use of testimony from people directly involved in the movement. Because the children and teenagers in these texts describe their own experiences, they place the reader in a unique position of bearing witness. Testimonies from these individuals help readers connect with the past in several ways. First, they emphasize individual agency, "the *sine qua non* of narrative."[6] Testimonial accounts show that the individual actions of ordinary people were central to (the) civil rights movement, making it easy for readers to empathize with these individuals. Second, testimonial accounts retrieve lost experiences, providing an "antidote to popular amnesia."[7] By giving readers access to grassroots activists whose activities were frequently erased from the historical record, these texts provide a counter-history to popular versions of the past, expanding traditional chronology by reaching back to the 1930s and forward to the present. This is a truer, more complex story, one that prevents us from equating the movement solely with what has been called its classical phase, namely the major achievements of the late 1950s and 1960s.[8] Whereas "top-down" history focuses on the work of a few great leaders of the civil rights movement, testimony keeps our attention on "struggle 'on the ground,'"[9] asking us to connect with ordinary individuals caught up in extraordinary events rather than exceptional individuals. Third, testimonial accounts evoke a social-emotional connection or what has been called an *emotional investment*.[10] Readers develop strong feelings of frustration, fear, anger, and hurt as they read risky historical texts. These feelings connect us to the people we are reading about. In addition, dealing with complex social issues found in testimonial accounts requires grappling with difficult moral issues. Young readers are faced with the question: what is the right thing to do?

Claudette Colvin: Twice Toward Justice (2009) and *Marching for Freedom: Walk Together, Children, and Don't You Grow Weary* (2009) both present children with opportunities to engage with risky historical text. In my discussion of each text, I will highlight the features commonly associated with testimonial literature: individual agency, retrieval of lost experiences and the creation of a counter-history, and social-emotional connections necessary for forming feelings of compassion and caring. Testimony about securing civil rights is an essential part of each historical narrative; readers are therefore positioned to develop a "rich meaning of the concept of 'citizen'"[11]—a concept with implications for our lives today.

Claudette Colvin: Twice Toward Justice

Winner of the 2009 National Book Award for young people's literature, Phillip Hoose's *Claudette Colvin* is a historical narrative that mixes current testimony from Colvin, who protested segregated seating on buses in Montgomery, Alabama in 1955, with commentary and background information by the author. Fifteen-year-old Claudette was a high-school student when she refused to give up her seat on a bus to a white woman. Despite the fact that she did this nine months before Rosa Parks, she was passed over by the black community because she was not the "right" person they were looking for to be the focus of a legal battle against segregated buses. Nevertheless, Colvin became one of the plaintiffs in the *Browder v. Gayle* court case that successfully challenged the constitutionality of Alabama's state and local laws requiring segregation on the buses. By allowing Colvin to tell her own story, Hoose rescues her account from historical neglect. Not surprisingly, recent articles about this book emphasize this rescue mission with such titles as "From Footnote to Fame in Civil Rights History"[12] and "The Greatest Story Never Told."[13] Hoose's counter-history has important implications for historical understanding.

This powerful story of individual agency tells how one adolescent girl took a stand against what she knew was wrong. Colvin tells us about her firm conviction to do something:

> I was done talking about 'good hair' and 'good skin' but not addressing our grievances. I was tired of adults complaining about how badly they were treated and not doing anything about it.... I was tired of hoping for justice. When my moment came, I was ready.[14]

When she refused to give up her seat and the driver called the police to evict her from the bus, the young activist remained firm, refusing to get up. She tells us,

> I kept saying over and over, in my high-pitched voice, 'It's my constitutional right to sit here as much as that lady. I paid my fare, it's my constitutional right!' I knew I was talking back to a white policeman, but I had had enough.[15]

For her actions, Colvin was handcuffed; taken to jail; tried in court; convicted of disobeying the segregation laws, assaulting a policeman, and disturbing the police; and handed over to the custody of her parents. After that, her story was largely ignored and forgotten.

Nine months later, when Rosa Parks refused to give up her seat on a bus and was chosen to be the focus of the Montgomery bus boycott efforts, Colvin reports feeling "left out" and "hurt"[16] but she still thought that maybe Parks, an adult, was the right person for the job. After the boycott had been in operation for two months, Colvin was still ready to play an active role. When she was contacted by attorney Fred Gray and asked to be one of the plaintiffs in a case challenging the constitutionality of segregated busing in the state of Alabama, she immediately agreed. As she tells it,

> I felt that if they really needed someone, I was the right person. It was a chance for me to speak out. I was still angry. I wanted white people to know that I wasn't satisfied with segregation. Black people, too.[17]

Through her testimony, readers learn that Colvin was a willing and active participant throughout the year-long boycott.

Though Colvin was not the chosen "face" of the now-famous boycott in 1955–1956, she was one of several activists standing up against racial injustice on the Montgomery buses from the 1920s to 1950s. When we lose these stories, we forget about "the other no's, the earlier no's, prior anchorings, some of which go back into previous decades."[18] And when we forget these stories, we see the work of the bus boycott largely as the work of men such as Martin Luther King, Jr., Ralph Abernathy, and E.D. Nixon, marginalizing or erasing the activism of women such as Jo Ann Robinson, Geneva Johnson, Viola White, Aurelia Browder, and Mary Louise Smith, the other teenager who refused to give up her seat on a bus. To correct this omission requires a transformative history, one that includes those who have been excluded.[19]

Retrieving lost history is particularly crucial for children's literature, the foundation of young people's understanding of history. As Herbert Kohl demonstrated many years ago, the story of the Montgomery bus boycott was in the past largely told as the story of Parks, a supposedly poor, yet impulsive woman who one day suddenly decided to challenge the system. This story fails to connect her to a large, vibrant, well-organized black community that sustained her throughout the boycott. It is, in Kohl's words, a story that "misrepresents an organized and carefully planned movement for social change as a spontaneous outburst based on frustration and anger."[20] And while more recent children's books about Parks and the Montgomery bus boycott correct this misunderstanding,[21] Colvin's actions should be acknowledged as a significant part of the Montgomery bus boycott and her thoughts a significant perspective on these events.

To correct past omissions, Hoose retrieves Colvin's story and places her squarely within the civil rights movement. He ends the first chapter of his book as follows: "She piled her textbooks on her lap, smoothed her blue dress, and settled back for a five-block ride that not only would change the course of her life but would spark the most important social movement in US history."[22] Such a history runs counter to less-inclusive textbook versions focusing only on famous men and runs counter to older historical accounts that do not acknowledge the pervasive role of community involvement.

Readers find it easy to connect with Claudette Colvin, the moody, outspoken teenager. We understand her anger at students in her high school who turned against her and even taunted her with "It's my constitutional right! It's my constitutional right!"—the sentence she continued to utter as police officers forcibly removed her from the bus. We understand her outrage at being passed over because she was too young, too emotional, and too feisty to be the central figure of the boycott. We understand why, when hearing about Parks's refusal to give up her seat on a bus, she states, "I was thinking, Hey, I did that months ago."[23] And if Colvin cried after losing her court case, a case that was not totally absolved on appeal, we forgive her for being emotional. She tells us, "I cried a lot, and people saw me cry. They kept saying I was 'emotional.'"[24] When Colvin tells us how she felt, we become her empathetic listeners.

Besides appealing to our emotions, Colvin's story raises important questions for young readers. Why didn't the Constitution protect black citizens of Montgomery from the daily humiliation of segregated busing? Why did it take both social action (a bus boycott) and litigation (*Browder v. Gayle*) to stop segregated busing? Why wasn't either social action or litigation enough? The combination of strong emotional feelings and significant social issues draws readers into this past event and makes them care about what happened. As author and critic Marc Aronson notes, Colvin's voice is

> so much closer to the teenage experience—of being liked or not liked, trusted or not trusted, making mistakes in your personal life, but also having the courage and passion to stand up for what you believe is right—than a perfect adult exemplar like Rosa Parks.[25]

When this voice is connected with facts about the past, the result is a believable, convincing narrative testimony—what Hoose refers to as "braiding" a personal life story with factual information.[26]

Marching for Freedom: Walk Together, Children, and Don't You Grow Weary

The 1965 march from Selma to Montgomery brought to national attention how state officials in Alabama systematically denied black citizens their right to vote. This denial was enforced through poll taxes that retroactively applied to each year a person was eligible to vote, stringent literacy tests that were given only to black citizens, and acts of outright hostility and violence. At the same time that black citizens in the South were gaining the right to integrated schooling and integrated busing, the denial of voting rights meant that much remained to be done. Civil rights leaders considered Selma, Alabama to be the right place to challenge state officials. Selma's racist, quick-tempered Sheriff Jim Clark and Alabama's racist governor George Wallace would surely bring matters to a head. Accordingly, Dr. King and other civil rights leaders turned their attention to Selma and the issue of voting rights. As tensions mounted, leaders decided to organize a march from Selma to Montgomery to bring their demands to the state capitol and, through the news media, to the nation at large.

Elizabeth Partridge's *Marching for Freedom* focuses on the experiences of black children and teenagers who give testimony about their participation in the march. This focus serves to "take the past off its pedestal,"[27] provide "an entry point for examining a spectrum of attitudes towards the marches,"[28] and "perfectly balance and complement the contributions of adult figures…that typically dominate the historical accounts of this event."[29] In the process of presenting multiple testimonial accounts of the Selma-to-Montgomery march, Partridge—like Hoose—alerts readers to the role of individual agency; retrieves lost experiences and creates a counter-history; and promotes social-emotional connections, which form the basis of compassion and caring. After reading this book, readers might well reflect on the implications of this event for today's world. As Leonard Marcus points out in his review, "Partridge's stirring history poses another, more immediate, question for a thoughtful reader: Where are today's Selmas and what might a young person do about them?"[30]

As those who were children and teens at the time of the march testify in *Marching for Freedom*, their participation required acknowledging and conquering fear while, at the same time, embracing a strong social purpose. Lynda Blackmon, who was fourteen-years-old at the time, recalls her growing sense of purpose: "The movement was like a fire inside that just kept spreading and spreading and spreading….It was not a fire that you wanted to put out. It was something you wanted to increase and let burn."[31] As the march began, Blackmon stated that she was ready to confront those who had previously assaulted her and denied her the rights she deserved: "I wanted him [Governor Wallace] to see my shaved head and I wanted him to see my face…'cuz it was still swollen and I still had bandages on it."[32] Similarly, Charles Benner recalls overcoming his fear in order to act: "Not that any of us were so brave we weren't scared.…We were scared to death. We acted in spite of the fear."[33] Again and again in *Marching for Freedom*, young people assert their willingness to participate because they felt they were reaching for a higher goal—a better life for themselves and their families. Charles Moton, a thirteen-year-old, summed it up this way: "When I grow up, I want to be a carpenter. And be able to vote. I want my children not to have to be in this mess like we are in now."[34]

While the testimony makes it clear that youngsters were willing participants in the struggle for voting rights, it needs to be acknowledged why their participation was necessary. Years of litigation had proven the judicial process to be ineffective, making social action necessary.[35] Children, who were not the breadwinners of their families or the heads of households, were more willing and able to participate than adults. As a result of their efforts, "the protest movement brought the problem to a head and to the attention and conscience of the nation."[36] In this effort, children and teenagers thus played a pivotal role.

An account of the experiences of young people raises different questions than an account focusing on the experiences of adult civil rights leaders. Few if any of us recognize the names Joanne Blackmon, Lynda Blackmon, Charles Bonner, Charles Mauldin, Bobby Simmons, Sheyann Webb, or Rachel West—youngsters who participated in the Selma-to-Montgomery march. At the same time, most of us immediately recognize the names of the adult participants— King, Coretta Scott King, Ralph Abernathy, John Lewis, and Andrew Young. To investigate the participation of children and teenagers, authors ask questions such as the following: what were children and teenagers doing to support the movement to extend voting rights in the South? Why? How did they and their parents feel about their involvement? How successful were their efforts? The resulting narratives of young people's activism provide different but complementary accounts to other historical narratives. These newer books show that historical accounts reflect the questions authors ask about the past.[37] Partridge alerts readers to her perspective on the first page: "The first time Joanne Blackmon was arrested, she was just ten years old."[38] This focus on youth is consistently maintained throughout the book.

More complex accounts of the Selma-to-Montgomery march incorporate the experiences of young people into the historical narrative. It doesn't place their experiences as a sidebar or an ornamental add-on. Instead, the actions of children—children who were willing to face physical danger and even jail—become an essential part of our historical memory. Such a counter-history, a more inclusive one, reinterprets the past from the perspective of the present. This is a natural and continuous part of historical thinking, a critical process that youngsters need to acquire in order to become effective citizens.[39]

The feelings of young marchers in 1965—feelings of intimidation, fear, outrage, and terror— were held in check by feelings of hope, inspiration, and determination to have a better, more dignified life in the future. Charles Mouldin, a high-school student, describes how he balanced his feelings:

> There's a type of coolness that you develop, a steeling of the nerves so that you can accept whatever happens.…There was no going back, and so you're willing to accept whatever it takes. That's what we were equipped with, just a sense of moral indignity.[40]

While readers have not experienced what Mouldin or the other marchers experienced, they know about strong feelings and they understand why it is sometimes essential to hold them in check because of a higher purpose. The emotions evoked by the marchers also connect us to the events that provoked them. We can ask questions about social issues the marchers were dealing with—issues such as the following: why didn't the Constitution ensure black citizens their right to vote? Why weren't their rights protected? Why did state officials like Sheriff Jim Clark feel empowered to attack black marchers?

The story of the Selma-to-Montgomery march has clear implications for the present. Our Selmas today are the stories of people who have been denied freedom and opportunity that is rightfully theirs. Consider the story of American immigration. In *Denied, Detained, Deported* (2009), Ann Bausum argues that the stories of US immigration denied "offer counterweight to the large and better-known narrative of our nation's more positive immigration history."[41] How and why was this allowed to happen? Why are some people allowed to immigrate while others are excluded? As Bausum rightly concludes, the way to understand this issue is through the stories of individuals. These stories—like those of civil rights activists—are made more engaging and vital through testimony.

Bearing Witness

Testimonial accounts of difficult and painful social events—those of a single individual like Claudette Colvin or groups of individuals like the Selma-to-Montgomery marchers—place readers in a unique situation of bearing witness, responding with empathy, and perhaps passing what was told to them on to others. The immediacy of testimony evokes an emotional response of caring and concern, while the events described raise enduring questions about social issues that should not be ignored. Readers of *Claudette Colvin* and *Marching for Freedom* encounter strong emotional content—feelings of fear and frustration—but they also witness a strong commitment to social justice. The impact of testimony is strong, so strong it might just convince the child I mentioned at the beginning of this chapter that the civil rights movement not only really happened but that it continues to affect the lives of Americans living today.

Teaching Approaches to *Claudette Colvin* and *Marching for Freedom*

Discussion Questions

1. Why is it important for children to connect to stories about the civil rights movement? What is at stakes in their ability to develop an accurate and compassionate historical memory?
2. How are testimonial accounts different from other historical accounts? What are the advantages and disadvantages of relying on testimonial accounts for historical understanding?
3. What books from your youth do you consider "risky historical text"? Do you think this term adequately describes books about young people's activism in the civil rights movement? What, exactly, are the "risks" involved in reading these texts—or *not* reading them?
4. In his review of *Marching for Freedom*, Leonard Marcus argues that we need to consider this question: "Where are today's Selmas and what might a young person do about them?" What do you think are the significant issues of equality, freedom, and tolerance right now? Are they located in specific areas of the country? How can young people work toward solutions to these problems?

Research and Writing Projects

1. With a partner or in a small group, read one of the following testimonial accounts of the civil rights movement written expressly for children: *Through My Eyes* by Ruby Bridges (Scholastic, 1999), *We've Got a Job: The 1963 Birmingham Children's March* by Cynthia Levinson (Peachtree, 2012), *Oh, Freedom! Kids Talk About the Civil Rights Movement with*

the People Who Made It Happen by Casey King and Linda Barrett Osborne (Knopf, 1997), *Claudette Colvin: Twice Toward Justice* by Phillip Hoose (Farrar, Straus and Giroux, 2009), or *Marching for Freedom: Walk Together, Children, and Don't You Grow Weary* by Elizabeth Partridge (Viking, 2009).

After reading the book you selected, prepare a multimodal presentation that addresses the following questions: which examples of individual agency stand out to you? What historical events and experiences did you learn about for the first time? How does this change or inform your understanding of the civil rights movement? What emotional feelings did you have as you read the book? Did testimonial accounts promote feelings of compassion and caring?

2 Each of the children's books listed above contains photographs documenting the events of the civil rights movement. Select several of these photographs to study. Using the Teacher's Guide for *Analyzing Photographs & Prints*, make a three-column chart to record your thoughts. Tell what you observe, reflect, and question. (A chart with sample questions can be found on the website of the Library of Congress. Look for a guide for using primary sources at *loc.gov/teachers*.) Use what you learned from examining these photographs to expand a textbook or Wikipedia account of the event.

3 In two accounts written for children, Russell Freedman has emphasized the importance of ordinary people to the success of the civil rights movement. Read *Freedom Walkers: The Story of the Montgomery Bus Boycott* (Holiday House, 2006) and/or *Because They Marched: The People's Campaign for Voting Rights That Changed America* (Holiday House, 2014). These books enrich historical accounts by retrieving stories that are lost or not well known in order to enrich our understanding of past events. Conduct a series of interviews (field research) with family and community members to determine what they know about both of these events. From where did they get their information? How does the information in these two texts compare to the general or consensus memory of the civil rights movement in your community?

Notes

1 James Damico and Laura Apol, "Using Testimonial Response to Frame the Challenges and Possibilities of Risky Historical Text," *Children's Literature in Education* 39.2 (2008): 141–158.
2 Neil O. Houser, "Critical Literature for Social Studies: Challenges and Opportunities for the Elementary Classroom," *Social Education* 63.4 (1999), 212.
3 Elizabeth Roberts Baer, "A New Algorithm in Evil: Children's Literature in a Post-Holocaust World," *The Lion and the Unicorn* 24.3 (2002), 384.
4 Katharine Capshaw Smith, "Forum: Trauma and Children's Literature," *Children's Literature* 33 (2005), 116.
5 Kenneth Kidd, "A is for Auschwitz: Psychoanalysis, Trauma Theory, and the 'Children's Literature of Atrocity,'" *Children's Literature* 33 (2005), 133.
6 Jacquelyn Dowd Hall, "The Long Civil Rights Movement and the Political Uses of the Past," *Journal of American History* 91.4 (2005), 1262.
7 Allison Berg, "Trauma and Testimony in Black Women's Civil Rights Memoirs: The Montgomery Bus Boycott and the Women Who Started It, Warriors Don't Cry, and From the Mississippi Delta," *Journal of Women's History* 21.3 (2009), 85.
8 Hall, "The Long Civil Rights Movement," 1262.
9 Adam Fairclough, "Historians and the Civil Rights Movement," *Journal of American Studies* 24.3 (1990), 392.
10 Damico and Apol, "Using Testimonial Response."
11 Richard H. King, "Citizenship and Self-Respect: The Experience of Politics in the Civil Rights Movement," *Journal of American Studies* 22.1 (1988), 21.
12 Brooks Barnes, "From Footnote to Fame in Civil Rights History," *The New York Times*, November 26, 2009.

13 Marc Aronson, "The Greatest Story Never Told," *School Library Journal* 56.1 (2010): 30–33.
14 Phillip Hoose, *Claudette Colvin: Twice Toward Justice* (New York: Farrar, Straus, and Giroux, 2009), 27.
15 Ibid., 32.
16 Ibid., 61.
17 Ibid., 74.
18 Paul Hendrickson, "The Ladies Before Rosa," *Rhetoric and Public Affairs* 8.2 (2005), 288.
19 James A. Banks, "Transforming the Mainstream Curriculum," *Educational Leadership* 51.8 (1994): 4–8.
20 Herbert Kohl, "The Story of Rosa Parks and the Montgomery Bus Boycott Revisited," in *Should We Burn Babar?: Essays on Children's Literature and the Power of Stories*, ed. Herbert Kohl (New York: New Press, 1995), 35.
21 See, for example, Russell Freedman's *Freedom Walkers* (2006).
22 Hoose, *Claudette Colvin*, 9.
23 Ibid., 61.
24 Ibid., 45.
25 Aronson, "The Greatest Story Never Told," 33.
26 Hoose, *Claudette Colvin*, 107.
27 Leonard S. Marcus, "Children Who Changed the World," *The New York Times*, January 14, 2010.
28 Elizabeth Bush, "Marching for Freedom: Walk Together, Children and Don't You Grow Weary (review)," *The Bulletin of the Center for Children's Books* 63.5 (2010), 210.
29 Jonathan Hunt, "Marching for Freedom: Walk Together, Children, and Don't You Grow Weary (review)," *The Horn Book Magazine* 85.6 (2009), 700.
30 Marcus, "Children Who Changed the World," 12.
31 Elizabeth Partridge, *Marching for Freedom: Walk Together, Children, and Don't You Grow Weary* (New York: Viking, 2009), 12.
32 Ibid., 37.
33 Ibid., 16.
34 Ibid., 20.
35 David J. Garrow, *Protest and Selma: Martin Luther King, Jr., and the Voting Rights Act of 1965* (New Haven, CT: Yale University Press, 1978).
36 Burke Marshall, "The Protest Movement and the Law," *Virginia Law Review* 51.5 (1965), 791–792.
37 Peter Lee and Denis Shemilt, "'I Just Wish We Could Go Back in the Past and Find Out What Really Happened': Progression in Understanding about Historical Accounts," *Teaching History* 117 (2004): 25–31.
38 Partridge, *Marching for Freedom*, 1.
39 B.A. VanSledright and Peter Afflerbach, "Assessing the Status of Historical Sources: An Exploratory Study of Eight U.S. Students Reading Documents," in *Understanding History: Recent Research in History Education: Vol. 4 International Review of History Education*, ed. Rosalyn Ashby, Peter Gordon, and Peter Lee (London: Routledge Falmer, 2005).
40 Partridge, *Marching for Freedom*, 26.
41 Ann Bausum, *Denied, Detained, Deported: Stories from the Dark Side of American Immigration* (Washington, DC: National Geographic, 2009), 10.

3

"TOMORROW'S GREAT MEETING PLACE"

Collective Autobiographies of the Civil Rights Movement

Elizabeth Rodrigues

> It is essential to resist the depiction of history as the work of heroic individuals in order for people today to recognize their potential agency as a part of an ever-expanding community of struggle.
>
> Angela Y. Davis[1]

In a 2014 interview published in *The Nation*, civil rights activist and scholar Angela Davis reminds us that what affects the meanings and legacies of the US civil rights movement is the form, as well as the facts, of the stories we tell about it. More to the point, it matters whether scholars and writers depict the civil rights movement as the story of a life or of lives. As reactions to Ava DuVernay's 2014 film *Selma* make clear, imagining the movement through the lives of its many activists constitutes not just an aesthetic shift but also a direct challenge to traditional historical narratives that privilege the contributions of well-known individuals. DuVernay's revision of the original script, her decision to add twenty-seven (mostly female) characters, led some commentators to claim that the resulting narrative diminished the contributions of its presumptive (male) protagonists—Martin Luther King, Jr. and Lyndon B. Johnson.[2] Indeed, this "diminishment" is precisely the point for a history that imagines the civil rights movement as the story of a life is formally constrained from the outset—to a beginning and ending that is limited to biological life, to a perception of individual agency as the determining force in social change, and to the effect of portraying the selected life as exceptional and so implying that its achievements are unrepeatable. This chapter considers how collective autobiography reimagines the narrative form of the civil rights movement through its exchange of the third-person, biographical, "he"/"she" narrative of civil rights as a hero-driven movement for first-person, "I" and "we" narratives that insist on the contingencies, conflicts, and continuing trajectories of activism that interracial organizing of the 1960s seeded.

The narrative form of movement representation is epistemologically consequential: it affects not just our analysis of US history but also our understanding of present-day political organizing around racial and economic justice. Jacquelyn Dowd Hall, in her landmark essay "The Long Civil Rights Movement and the Political Uses of the Past," argues that "the dominant narrative of the civil rights movement…embedded in heritage tours, museums, public rituals, textbooks, and various artifacts of mass culture—distorts and suppresses as much as it reveals."[3] Kathryn Nasstrom provides a concise version of this dominant narrative:

> The civil rights movement began in the mid-1950s, its origins marked by the U.S.

Supreme Court's landmark 1954 ruling against racial segregation and by the Montgomery Bus Boycott of 1955–1956, when fifty thousand black citizens refused to ride the city's buses and eventually brought an end to segregated transport. The events in Montgomery inaugurated a decade of collective action, inspired by the charismatic leadership of Martin Luther King Jr. and sustained by the heroism, dignity, and sacrifice of African Americans. Animating the movement was a powerful moral vision of nonviolent direct action and the goal of an interracial democracy. From Montgomery the grand narrative moves forward by a series of dramatic episodes, chief among them the desegregation of Central High School in Little Rock, the lunch counter sit-ins, the Freedom Rides, the Birmingham campaign, the March on Washington and King's "I have a dream" speech, and the voting rights march from Selma to Montgomery. Key legislative victories were secured during this wave of protest, notably the Civil Rights Act of 1964 and the Voting Rights Act of 1965....Black Americans and the nation as a whole took a decided step forward. In the mid-1960s...the movement began to unravel, and 1968 brought the symbolic end of the movement with the tragic assassination of Martin Luther King. The Black Power era serves as a "tragic epilogue" to the grand narrative, lacking the moral clarity of the earlier movement and without its efficacy.[4]

This version of the story, beginning with *Brown v. Board* and ending with the passage of the Voting Rights Act, implicitly contends that action taken through legal, governmental (and specifically federal) processes constitutes the defining achievements of the movement. This narrative further implies that the movement is over because its leader has been assassinated and the law has been changed, implying that formal equality before the law constitutes the scope of activist ambition. Furthermore, all that followed the anti-segregation work of King and the Southern Christian Leadership Conference (SCLC) in the mid-1960s is presented as a decline into divisive rhetoric and threatened violence.

The scholarship of historians such as Hall, Nasstrom, and Peniel Joseph calls attention to the political effects of this declension narrative of civil rights history, arguing that its blindness to continuing trajectories of activism has had a role in creating a public sphere that seems stalled on the issue of racial equality.[5] In its place, Hall proposes the "long civil rights movement," with roots in the Double V campaign of World War II and branches in the Black Power Movement, women's/womanist movements, and nationalist movements among Asian Americans and Chicanas. In historical and political terms, this longer narrative is *harder*: "Harder to celebrate as a natural progression of American values. Harder to cast as a satisfying morality tale. Most of all, harder to simplify, appropriate, and contain."[6] Questioning the straightforward narrative models of developmental progress and the morality tale, Hall suggests that new stories of the movement will need new forms of narrative to capture the thematic and temporal complexity of social change.

Literary critics have begun to look for this harder narrative of the long civil rights movement in the formal innovations of post-1960s African American literature and in autobiographies of movement activists. Christopher Metress, Sharon Monteith, and James Robert Patterson have considered how contemporary novels engage in the project of extending the temporal trajectories of the movement, re-formulating concepts of black leadership, and challenging plot-driven representations of social change that make progress seem destined and inevitable.[7] Margo Perkins has also contributed a book-length study of three individual activists' autobiographies, highlighting how their portrayals of black women's experiences in the 1960s and 1970s lay the groundwork for the critique offered by long movement scholarship.[8] So far, though, literary scholars have not considered the mode of collective autobiography, a form that embodies the polyvocality, horizontality, and extended temporality that the lens of the long civil rights movement brings into focus.

In terms of the historical content each offers as well as the formal structures each proposes, *Deep in Our Hearts: Nine White Women in the Freedom Movement* (2000) and *Hands on the Freedom Plow: Personal Accounts by Women in SNCC* (2010) illustrate collective autobiography as the central narrative form of the long civil rights movement. Both volumes revise the subjectivity, emplottedness, and temporality of the movement's dominant story. As collections of women's civil rights memoir, *Deep* and *Hands* negotiate subjectivity in the contexts of individual identity and collective identification, juxtaposing the "I" with the "we" as emerging movements attempt to re-assemble a "we" out of "I"s. Through the varied and contingent paths to activism that these narratives represent, they replace the figure of the exceptional leader and destined movement with ordinary citizens transformed through commitment to action. In addition, by highlighting the intergenerational nature of movement activism and the relational dynamic of activist identity, these narratives represent a story that is very much ongoing and unfinished. I use the term "collective autobiography" to designate *Deep* and *Hands* as textual forms. Collectivity implicitly intervenes on the typical generic conventions of autobiography, which may be glossed as a story about the self, told by the self, that tends to, in varying degrees, reify the agential Western subject.[9] Through collective autobiographical form, these works constitute an intervention in both the individual-centric historiography of the movement and a larger culture of individualism struggling to remember and re-formulate collective modes of political action.

Collective Autobiography as Historiographical Intervention

Both through their form and content, *Deep* and *Hands* arise from and contribute to what Nasstrom aptly describes as "a dialogue between memory and history."[10] These collective and collaborative autobiographical projects speak back to the oversights and over-reaches of previous historical narratives. Women's experiences were largely absorbed into the broad, hero-centric narrative of early histories of the movement. As Winifred Breines has observed, the white male memoirs of new left leaders celebrate the early 1960s and express almost nothing but pessimism and condemnation of the developments of the late 1960s.[11] They also emphasize the importance of leadership decisions and include little or nothing on the day-to-day work of field activists. The work of feminist historians, such as Breines and Sara Evans, called attention to the range of women's contribution to the movement and the differences of their experience. Through this work, another important angle of difference and analysis became apparent—the difference between black and white women's experiences.

Documenting women's experiences has spurred critical revision of the civil rights narrative. *Deep* and *Hands* explicitly and implicitly constitute substantial revisions to the consensus narrative of the civil rights movement. By centering the experiences of black, white, and Latina women, these books highlight the need for more nuanced attention to the subjectivity, emplottedness, and temporality of movement narrative. Both collections focus on the experiences of women in the Student Nonviolent Coordinating Committee (SNCC), each working to chisel the monolithic designation of "women's experience" into a cascade of specific experiences that illuminate and challenge the assumptions of movement historiography and solidarity-based activism.

While both employ the mode of collective autobiography to challenge assumptions, they offer very different perspectives. *Deep* is composed of nine autobiographical narratives that focus on complicating the perception of white women's work in the movement. Collaboratively edited by all nine contributors, it paints a portrait of white women's civil rights activism as regionally and socioeconomically diverse, complicating the grand narrative in form as well as in content. *Hands* takes the project of inclusive and expansive representation much further. The five editors, all activists themselves, foreground such inclusion in the introduction: "The fifty-two women speaking in this book represent a wide variety of movement participants—black, white, and Latina; young and old; southern and northern—a reflection of the composition of the Movement itself."[12] The inclusion of the category of Latina indicates that a binary notion of racial identity has been revised as multiracial. Although no Asian American activists' personal narratives are included, there are reports throughout the book that they were indeed present, if in small numbers.[13] Mary Varela, cited in previous movement historiography, such as Evans's *Personal Politics*, is here named as Maria Varela.[14] *Hands* continues to propose another iteration of the SNCC women's "we" through its paratextual framing of the narratives it collects. It divides its fifty-five narratives by fifty-two women into nine parts that span the pre- and post–Voting Rights Act divide temporally and cross the North/South divide geographically. These parts suggest a beginning and ending point for the *broader* story that these individual narratives constitute, the new beginning and ending suggesting that the productive recognition of racial difference structures and enables an ongoing history of activism.

The "I" of Activism and the "We" of Movement

In "Uncovered and Without Shelter, I Joined This Movement for Freedom," Bernice Johnson Reagon offers a brief but provocative meditation on the choice between the first-person singular and plural in the language of civil rights activism. As she begins to lead fellow activists in "I'll Overcome," a song she knows is a movement anthem and one that she is familiar with as a church hymn, she is stopped by a more experienced activist, who tells her, "We don't say 'I'll overcome'; we say, 'We shall overcome.'" Reagon goes on to reflect,

> I would work out later that while *we* might express a collective, it was not always a wise replacement for *I*. When Black people sang 'I'll Overcome' in a group, the collective was expressed, because with all present singing 'I,' the group was there, formed by individuals stating their commitment or condition.[15]

In "Getting Out the News," Mary E. King echoes Reagon's insistence on the importance of "I" and "we" as relational, rather than mutually exclusive, stances toward the struggle for freedom:

> Although nonviolent movements require group discipline, they also rest on personal commitment, making such mobilizations inherently averse to top-down command structures. Since the decision to accept the penalties for nonviolent resistance cannot be externally imposed, and no one can force another person voluntarily to accept reprisals for their acts of noncooperation such as civil disobedience, the judgment of a group begins with the conviction of the individual.[16]

These statements speak to the complexity of activist subjectivity and movement historiography, for collective action is invariably driven by individual commitment. Following the analytical lead of these two writers, we can see collective civil rights autobiography as a continuing interrogation of the "I" and the "we" of the civil rights movement, which demonstrates the continued political importance of both the personal and the collective through their exploration of subjectivity.

Collective civil rights autobiography stages a continual, and productive, contestation of the right to speak in the first-person plural. The proposed "we" of the interracial civil rights movement of the early 1960s was, by some accounts, as broad as all humanity, rhetorically grounding its political project in universalist tenets. Yet over time, this broad claiming of a movement "we" proved to obscure important differences of gender, race, and class. The overreaching "we" becomes the peril of social movements organized around identity categories, discursively reproducing elisions of difference. Memoirs by movement women not only call attention to the gendered nature of their experience but also provide a subjective analysis, offering unique insight into the divisions that threaten social movements. As Breines suggests, ending these silences through personal accounts serves a future-oriented political purpose: "The silences suggest the tender spots any future democratic, multiracial, and feminist movement committed to women's, peoples' of color, and gay and lesbian equality must address."[17] Breines envisions personal narratives as the foundation of future politics. The gap between promises of liberation and equality for this broad "we" and the lived experiences of women in the movement was the birthing ground of new projects of activism and new forms of activist subjectivity.

Deep engages in this process of revising the "I" of movement narrative by racializing white women's experiences in SNCC—forcing us to see the experience of these women as *white* women's experiences in SNCC rather than simply *women's* experiences in SNCC. The foreword by Barbara Ransby positions the book as a "narrative addendum to the work of scholars like David Roediger, Richard Delgado, and Noel Ignatiev, who have encouraged us to interrogate the historical and cultural meaning of whiteness."[18] Interesting continuities emerge when whiteness is self-consciously engaged as a racial and ethnic identity. In Constance Curry's "Wild Geese to the Past," this racialization reveals a surprising continuity between ethnic white experience and civil rights activism. Curry begins her essay by locating herself as an ethnic white: "I have been acutely aware of my Irish roots as far back as memory allows."[19] She quotes lines from a poem by an Irish revolutionary and states,

> I have often thought that these lines could have come straight from the Freedom Movement of the 1960s....the Irish struggle got planted deep in my heart and soul at an early age...and its lessons and music and poetry were easily transferred to the southern freedom struggle.[20]

Racializing white experience allows this point of political connection to emerge, a connection that also suggests a longer and more varied pre-history of activism.

While *Deep* reveals a number of shared dynamics across white women's experience, it also destabilizes any notion of a coherent white experience. Joan C. Browning's "Shiloh Witness" exemplifies previously obscured dynamics of white experience of the type that this collection uncovers. As a poor Southern white, Browning pays a high price for her involvement in the movement. Because of her activism, her scholarship to college is revoked. Needing to find a new way to finance her education, she writes to a Northern college to apply for their Southern civil rights scholarship, only to discover it is for blacks only: "They said they had never heard of a white southern civil rights activist."[21] The tone of this passage is not to question that such a scholarship would be reserved for blacks but to register that, even in the discourse of supposed political allies, her unacknowledged position renders her invisible.

Hands continues the work of diversifying the subjective positions of activism, using the collective form to allow divergent and sometimes discordant voices to co-exist. Part 1 of *Hands* consists of a single narrative, Gwendolyn Zoharah Simmons's (aka Gwendolyn Robinson) "From Little Memphis Girl to Mississippi Amazon." The editors explain their decision to highlight this narrative as a gateway text because "it spans several years of SNCC history and incorporates themes found in the remaining fifty-four contributions."[22] They further describe the narrative as chronicling "[Simmons's] personal growth from a gradual and somewhat timid entrance into activism to becoming a self-assured project director."[23] By privileging this narrative as a first and stand-alone section, the editors suggest that in some crucial way, it represents the kind of story *Hands* is bringing to light. Simmons is presented as an activist whose commitments to and ultimate achievements in the movement emerged not from a foreordained sense of fate but somewhat accidentally.[24] The activist, in this portrait, becomes exceptional through participation in collective action rather than being innately exceptional. By opening with this single story of a black activist, a self-proclaimed "Amazon" who confronted sexism along with racial tensions as project director in Mississippi, *Hands* recovers the black woman activist as the central agent of the civil rights movement and creates an activist "I" whose achievements arise out of unexpected decisions and contingencies as much as stated ambition.

"Black Power: Issues of Continuity, Change, and Personal Identity, 1964–1969," the final section of the collection, embodies an intersectional approach to identity that marks how movement activism spurred political projects of self-reflection. "Black Power" is thus not a divisive claiming of group exceptionality but rather the basis of future coalitional activism. Of the four narratives in this section, only the final one is by a black woman. Of the other three, two are by Latinas, and one is by a white Jewish woman. Placing these narratives by non-blacks in a final section ostensibly on Black Power suggests that the politics of Black Power remain relevant because of the productive evaluations of difference they helped to surface. Elizabeth (Betita) Sutherland Martinez's "Neither Black nor White" opens the section. Her perspective on debates concerning whites participating in the movement gently critiques the limits of their racial vision and reframes them as harbingers of identity politics: "As far as anyone seems to remember, we [Martinez and Varela] were classified as white, even though I did not consider myself either white or black."[25] She describes writing and circulating among SNCC leadership a position paper in June 1967 titled "Black, White, and Tan." She received even less response than King and Hayden received to an earlier position paper they had written about women's role in the movement. After leaving SNCC, Martinez begins a period of activism based on her identity as a Chicana, a period she describes entering "as an individual" tasked with "finding myself in new, Chicana ways."[26]

For Martinez, this process of turning to self leads to a revised sense of identification with blacks. She portrays this process as an ongoing dialogue with herself. Traveling to Mexico,

> [a] voice inside me said, 'You can be Martinez here. It feels like home!' Later, another voice would say… 'The brown people were born colonized, not enslaved like blacks, but white supremacy dominates both.' 'So the two prisons are really one. And the fight is really one,' said the last and loudest voice.'[27]

Martinez talks to herself in the same way that the book speaks through her. The culminating statement of this dialogue, the "last and loudest voice," is the one who uses individual difference as a path to recognition of shared oppression. This recognition, Martinez claims, is "tomorrow's great meeting place."[28]

Both at the level of form and the level of the individual narrative, *Hands* also highlights the relationality of identity—the degree to which individuals are defined through their relationships to others rather than being the independent creators of selves. Although it is now a commonplace of literary criticism to point out that all autobiographical narratives are, at some level, relational, *Hands* foregrounds the relationality of identity as central to its narrative project. Through this emphasis on interconnectedness, it counteracts leader-centric portraits of the movement. However, at the same time as this collection emphasizes that individuals are shaped by collective identities and communities, it also reflects upon the complicated relationship between the "I" and the "we" of social movements, suggesting that collective identity never supersedes individual identity as a site of commitment but must work in tandem with it.

The collective autobiography of *Hands* also revises many of the defining characteristics of what has been called the generational autobiography of the 1960s. John Hazlett proposes the concept of the generational autobiography in his reading of memoirs by the white male leaders of 1960s left movements as

> a narrative of the generation as told by one who defines the self in terms of generational identity….often, the texts slip back and forth between the 'I' and the 'we' so fluidly that the distinction between the autobiographer's personal story and the collective history of the generation to which he or she belongs is completely blurred.[29]

As feminist theorists and historians have observed, the slippage from "I" to "we" is always a political act. As Hazlett explains, "the generational autobiographer's own story is meant to serve as the narrative that will ultimately define the public identity of the author's peers" and "contemporary readers inevitably perceive them, whether sympathetically or unsympathetically as bids for power."[30] The genre tends, in Hazlett's view, to develop dialogically, with each wave of autobiographies implicitly or explicitly responding to the last. Generational autobiography rarely presents a coherent portrait and is instead characterized by internal debate over the representative generational identity. This frame of reading illuminates the central dynamic of *Hands*. As generational autobiographies, they participate in an ongoing dialogue over how the experience of working in the civil rights movement will be described, defined, and leveraged in future political projects and historical accounts.

Hands revises several of the tropes Hazlett finds characteristic of generational autobiography of the 1960s. Formally, they forestall the substitution of self for generation through the incorporation of multiple authors writing and re-writing the definition of an era. By making the identities they compose explicitly relational, they challenge the concept of a single representational identity of a generation and force us to grapple with the heterogeneity of the historical moment. On a narrative level, these texts do not conform to the arc of the conversion narrative, which involves an epiphany in which prior beliefs are discarded and a "violent casting off of the narrator's old self" occurs.[31] The memoirists of *Hands* acknowledge the heartbreak (for whites asked to leave SNCC) and disillusionment (of blacks frustrated with the lack of real change interracial activism achieved) but never disavow the selves that undertook the political work that for them defines the generation. The collection speaks from and to a different historical moment; the failures and frustrations are distanced, and the need to reclaim and repackage the legacy of that period in order to inspire future generations of activism is paramount.

The trope of generational autobiography most unsettled by *Hands* is the trope of the generation as self-consciously exceptional and isolated from the generations before and after it. *Hands* gives us a portrait of the movement largely composed of young people, many of whom recall having a sense of themselves as being part of a unique and history-making generation, but never solely defined by youth, rebellion, or a sense of exceptionality. One relationship spotlighted by these collections is that of child to parent, a source of influence that works in both directions. Carolyn Daniels begins her narrative this way: "I got involved in the movement and SNCC because of my son, Roy."[32] Many other narratives start by situating the subject in relation to familial elders. Zoharah Simmons, for example, begins "From Little Memphis Girl to Mississippi Amazon" with an extended passage that attributes her sense of a black woman's role in history to a matrilineal practice of storytelling: "Grandma Lucy told my grandmother the stories of slavery as she grew up. My grandmother told them to me. I have told them to my daughter."[33] Her subjectivity is profoundly shaped by the relationship formed through this storytelling. At the same time as it empowers her, though, her relationship to her grandmother complicates her relationship to the movement. She seeks to avoid becoming involved in the movement so as not to jeopardize her college scholarship and disappoint her grandmother, who takes great pride in her granddaughter's educational accomplishments and believes higher education is essential to her future. Simmons writes, "Her parting words to me were to not get into any trouble with boys or to let anything pull me away from my school work. I promised!"[34] Thus, when she is required to contact her grandmother after being put on probation by college administrators for being arrested during a sit-in, "Making that call was one of the worst moments of my life....She said I had disgraced the family and reminded me that I was the first person in our family ever to be arrested."[35] This comes as a confusing surprise:

> Hadn't she told me the stories about Grandma Lucy during slavery and her own struggles as a sharecropper with unscrupulous white landowners?...Why wasn't she proud that I was standing up to them and fighting for what was rightfully ours?...I was heartbroken.[36]

The depth of Simmons's sadness speaks to the power of this relationship in her life and emphasizes that activists never acted in a vacuum of self-appointed destiny but always within contexts of family and relationship.

Cathy Cade's "Caught in the Middle" demonstrates the centrality of the parent-child relationship to understandings of activist work. "Caught" alternates between Cady's own present-day narrative of her experiences in the Albany Movement of 1963, her field notes and letters to her parents (one from jail) during that period, and an extensive excerpt from her father's journal of his trip to Albany to try to get her out of jail and convince her to come home. This collage of sources vividly depicts the activist as young person, still composing her own identity in terms of her relationship to her parents. Cade's letters to her parents are striking for their difference in tone from her field notes. Her field notes have a tone of ambivalence and generally stick to chronicling events as they proceed, taking special note of arrests and acts of violence. By contrast, the letters from jail downplay danger and stay "on message." She switches between the voice of adolescent daughter, writing, "I'm fine, am losing weight!"[37] and activist-educator, admonishing her parents to support SNCC's work because "[i]f this frustration and anger isn't organized and channeled, even more violence will occur with no beneficial results for the Negro community."[38] The shift in tone highlights the performative dimension of activist identity, demonstrating it is not a unique feature of retrospective narrative but a persistent marker of the relational dynamic of identity. At the time, parents were a key audience. Cade's narrative ends with a reflection not only on how the events of that summer shaped her relationship to her father for the remainder of his life but also on how he shaped her relationship to her own experiences. Reviewing her letters and his notes after having become a mother herself, Cady finds herself much more sympathetic to a father who, focused at the time only on his daughter's safety and apparent rejection of his values, seemed clueless about what she was trying to do.

The "I" of activism is never self-contained. Nor is it foreordained. Through their depictions of the role of contingency in shaping individual and collective destiny, these collections challenge the dominant emplotment of the activist life story and the story of the movement. To examine plot as an element of narrative form is to call attention to how the process of constructing stories is a site of critical agency in which new understandings of and relationships to the past emerge. Following historian and theorist Hayden White, this reading understands narrative as always being an intervention, selecting and privileging certain events as significant and causally linked steps between a beginning and an end, and as always seeking to construct and convey a moral order structuring the unfolding of historical events. These acts of selection and interpretation constitute what White terms "emplotment" and implicitly form arguments about the nature of the people, events, and processes they represent.[39] Understanding how the underlying narrative forms of historical representation construct cause, effect, and agency is a critical task for students of civil rights literature. As David Scott proposes with respect to postcolonial critique, analysis of narrative form is central to continuing the creative social work of the civil rights movement because "the relation of pasts, presents, and futures is a relation constituted in narrative discourse."[40] Understanding the role of contingency both in the lives of individual activists and in the progress of the movement as a whole helps to dismantle certain implications of the dominant civil rights narrative by changing its plot structure. Emphasizing contingency and the repetitive work of activism rather than climactic moments challenges the idea that progress is an inevitable result of the passage of time, that certain individuals are natural leaders upon whose shoulders the responsibility for activism lies, and that individual effort is adequate to address structural injustice.

For some activists, the choice to become involved with the movement does feel like the next logical step in a destiny laid out by familial example or internal desire, but remaining active with the movement requires relinquishing the expectation of control over one's life. In "Freedom-Faith," Prathia Hall indicates that she identified strongly with activism as a destiny, writing, "I had been born and raised for the struggle for human justice, freedom, and equality."[41] She leaves her hometown of Philadelphia to go south "convinced that was God's work and also my sacred calling."[42] The language of being "born for" and having a "calling" imbues her participation with the sense of a plot being played out. Yet, living this plot requires embracing radical uncertainty. Through her work, she develops a guiding concept of "freedom-faith," learned from local black women in the community in which she works: "The primary lesson that I received from those black sages was that of faith for living in life-threatening circumstances....The freedom-faith fueled the fight."[43] Placing faith not in a successful outcome or personal safety but in the need for justice, these activists illustrate the alternate emplotment of contingency. In "Resistance U," Faith Holsaert articulates a similar moment-to-moment understanding of movement work:

> As I sat on my folding chair [at her first mass meeting], only three of whose legs rested on the uneven ground, I thought, *This is what our work is: moment added to moment, sandwiches and scary car rides, citizenship lessons added to citizenship lessons, staff reports week after week.*[44]

The image of the three-legged chair conveys the precarious mixture of a sense of rootedness in interpersonal relationships and the reality of permanent uncertainty, which is also a source of potential. Her description focuses on the incremental nature of steady work, not milestones in a grand narrative. The movement, in this view, is not a story to be completed but a practice to be lived and documented.

Browning's "Shiloh Witness" provides an alternate view, widely shared among the subjects, that she was thrust into the movement unexpectedly as a result of actions she did not know would come to define her life. Her stark reflection illustrates that small decisions can lead to big commitments and life-altering consequences. The fault lines of Browning's subjective position as a poor white woman within the black freedom movement are formally reflected in her emphasis on the contingencies and consequences of her decisions. She writes of her decision to attend a black church, the act that gets her scholarship revoked: "If asked today to choose between attending that church and completing my education, I am not sure which choice I would make."[45] This offers a pointed and poignant contrast to narratives of other activists who describe their entry into activism as recognition of something fated and inevitable. It also highlights how the cost and rewards of activism are split differentially along class lines. Other activists from more well-connected and financially stable family backgrounds were able to parlay their social iconoclasm into prestige and careers. Browning represents her choice to leave the well-traveled path of typical white Southernness as the defining choice of her life: "The personal history I was writing made me an outcast in a white southern society, while my white skin sometimes separated me from black people. I became, at once, irrevocably, racially homeless."[46] The agency she exerts in this choice contrasts sharply with her lack of choice about her skin color. Her choice to live as an anti-racist Southerner, metaphorically figured as writing a life history, cannot be productively reconciled with her whiteness, figured as a skin that separates her from the people with whom she was politically and morally aligned. She cannot cast her participation in the movement as fate or any kind of coherent narrative, for it has led to a life of contradictions and unresolved questions of identity.

Browning's experience is far from singular; many of the activists find themselves economically and morally separated from the dominant narratives of middle-class life. Many subjects recount being forced out of college, either through disciplinary action or through the demands of the movement on their time. Annette Jones White finds herself expelled from Albany State University after being arrested, even though she was such a model student that she had been named "Miss Albany State." While White is able to resume her education at Spelman College, the experience of finding herself on the outside of the institution she had once represented underlines the recognition that individual merit does not exempt one from the social rules of the racial status quo.[47] Others find that they can no longer associate themselves with the self-centered focus on career achievement after their intense experience of meaningful work in the movement. As Mary E. King, with a tone of pride rather than loss, claims at the close of her narrative,

> Having experienced the exhilaration of working on issues much grander than my own desires—while usually feeling that I was doing more for myself than anyone else, because of the intertwining of belief and purpose—I later found it almost impossible to think of what would 'help a career.'[48]

Even when spared from the worst consequences of their activism, which, it must not be forgotten, included physical injury and death, these activists find themselves forging a new plot of selfhood that puts them in conflict with the society in which they had been raised.

The continuing growth of activist identity constitutes a temporal challenge to the consensus civil rights narrative, which posits that the movement was roughly contained to the decade between *Brown v. Board* and the passage of the Voting Rights Act. These women's narratives suggest a much more complex timeline. In the mosaic of widely varying experience these narratives form, there is no clear-cut beginning or ending but instead multiple histories of relationship, reflection, and resistance. For some, however, leaving SNCC did indeed signify the end of the movement. A deeply felt sense of loss pervades some of the narratives in both collections, humanizing the activists and illustrating that activist subjectivity is complex and affectively demanding. While early historical analysis, for example, posits that second-wave feminism was launched by activists who moved between civil rights and new left organizations, for many individuals, it was not a smooth transition between civil rights and feminist activism. Their participation in the movement awakened them to sexist dynamics in the culture at large but also left them feeling aged and exhausted by the struggle against racism. Elaine DeLott Baker describes this trajectory in her narrative, "They Sent Us This White Girl." After volunteering in Mississippi, she returns north to New York City where student activists at Columbia urge her to get involved. Though only a few years older than them, Baker perceives them as "so young and immature" and feels she had "exhausted my interest in politics as personal adventure."[49] In a comment on how the assumptions of historical research can overlook the realistic limits of human beings, she states,

> I have been asked by feminist historians why more of us who are considered to be 'early feminists' did not go on to leadership positions in the women's movement….To shift my identity, commitment, and energy from the freedom struggle to the women's struggle was

not something I could do, especially at a time when I was still grieving over my separation from the movement. The freedom struggle was flame; all else was shadow.[50]

For some, the desire for social change was not straightforwardly transferable between causes, and individuals were not unlimited founts of energy and hope. In "My Real Vocation," Dorothy M. Zellner writes that

> [l]eaving SNCC was one of the most painful things that ever happened to me. It meant not only the loss of my life's work, but it was also the end of my five-year proud association with SNCC, the most creative, funny, innovative, daring, fearless group of people I ever met.[51]

Those who had the deepest commitment to the civil rights movement were the most likely to be hurt and confused by the end of their participation in it. As Baker and Zellner attest, the emotional dynamic of grief and loss pervades their perception of other contemporary political developments.

For many others, though, movement work was just the beginning. In "We Turned This Upside-Down Country Right Side Up," Joann Christian Mants claims such a trajectory: "As I look back I see that the commitment is there, wherever I might live. It is a continuous thing, not just for Albany, Georgia. The movement continues wherever you find yourself."[52] Even a cursory browsing of the biographical endnotes that accompany each narrative confirms that the activists have found themselves in a variety of projects that grew from their tested commitment to justice, including peace activism, fighting mass incarceration, and labor organizing. In place of a traditional career, Mary E. King describes a continuing commitment to the contingent unfolding of work for justice as defining her life after the movement: "My search has been to find again the unity that was part of my movement experience, when we were able to bring ideas into action at the same time that we let our actions give rise to new concepts."[53] Jean Wiley structures her narrative as a "Letter to My Adolescent Son," in which she seeks to extend the movement's legacy by instilling in him a knowledge of her work in SNCC so that he can find his "rightful place within our struggle" for "[t]he struggle continues. It must."[54]

Revising the First-Person Plural

If, as many of the activists whose personal narratives make up these collective autobiographies attest, one of the primary goals of the movement was to create a new world, one of the requisite tasks before literary critics is to examine the narrative modes through which the making of this new world is to be imagined, represented, and understood. As retrospective narratives that are necessarily as much about the present as they are about the past, these collections are both a result of and a contribution to a decades-long process of revising the first-person plural. In both their emphasis on polyvocality and their self-conscious attempt to bring previously hidden narratives of activist experience and political commitment to the surface, these collections constitute a unique form of civil rights memoir that uses the political and theoretical tools of feminisms to intervene on their narratives of identity. Individual-centric narrative forms enact a double erasure on civil rights history, obscuring not only the contributions of other individuals but also the ongoing mechanics of social change. These twenty-first-century narratives of 1960s activism offer models of activist identity that emphasize the multiple routes to and trajectories of engagement with social movements. These activist selves form narratives of political commitment that revise the past in order to speak directly to the current political moment and to activists-in-the-making.

These collections provide students of the movement an invaluable opportunity to parse and interpret the primary sources of activists' autobiography, constructing their own interpretive narratives of a history very much alive in their own day.

Approaches to Teaching Collective Autobiography and the Civil Rights Movement

Deep and *Hands* offer a range of entry points for discussion and flexible options for incorporation into classroom activity or written work. While the collections are likely too long to be assigned in full, selections can be used to form a coherent group of readings or to complement other texts. What follows are suggestions for approaching and contextualizing selected essays.

Structuring Reading Selections

1. Select one narrative from each of the nine sections of *Hands* in order to capture a range of experiences that vary by geographic region and time.
2. Focus on one section of *Hands* to offer an in-depth look at one region and period of movement activism.
3. Juxtapose two long narratives from *Deep*, one from a woman who grew up in the South and the other in the North.

Discussion Questions

1. Brainstorm a list of things you already know about the civil rights movement. Where did you get this knowledge? What, specifically, in the narratives you have read, added to or even contradicted your understanding?
2. Perform an in-class close reading that compares retrospective narrative to incorporated documents that activists used to record their experiences in real time. In what ways does the plot constructed retrospectively revise the experiences of the moment? *Suggested examples*: Joan Trumpauer Mulholland's "Diary of a Freedom Rider," Cathy Cade's "Caught in the Middle," and Judy Richardson's "SNCC: My Enduring 'Circle of Trust.'"
3. How is leadership portrayed? What models of leadership do these texts highlight?
4. Compare selected narratives to present-day representations of activism—for example, blog posts or news articles concerning Black Lives Matter or Antifa.

Research and Writing Projects

1. Compare the experiences of two activists whose experiences are in some way divergent in terms of race, age, geographical location, or socio-economic position. How do these differences influence the story the narrator tells about the civil rights movement? *Suggested pairings*: Gwendolyn Zoharah Simmons's "From Little Memphis Girl to Mississippi Amazon" and Mary E. King's "Getting Out the News," Joan C. Browning's "Shiloh Witness" and Emmie Schrader Adams's "From Africa to Mississippi," and Janie Culbreth Rambeau's "Ripe for the Picking" and Joyce Ladner's "Standing Up for Our Beliefs."
2. Compare the plot dynamics of one or more autobiographical narratives to another representational form such as fiction, film, or journalism. First, identify what each narrative presents as the beginning, middle, and end of the story. Then, pay close attention to what forces or events seem to be moving the plot from one stage to the next. Form an interpretive argument about how this plot structure influences perception of the movement.

3 Locate newspaper articles from the 1960s concerning sit-ins, freedom rides, or voting registration drives. Compare these articles to selected narratives in *Deep* and/or *Hands*. The library will likely have relevant resources, or the online archives of newspapers, such as *The New York Times* and *The Guardian*, could be consulted.
4 Note all geographical places mentioned in selected narratives and mark them on a map (print or digital). What does the geographical range of activism suggest about the nature of the movement? Does it challenge your expectations or confirm them?

Notes

1 Frank Barat, "A Q&A with Angela Davis on Black Power, Feminism and the Prison-Industrial Complex," *The Nation*, August 27, 2014.
2 Brittney Cooper, "Maureen Dowd's Clueless White Gaze: What's Really Behind the *Selma* Backlash," *Salon*, January 21, 2015.
3 Jacquelyn Dowd Hall, "The Long Civil Rights Movement and the Political Uses of the Past," *The Journal of American History* 91.4 (2005), 1233.
4 Kathryn L. Nasstrom, "Between Memory and History: Autobiographies of the Civil Rights Movement and the Writing of Civil Rights History," *The Journal of Southern History* 74.2 (2008), 330.
5 See Joseph's "Waiting till the Midnight Hour: Reconceptualizing the Heroic Period of the Civil Rights Movement, 1954–1965," *Souls* 2.2 (March 2000): 6–17.
6 Hall, "The Long Civil Rights Movement," 1235.
7 See Metress's "Making Civil Rights Harder: Literature, Memory, and the Black Freedom Struggle," Monteith's "Revisiting the 1960s in Contemporary Fiction: 'Where Do We Go From Here?'", and Patterson's "Exodus Politics: Civil Rights and Leadership in African American Literature and Culture."
8 Margo V. Perkins, *Autobiography as Activism: Three Black Women of the Sixties* (Jackson: University Press of Mississippi, 2000).
9 Sidonie Smith and Julia Watson, *Reading Autobiography: A Guide for Interpreting Life Narratives* (Minneapolis: University of Minnesota Press, 2010), 2.
10 Kathryn L. Nasstrom, "Between Memory and History," 333.
11 Winifred Breines, "Sixties Stories Silences: White Feminists, Black Feminists, Black Power," *NWSA Journal* 8.3 (1996), n.p.
12 Faith S. Holsaert et al., *Hands on the Freedom Plow: Personal Accounts by Women in SNCC* (Urbana: University of Illinois Press, 2010), 1.
13 Ibid., 16. See this page for an example of narratives from Asian Americans.
14 Sara Evans, *Personal Politics: The Roots of Women's Liberation in the Civil Rights Movement and the New Left* (New York: Knopf, 1979).
15 Ibid., 123.
16 Ibid., 341.
17 Breines, "Sixties Stories Silences."
18 Constance Curry et al., *Deep in Our Hearts: Nine White Women in the Freedom Movement* (Athens: University of Georgia Press, 2000), viii.
19 Ibid., 3.
20 Ibid., 4.
21 Ibid., 78.
22 Ibid., 7.
23 Ibid.
24 In the narrative, Simmons provides the details of this contingency: her promotion to project director was completely unplanned as the man originally assigned as director had to leave the state to avoid imprisonment.
25 Curry et al., *Deep in Our Hearts*, 535.
26 Ibid., 537.
27 Ibid., 536–537.
28 Ibid., 537.
29 John Hazlett, "Generational Theory and Collective Autobiography," *American Literary History* 4.1 (1992), 85.
30 Ibid.
31 Ibid., 87.

32 Holsaert et al., *Hands on the Freedom Plow*, 153.
33 Ibid., 9.
34 Ibid., 14.
35 Ibid., 19.
36 Ibid.
37 Ibid., 198.
38 Ibid., 199.
39 Hayden White, "The Value of Narrativity in the Representation of Reality," *Critical Inquiry* 7.1 (1980), 19.
40 David Scott, *Conscripts of Modernity: The Tragedy of Colonial Enlightenment* (Durham: Duke University Press, 2004), 7.
41 Holsaert et al., *Hands on the Freedom Plow*, 172.
42 Ibid., 173.
43 Ibid., 176.
44 Ibid., 188. Emphasis in original.
45 Curry et al., *Deep in Our Hearts*, 63.
46 Ibid.
47 Holsaert et al., *Hands on the Freedom Plow*, 107.
48 Ibid., 342.
49 Curry et al., *Deep in Our Hearts*, 282.
50 Ibid., 280.
51 Holsaert et al., *Hands on the Freedom Plow*, 325.
52 Ibid., 139.
53 Ibid., 342.
54 Ibid., 523.

4

"GOD DECREED IT SO"

The Rhetoric of Destiny in 1963

Corrine E. Hinton and Tonya M. Scott Hill

During the classical phase of the civil rights movement, after enduring unprovoked acts of violence, humiliating Jim Crow policies, and exclusion from much of the nation's political structure, many African Americans struggled to reconcile their feelings about faith, freedom, and fate. In 1963, inundated with several different paths to racial justice, many activists found themselves standing at a crossroads—unsure which path (and who) would lead them to equality and prosperity. Stepping into this uncertainty were various authors, politicians, and activists who manipulated *destiny* as a rhetorical device to advocate their own vision of the future. In James Baldwin's "Down at the Cross," Alabama Governor George Wallace's Inaugural Address, Martin Luther King, Jr.'s "Letter from Birmingham Jail" and "I Have a Dream" speech, and John F. Kennedy's "Undelivered Remarks," the writer/speaker applies various constructs of destiny as a cornerstone of their own philosophies of equality, freedom, and faith. Using Critical Race Theory (CRT), this chapter examines how each of these important figures advances his own ideas by purposefully blending and blurring religious, historical, and national characterizations of destiny, thereby intentionally wielding these rhetorical manipulations both as demonstrations of their own power and as provocations for readers and listeners to reaffirm, advance, and capitalize on the destiny promised to them.

While the rhetoric of destiny imbues the discourses of equality, freedom, and faith, the perspective of CRT provides the theoretical vantage point. In "Working with Difference," Gary Olson defines CRT as

> an intellectual movement dedicated to interrogating how dominant society constructs and represents both race and racism. [CRT] pays particular attention to how power and domination are always inherent in racial relations and to how society's governing institutions, especially the law, enforce a regime of domination and subordination on all people vis-à-vis their race.[1]

In the US, issues of race, power, and domination are omnipresent. Because racism is so deeply rooted in the nation's history, it is "normal, not aberrant, in American society" and functions as a foundational notion in CRT.[2] Thus, race issues permeate American society and culture, binding themselves to the way we negotiate justice, morality, equality, freedom, and faith. In an article focusing on black spirituality and CRT in higher education, Howard Thurman contends:

The linkage between the Black experience, Christian theology, and systemic racism finds common ground with CRT, which seeks to expose the nature of race in America and the importance of people of color resisting hegemony while expressing their authentic voice to tell their own stories.[3]

Indeed, the texts of Baldwin, Wallace, King, and Kennedy articulate distinct (and often disparate) visions for America's future, visions steeped in religious, historical, and national interpretations of destiny that expose the marginalization or mongrelization of the black voice and empower audiences to seize their promised destiny. Combining ideologies of traditional Christian destiny with those of racial (dis)empowerment and national destiny, these four voices propose diverse paths to freedom and equality, all of which seemed to be blessed equally by God during a time when most of the country held tight to their religious (and primarily Christian) beliefs. A review of the places from which these multiple constructions of destiny emerged is necessary to understand how these differing approaches further complicated the decision-making of blacks and whites in the 1960s.

Destiny Emerged, Destiny Converged

While the Bible clearly spells out the destiny of a Christian, the interpretation of that destiny poses some challenges. In Romans 8, Paul says, "[W]e are the children of God: / And if children, then heirs; heirs of God, and joint-heirs with Christ; if so be that we suffer with him, that we may be also glorified together."[4] Thus, the role of Christians, as God's chosen people, is to be like God as the heirs to His Kingdom, and as God's first heir, Christ is to be "the firstborn among many brethren" who should live up to being Christ-like and therefore Godlike.[5] Theology scholar Douglas Davies explains, "Human destiny lies in being transformed into the likeness of Jesus in some moral sense, and in a process that will be completed after death in the new order of heaven."[6] The Christian destiny, then, is to ensure our glorified places in the family of God in His Kingdom, but also important to note is what Romano Guardini refers to as the "eschatological character" of Christian Providence.[7] Destiny is God's direct guidance for every Christian "when in faith and love a man shows God's care and concern for His Kingdom," and it can only be fully realized after death.[8] What, then, is to be done about one's time on earth? How does man show "care and concern" for God's Kingdom before he enters it? The answer to this quandary is the premise behind the fusion of social justice and Christian theology. In *Faith, Hope, and Love*, Swiss theologian Emil Brunner explains the Christian commitment to the world this way: "He is not concerned primarily about his own personal salvation; he is concerned about God's concern, which is for the world. His hope therefore must be both personal and universal."[9] In other words, Christians can do right by God by doing right by their people on earth—an idea that formed the perfect platform for infusing social constructions of freedom, justice, and equality into religion as "natural rights" sanctioned by God.

Freedom and destiny are never far apart in conversation or in scholarship; in his aptly titled *Freedom and Destiny*, Rollo May asserts that the two "give birth to each other."[10] Early notions of the role of freedom in destiny focused on an individual's freedom to follow (or not follow) the destiny given to him by God. However, as social and historical conditions shifted, securing personal freedom became a necessary step in preserving one's Christian destiny and entrance into the Kingdom of God. This shift was distinctively American, employed first by the Puritans and then later by social justice advocates, including those in the civil rights movement. The New England Puritans, in search of freedom from oppressive rule and the freedom to practice their religion without persecution, often preached about sinners and social injustice. They saw themselves as "practical and as spiritual guides, and…in their church-state, theology was wedded to politics and politics to the progress of the kingdom of God."[11] The Puritans not only believed in the eschatological nature of destiny but also recognized that entrance into the Kingdom of God relied heavily upon righting the sins of mankind. The success of the new America relied on the success of her people in living morally—in terms of both religious teachings and socially acceptable practices. "Of all symbols of identity," writes Sacvan Bercovitch, "only *America* has united nationality and universality, civic and spiritual selfhood, secular and redemptive history, the country's past and paradise to be, in a single synthetic ideal."[12] This "single, synthetic ideal" was the construction of what would later become a national destiny or, as most Americans call it, the American dream.

The Declaration of Independence represents what is perhaps the first deliberate and explicit document characterizing a seemingly unique and universal American destiny: "all Men are created equal"; we have three "unalienable rights" of life, liberty, and the pursuit of happiness; and these rights are "endowed by their Creator." Note that the bestower of rights is just as important as the rights themselves. As the Declaration's writers emphasize, God sanctified the separation of the American colonies from British rule. True to their Christian roots, these writers (and traitors) knew that to gain support for what would surely result in bloody conflict, they must express their unity and do so with God's approval. As such, the document represents what is perhaps the first deliberate and distinctly *American* infusion of religion and politics with specific regard to the nation's destiny. Furthermore, the Declaration illustrated to the world America's first national identity. While the founders did not want to include enslaved black people as part of that identity, they did, according to historian Jim Cullen, portray all colonists, for political purposes, as slaves striving to be free from the oppressive British Empire.[13] This depiction, illustrating a destiny of freedom, becomes the first artifact of the American dream, an example that would prove quite useful for subsequent movements for social justice.

Some of what kept African Americans politically subjugated until the passing of the fourteenth amendment in 1868 was their exclusion from the collective American identity. If whites did not consider blacks legal citizens, then blacks did not have the right to pursue any of the Declaration's promises. Until emancipation, constructs of racial destiny prohibited social acceptance of blacks as equals to whites. Historian Michele Mitchell asserts that racial destiny began "between 1830 and 1850 when the American school of ethnology classified racial types," establishing a racial hierarchy based on innate characteristics deemed superior or inferior.[14] For decades, whites considered blacks debased human beings, exacerbated by claims that the race was hypersexual, violent, and primitive. These claims held steady in much of US society until well into the twentieth century. While the allegations of a biologically subhuman position based entirely on race were eventually deemed unfounded, Mitchell points out that "such allegations rationalized lynching and ritualized rape, legitimated segregation, and restricted employment opportunities."[15] Instead of shunning the idea of racial destiny, however, black activists embraced and refashioned it by creating a "more inclusive and flexible concept…[that] African Americans increasingly invoked…when speaking of themselves" in relation to the nation's collective destiny.[16] Originally meant to exclude them from positions of social and political status, racial destiny became important to the black community as its leaders positioned the race as instrumental to fulfilling the nation's destiny, a destiny affirmed by the very document from which they were originally excluded.

How did the black American notion of destiny evolve to incorporate Christian theology, social justice, and patriotism for a country that, for almost two centuries, had expressed little more than tolerance for its black people? Historian Andrew Manis describes black American Christianity as a "gumbo from a base or roux (a spirituality from African traditional religions) and various doctrinal ingredients from Evangelicalism, cooked together over the fire of racism, slavery, and segregation in America," with this combination of tradition, experience, and "prophetic consciousness" convincing blacks that "God's Kingdom meant justice '*on earth* as it is in heaven' or it meant nothing at all."[17] Like the New England Puritans, black Americans considered themselves "God's anointed children," and as such, "they came to interpret their covenant as obliging them not only to preserve Christian ideals, but to uphold the natural rights of man," the very same rights promised by the document declaring all men to be created equal.[18]

In the 1960s, the civil rights movement gained momentum as leaders exposed "the yawning gap between the cherished ideals of the Declaration and the appalling realities of American life."[19] For this strategy to be persuasive, particularly for gaining white support, activists had to first establish that such a gap existed and, second, convince others that ignoring this gap could have significant political and theological consequences. By claiming that segregation jeopardized fulfillment of American and Christian destiny, activists could promote an interracial, unified future; at the same time, they could evince the racial destiny of black Americans by claiming their necessary and ordained place in the progress of America. White segregationists confronted the specter of such a future by exploiting white fears of the impending degradation that would befall them (and all Americans) should blacks achieve social and political equality. These fears, as politicians like George Wallace would demonstrate, could be quelled by manipulating historical memory as well as the notions of Christian and national destiny.

James Baldwin, the Cursing of the Races, and Unification

Baldwin addresses the issues of freedom, faith, and destiny in his essay "Down at the Cross: Letter from a Region of My Mind," published in 1963 in the aptly titled *The Fire Next Time*. In "Down," Baldwin examines destiny as it pertains to white people, black people, Christians of both races, and the nation as a whole amidst dueling ideologies of nonviolent direct action (represented by King and the Southern Christian Leadership Conference) and black nationalism (represented by Elijah Muhammed and the Nation of Islam). Baldwin highlights his religious characterizations of destiny and declares that despite Christians' biblical tenets, no equality exists between blacks and whites in 1960s America. Baldwin directly confronts the differences of perspective on destiny. For whites, he argues, destiny relates directly to race: "White people hold the power, which means that they are superior to blacks (intrinsically, that is: God decreed it so)."[20] Baldwin frequently criticizes white notions of Christian superiority, describing the spread of Christianity in African and American Indian nations as a way for whites to induce power over others by presenting themselves as closer to God. In order to successfully employ this power, Baldwin asserts, white Christians had to find a way to be superior to blacks, even to black Christians. Accordingly, he addresses what many scholars call the fundamental doctrine that influenced the nature of race relations for centuries to come: the Hamitic theory. Baldwin explains the pervasiveness of this belief on black destiny:

> I knew that, according to many Christians, I was a descendant of Ham, who had been cursed, and that I was therefore predestined to be a slave. This had nothing to do with anything I was, or contained, or could become; my fate had been sealed forever, from the beginning of time. And it seemed, indeed, when one looked out over Christendom, that this was what Christendom effectively believed.[21]

God's cursing of Ham and the binding of Ham's descendants specifically to those of the black race provided many Christians with a divine ordinance that "allowed exploitation of the Negro for economic gain to remain undisturbed by any Christian doubts as to the moral issues involved."[22] If God himself had cursed blacks, why should white Christians, in the eternal service of God, do anything to rebuke his orders? By supporting the ascension of blacks to that of whites, Christians were violating what they perceived to be God's will. Second, the Hamitic theory gave even greater weight to the pre-emancipation concept of racial destiny. From both a Christian perspective and a scientific perspective, African Americans were inferior in every way to whites. God affirmed it; scientists confirmed it. To overcome this perverted notion, white Christians would have to believe in something greater than God's curse—they would have to believe in God's love.

The Hamitic theory affected black ideologies of faith and destiny. Baldwin questions God's intentions, or, rather, he questions the intentions of white Christians' interpretations of God's word: "if His love was so great, and if He loved all His children, why were we, the blacks, cast down so far?"[23] But whites were not the only ones who believed in blacks' inherent inferiority. Baldwin remembers having a difficult time understanding why his parents refused to encourage his dreams that he could do anything a little white boy could do. The limitations placed on blacks by their own people, admittedly the result of decades of atrocious treatment and debasement, were, Baldwin posits, also related to black destiny. Sadly, what also awaited the black American child during much of the twentieth century was violence and humiliation: "Every effort made by the child's elders to prepare him for a fate from which they cannot protect him causes him secretly…to begin to await…his mysterious and inexorable punishment."[24] Baldwin admits, "One did not have to be very bright to realize how little one could do to change one's situation."[25] While Baldwin suggests that love cannot prompt change, he asserts that fear can—a realization he investigates through his meeting with the Honorable Elijah Muhammad.

Baldwin portrays the Nation of Islam as having its own ideologies of destiny, one cornerstone of which was a black-only revolution as a way to fulfill black destiny. Activists following Elijah Muhammad and his teachings believed that the fulfillment of black destiny required the destruction of the white man. These teachings, Baldwin says, inspired fear on the part of white police officers, fear that Baldwin "was delighted to see."[26] While white Christians believed God had cursed the black race, black Muslims of the Nation of Islam believed the opposite, offering "historical and divine proof that all white people are cursed, and are devils, and are about to be brought down."[27] In particular, Baldwin tells us, the Nation references Germany's role in Europe—especially the tenuous power over the Jews that certain German forces enjoyed—and the attempted French takeover of North Africa in 1956.[28] These historical references were rhetorical fodder for the Nation of Islam, advancing the Nation's own manipulation of racial destiny to empower its supporters.

Baldwin questions and ultimately rejects the Nation's vengeance-based solution. He believed that black progress hinged on whites being able to accept blacks as religious, social, and physical equals. In order for progress to occur, Americans cannot simply make extrinsic changes (anti-discrimination public policies, equal employment opportunities, and desegregated schools, for example); individuals must make intrinsic, fundamental changes in their hearts and minds. Indeed, great strides are possible only if

> the relatively conscious whites and the relatively conscious blacks…insist on, or create, the consciousness of the others…[then] we may be able, handful that we are, to end the racial nightmare, and achieve our country, and change the history of the world.[29]

Thus, unification is not the path to the American dream so much as an end to the American nightmare—an end that is another beginning.

George Wallace and Necessary Segregation

In his inaugural address delivered on January 14, 1963, Governor George Wallace focuses on what he believes are his fellow Alabamians' central concerns: duty, industry and trade, the overreaching power of the central government, and segregation. He weaves together these concerns with the common threads of individual freedom and ethnic nationalism. Scholars have thoroughly examined the governor's address, famously known as the "segregation now… segregation tomorrow…segregation forever" speech, so the focus here will not be on the speech in its entirety but rather one of the final sections of the speech that uses destiny to tie various themes together. The word *destiny* appears in Wallace's remarks just one time:

> Let us, as Alabamians, grasp the hand of destiny and walk out of the shadow of fear…and fill our divine destination. Let us not simply defend…but let us assume the leadership of the fight and carry our leadership across this nation. God has placed us here in this crisis… let us not fail in this…our most historical moment.[30]

Wallace personifies destiny for illustrative value as one who leads and can be led in an attempt to fulfill a "destination" that has been "divinely" determined. His statement begins with the illusion of unification: "Let *us*, as Alabamians." In using the first-person plural, Wallace both defines the group ("Alabamians") and includes himself within that group: thus, the "destiny" to which Wallace alludes is one that he and his fellow Alabamians share. These fellow Alabamians, however, are a distinct subset of all Alabamians. The racially-unified white "destiny" Wallace implies is contingent upon multiple destinies. Wallace manages to both unify and divide the citizens of his state by intertwining historical, national, religious, and racial ideologies in other distinct moments earlier in his speech.

The first moment occurs directly after the opening quote by General Robert E. Lee when Wallace references another pinnacle of the Confederacy: Jefferson Davis, the President of the Confederate States of America. Wallace conjures his fellow Alabamians' historical and national memory of a treasured time as he takes "an oath to my people." Wallace's use of the possessive suggests ownership of or kinship with his fellow Alabamians. White Alabamians would likely interpret this ownership positively, like a shepherd safely leading his flock to green pastures. Those outside this primary constituency, and certainly black Alabamians, would have been more likely to understand Wallace's oath as one that either (a) did not include them as *his* people and thereby excluded them from such protection or (b) one that likened itself to forced ownership, an enslaving of "my people" who may not necessarily have had the desire to be included in Wallace's flock. Further in that paragraph, Wallace reinforces the latter interpretation, saying, "Let us rise to the call of freedom-loving blood that is in us and send our answer to the tyranny that *clanks its chains* upon the South."[31] References to the Confederacy, to the "Great Anglo-Saxon Southland," to freedom, to slavery, and to segregation—all in one powerful paragraph—firmly establish Wallace's position and loyalty to white Alabamians, not all Alabamians.

Wallace justifies segregation as necessary both nationally and spiritually. Maintaining separate "racial lives," Wallace argues, stems from the same reasoning as maintaining separate political lives. While we live united, each person comes from a "separate political station…respecting the rights of others to be separate and work from within their political framework"; similarly, Wallace argues, "Each race, within its own framework has the freedom to teach…to instruct…to develop…to ask for and receive deserved help from others of separate racial stations."[32] To reinforce this ideology, Wallace taps into his listeners' historical and national identities, maintaining, "This [separatism] is the great freedom of our American founding fathers," a freedom in danger should the country move toward unification. To Wallace, then, freedom can only be attained through maintaining and respecting separation of the races; otherwise, the nation risks becoming "a mongrel unit of one."[33] Advocating for unification would not only fly in the face of democracy (by supporting this "doctrine of communist amalgamation") but would also result in the surrendering of "our freedom of race and religion." Dan T. Carter, renowned Wallace scholar, argues that Wallace's positioning of anti-civil-rights rhetoric with communism was deliberate and served two purposes: on the one hand, "it allowed him to use Cold War fears of international Communism to discredit the civil rights movement," and, on the other, it allowed Wallace to connect political action with the "religious struggle of conspiracy and betrayal in which the forces of light must constantly struggle against those of the darkness."[34] So begins Wallace's methodical distortion of the American dream: achieving the country's national destiny can only be realized if everyone (blacks and whites) ensures the purity (segregation) of the country's political *and* racial structures.

Reinforcing his message that separation of the races is the only way to maintain individual freedom and dedication to the Christian faith, Wallace continues with an invitation to black Alabamians: "We invite the negro citizens of Alabama to work with us from his separate racial station…as we will work with him…to develop, to grow in individual freedom and enrichment." Several key moves are important to examine in this statement. First, "we" implies that Wallace belongs to the group extending the invitation. When considering the act of invitation through the lens of power dynamics, power lies with the one extending the invitation rather than the one accepting it as the action suggests one who *has* offering something to one who *has not*. Second, Wallace, for the first time in his address, clearly separates an in-group "us" from an out-group "them." Wallace implores black Alabamians "to work with *us*," an in-group to which black Alabamians do not belong (our emphasis). Rather than choosing the third-person plural "them," Wallace chooses instead the third-person singular "him." He does so in an effort to appear as if he is *not* separating his constituency into an "us" versus "them" dynamic by choosing the more personal, less threatening usage of the singular pronoun to represent all black Alabamians. Such a choice would both lessen the perceived threat that blacks were to whites and demonstrate the black Alabamians' humanity. Finally, Wallace ensures that the notion of whites working "with" blacks does not come from a place of racial unification but rather from each race's "separate…station." Then, Wallace suggests to black Alabamians that white Alabamians desire nothing more than to ensure the physical, mental, personal, and financial health of both races. This desire, Wallace asserts, "is the basic heritage of my religion, of which I make full practice…for we are all the handiwork of God."[35] Wallace's remarks are reminiscent of another infamous Southern white segregationist politician—Theodore Bilbo. In the preface to *Take Your Choice: Separation or Mongrelization*, Bilbo professes, "This book is not a condemnation or denunciation of any race, white, black or yellow because I entertain no hatred or prejudice against any human being on account of his race or color—God made them so" before he declares that avoiding mongrelization of the races is necessary for the success of each race individually as well as the children of all races for generations to come.[36] In his inaugural speech, Wallace appeals to both black and white Alabamians' firm Christian traditions of charity to support a "separate but equal" stance that will, despite all evidence to the contrary, yield growth and prosperity for all.

Wallace positions God at the helm as the one who has purposefully placed whites and blacks in this exact moment in time, a moment Wallace characterizes as a "crisis." This "crisis," given the themes highlighted in his speech, could refer to the state's suffocation by a strong central government, the result of which is the inevitable loss of individual rights. Among those rights in danger, Wallace says, is the right of each race to remain separate from the others. Throughout his 1963 gubernatorial address, Wallace calls upon the historical memory, national reverence, and religious beliefs that he attributes to all Alabamians to persuade them (and the thousands of others who would hear his address) to support segregation as the only destiny for those who desire both freedom and God's love.

A Letter and a Dream: Dr. Martin Luther King, Jr.

To understand why and how King used the rhetoric of destiny in both his "Letter from Birmingham Jail" and "I Have a Dream" speech, one must understand the ideologies from which he drew and those he wished to express to his audience. King accepted the messianic notion of Christian destiny, which focuses heavily on correcting the wrongs on earth in order to secure entrance into the Kingdom of God. In *Stride Toward Freedom*, King writes, "Any religion that professes to be concerned with the souls of men and is not concerned with the slums that damn them, the economic conditions that strangle them, and the social conditions that cripple them is a dry-as-dust religion."[37] And while he believed in the destiny of African Americans, King did not necessarily condone their race-specific position as a chosen people. In *Black Messiahs and Uncle Toms: Social and Literary Manipulations of a Religious Myth*, Wilson Jeremiah Moses argues that "[King] did not claim that black Americans were a chosen people or a master race, but he did feel that Providence had often made them pioneers in movements essential to the nation's development."[38] The treatment and denial of their rights compelled blacks to begin bearing the ignominious torch of the civil rights movement, a torch that simultaneously held people accountable for the Christian principle of right versus wrong.

King's criticisms of white Christians and their allowance of—and sometimes participation in—violence and degradation toward blacks compelled him to write "Letter from Birmingham Jail" on April 12, 1963. Several incidents during desegregation protests in Birmingham, Alabama increased the fervor of civil rights activists, so what better ways to bring them to a crescendo than to violate an injunction to protest on Good Friday and, upon incarceration, to write a letter responding overtly to white clergymen who argued that the civil rights protests were "unwise and untimely"? Robert Westbrook describes King's letter as "a powerful indictment of the shortcomings of timid moderation in the face of injustice, a sermon of chastisement—a shrewd, tough-minded, even militant political document."[39] "Timid moderation" is a criticism of the unfairly slow-moving acquisition of black civil rights, a criticism often applied to the political decision-making of then-President John F. Kennedy.

Using classical rhetorical form and wielding destiny as a rhetorical device, King obtains the intended effect of his "Letter." Edward Berry suggests that King's letter "achieves its distinctive and enduring rhetorical power because he was able to overcome in expressive form the historical, political, and deeply personal problem that inspired it—the problem of time."[40] He identifies three interrelated conceptions of time in King's letter, which he labels "'sacred,' 'personal,' and 'patriotic' time."[41] These conceptions of time intersect with the three discursive frameworks upon which the civil rights movement is based: unification, conciliatory, and protest. With rhetorical finesse, King addresses the "tragic misconception of time."[42] His explanation of this misinterpretation comes from biblical, personal, and national experiences and hints at their influence on the stages of the US civil rights movement. King writes that time delusion stems from

> the strangely irrational notion that there is something in the very flow of time that will inevitably cure all ills. Actually, time itself is neutral; it can be used either destructively or constructively. More and more I feel that the people of ill will have used time much more effectively than have the people of good will.[43]

According to King, people give time its power. Time passes by itself; it cannot accomplish anything else without people:

> Human progress never rolls in on wheels of inevitability; it comes through the tireless efforts of men willing to be co-workers with God, and without this hard work, time itself becomes an ally of the forces of social stagnation. We must use time creatively, in the knowledge that the time is always ripe to do right.[44]

King argues that in accordance with God's word, progress (and thus the destiny of equality and dignity) relies on men's steadfast pursuits. Furthermore, God gives men power over time with which they must do what is right for all His people—for all in society—in order to progress socially. King's concept of time is directly related to destiny, which begets equality, which begets dignity.

In "Letter," King carefully crafts ideas he would later echo and expand upon in his "I Have a Dream" speech, especially how national and racial destinies align through the achievement of racial justice even in the face of competing Christian ideologies. Frustrated with the contemporary Church as an "archdefender of the status quo," King begins to conceptualize for a Christian public the way in which supporting racial equality is a moral decision free from any dedication to an organized religion.[45] King writes,

> Even if the church does not come to the aid of justice, I have no despair about the future…. We will reach the goal of freedom in Birmingham and all over the nation, because the goal of America is freedom. Abused and scorned though we may be, our destiny is tied up with America's destiny.[46]

Alluding to the Declaration of Independence, King establishes the foundation upon which his central argument will rest: America cannot fulfill its purpose as a country until racial equality is achieved. King also makes clear that African American lives and futures do not exist separate from those of the country, nor is racial equality a right they will achieve without the support of the nation (as other civil rights camps would suggest); rather, the two are "tied up" together or "inextricably bound" as King would revise the phrasing for his iconic speech just four months later.[47] And although King champions a nation that can make progress without the support of organized religion (or rather, the positions of organized churches), it is *not* a nation that can do so without the support of God. As King approaches the end of his "Letter," he declares, "We will win our freedom because the sacred heritage of our nation and the eternal will of God are embodied in our echoing demands."[48] Thus, King consummates his message by calling once more upon the trinity of destiny: one nation, one God, and all people.

The first section of King's "I Have a Dream" speech that exercises his call to join political, theological, and racial destinies appears in the section on the nation's "promissory note." As in his "Letter," King uses the Declaration of Independence as a call to the nation's history:

> When the architects of our republic wrote the magnificent words of the Constitution and the Declaration of Independence, they were signing a promissory note to which every American was to fall heir. This note was a promise that *all* men would be guaranteed the 'unalienable Rights' of 'Life, Liberty and the pursuit of Happiness.'[49]

King strategically uses the all-inclusive, first-person plural "our" to amplify to whom the country, and thus the Declaration, belong. Additionally, "[h]is verbal bracketing of 'black men as well as white men' was a reprimand, reminding his audience of how America had failed to live up to the promises in the Declaration."[50] This section is the first point at which King begins the infusion of destinies, beginning with one that should encompass all Americans regardless of color: national destiny. As Manis explains, "King understood America itself as the unfulfilled dream….[and] found divine sanction for the dream in the self-evident truths of the Declaration of Independence."[51] Also, one could find this divine sanction in King's simple inclusion of the "heir" of the promissory note, a call back to Romans 8, verse 17, identifying Christ's followers as "heirs of God, and joint-heirs with Christ." While this connection may seem difficult to justify, consider King's considerable familiarity with the King James Version of the Bible. Hansen contends, "[H]e was so steeped in [it] that even his sentence structure was marked by a Biblical idiom."[52] "Heir" emphasizes the importance King placed on developing his theme of an interracial, interdependent national destiny. Shortly after, King remarks, "Instead of honoring this sacred obligation, America has given the Negro people a bad check."[53] Here, King reminds the audience of the ties that the Declaration of Independence has to Christianity, marking it as a "sacred obligation," hinting that rejection of the document's theological sacredness would have consequences not only to the nation's destiny but also to Christian destiny. King's reference to the Declaration and the ensuing metaphor of the bad check provides a firm foundation for the list of grievances that follows.

The strongest emphasis of King's rhetoric of collective destiny appears approximately midway through the speech:

> The marvelous new militancy which has engulfed the Negro community must not lead us to a distrust of all white people, for many of our white brothers, as evidenced by their presence here today, have come to realize that their destiny is tied up with our destiny. And they have come to realize that their freedom is inextricably bound to our freedom. We cannot walk alone.[54]

Note that King does not just acknowledge the role of whites in the journey toward social justice, he also affirms the role as one of predestination. He directly links the destinies of whites and blacks, illustrating that both sides are necessary in order to realize this collective national destiny, a belief many did not share. Since the movement's progress had slowed when the March on Washington took place, many activists began wondering if King's approach of emphasizing interracial cooperation was working. Responding to growing concerns for a black-only revolution, this section in particular "reaffirm[ed] his belief in racial integration within the protest movement" and "publicly rebuked those who were becoming skeptical of nonviolence and integration."[55] Crucially, this section appears prior to the famous "dream" anaphora; if whites did not feel especially acknowledged or part of the movement's progress, they may not have been as receptive to King's dream. And after rebuking their reneging of the natural rights of the Declaration, King knew he needed to assure white supporters and opponents alike. For those who had come to the March, King offered his embrace. For those who were still deciding or, much worse, committing acts of violence against African Americans, King offered his forgiveness. Cooperation was not just a message for whites: King also reminds his fellow African Americans that not all white people are untrustworthy and that they could not succeed alone. This division of power between white agency and black agency allowed King to begin anew, to build fresh from a level platform, now that he had put his white and black listeners on equal footing. Whereas the "promissory note" section provided a platform for a list of specific injustices, this section marks the point at which King focuses on forgiveness and the importance of moving forward together to praise God *and* to fulfill the American dream.

Kennedy's Final Words

In 1963, President Kennedy found himself in a precarious position: advancing an agenda for freedom and democracy in the communist-ruled Soviet Union with the recognition that his own country hypocritically failed to uphold such ideals with members of its own citizenry.[56] The significance of Kennedy's role in the advancement of black freedom during the civil rights movement has been hotly debated since the 1970s. We support the position of Kennedy scholars, such as Richard Reeves and Yasuhiro Katagiri, who assert that Kennedy's decision-making with regard to civil rights legislation was "driven…by a series of rapid-fire incidents" he could neither predict nor control and "dictated" by "Cold War restraints and his uneasy relationship with Congress."[57] Several events in the first half of 1963, however, prompted Kennedy to take a clear public position on civil rights by calling it a national and moral issue in his June 11, 1963 address to the nation and then, just eight days later, submitting civil rights legislation to Congress. Here, we will examine the way in which Kennedy's presidential rhetoric continued to progress in response to his revised approach to civil rights through integrating multiple notions of destiny in the speech he intended to deliver on the day he was assassinated in Dallas, Texas.

Kennedy did not intend for his undelivered address, formally titled "Undelivered Remarks for Dallas Citizens Council, Trade Mart, Dallas, Texas, 22 November 1963," to serve as a historic example of his civil rights views. Rather, the address is important primarily because it represents the President's final public words on the subject. The thirty-seven notecards for the speech, complete with handwritten notations by the President himself, position the country's national defense and security at the forefront. However, Kennedy establishes early one refrain of his address: the necessary relationship between learning and leadership in the advancement of progress. Kennedy notes,

> America's leadership must be guided by the lights of learning and reason—or else those who confuse rhetoric with reality and the plausible with the possible will gain the popular ascendency with their seemingly swift and simple solutions to every world problem.[58]

President Kennedy crafts this passage, which audience members and members of the press would have heard very early in the speech, not just as a tribute to the value of reason in general decision-making but also as justification for *his* decision-making, which critics had often censured for its sluggishness. The President did not intend this message only for the Dallas Citizens Council but for all political and public leaders pressuring him to find "simple solutions" to the "complex and continuing problems" of the country.[59] This early section of the address is also important because it establishes another item on the President's agenda—rhetoric serves little purpose without the strength to act.

Although Kennedy does not overtly address civil rights until the very end of his intended remarks, he planted rhetorical seeds throughout, setting himself up to do so in the final section of his speech. The final two paragraphs firmly establish Kennedy's two fundamental ideologies with regard to civil rights: (1) strength lies in restraint and nonviolent action, and (2) Americans are obligated to pursue equality for all:

> That strength will never be used in pursuit of aggressive ambitions—it will always be used in pursuit of peace. It will never be used to promote provocations—it will always be used to promote the peaceful settlement of disputes.
>
> We in this country, in this generation, are—by destiny rather than choice—the watchman on the walls of world freedom. We ask, therefore, that we may be worthy of our power and responsibility—that we may exercise our strength with wisdom and restraint—and that we may achieve in our time and for all time the ancient vision of "peace on earth, good will toward men." That must always be our goal—and the righteousness of our cause must always underlie our strength. For as was written long ago: "except the Lord keep the city, the watchman waketh but in vain."[60]

Because of Kennedy's ambiguity, his words could apply to any of the national concerns he has addressed in the talk (communism and the Soviet Union, for example) or the domestic concern of black equality. Kennedy probably intended both, but he veiled the latter using caution common to much of his civil rights rhetoric.[61]

Kennedy uses destiny to convince listeners that people must earn and maintain peace and freedom together. Kennedy begins the last paragraph with the first-person plural to demonstrate unity with his audience, but he qualifies that "we" in both time and space to reiterate a shared sense of responsibility. The "we" only applies to Americans, and it only applies to those with the capability (and responsibility) to act now in the name of freedom, in the midst of the Cold War and the civil rights movement. To amplify the weight of this responsibility, Kennedy explains they have been tasked "by destiny rather than by choice," implying some force outside of their control has put them in this moment to make decisions that will have an impact across the world and across "all time."

What force has delivered to them this destiny? For Kennedy, the response is primarily religious and secondarily, moral. Kennedy tells his listeners that they are "watchmen on the walls of world freedom," alluding to the quote from the Book of Psalms he will reference more explicitly in the final line of his speech. For context, the full quote from Psalms 127:1: "Except the LORD build the house, they labour in vain that builds it: except the LORD keep the city, the watchman waketh but in vain." The verse implies that without God's protection, those who have been charged with watching over a community and its people do so uselessly. Kennedy, then, tasks his people, the American people, with serving as the guards of world freedom. Interestingly, the speech was written originally as "watchman on the walls of freedom," but Kennedy, in his own hand, added the word "world." In the one sense, this addition strengthens his message of the country's prominent role in spreading freedom and democracy across the globe. However, "world" also weakens the phrase's value to the issue of civil rights *within* the country by shifting the focus from the domestic to the national. Given Kennedy's insertion of biblical passages, common in his rhetoric, we can assume that the primary deliverer of the destiny he references is God. Yet, Kennedy positions the notion of Christian destiny within that of both a historical sense of destiny ("in this generation" and "in our time and for all time") and a national one ("We in this country").

Kennedy sets a goal for the nation: to be the primary force driving toward the achievement of "peace on earth, good will toward men." Most listeners would recognize the phrasing of this goal as another one of Kennedy's attempts to align himself with his audience by using a biblical passage (Luke 2:14) common to all Christian traditions, but the quote also implies two moral obligations. The first, "peace on earth," speaks to a state of being that occurs only in the presence of harmony. Viewing this from its negative definition, *peace* is not discord; it is characterized by the absence of violence, of conflict, or of fear of violence. Thus, achieving peace, as a national goal, would require direct action to dispel conflict or violence. To do so, Americans would have to feel morally obligated to ensure peace across the globe, accepting the responsibility to support any action to uphold it. The second goal, "good will toward men," is not a state of being but rather a gesture; it is something we must offer rather than something we can create. "Good will" or rather "goodwill" stems from one's feelings, from one's humanity. For Kennedy, Americans cannot extend goodwill to those outside the country until we extend it to those within the country by ensuring freedom and equality for all. In what way are these goals related to the destiny confronting Americans in 1963? In *Freedom, Grace, and Destiny*, Guardini explains, "In destiny the world confronts a man as that which is given in order that from it he may bring forth the world which it is his task and responsibility to create."[62] Thus, the "destiny" that Kennedy claims has brought all Americans into such a critical position in time is one that taps into their religious, national, and moral natures and compels them to act.

Black *destiny*: its definition, its power, its means of attainment, its proponents, and its adversaries emerge through these exemplars and their artifacts. Based on King's "Letter," Robert Westbrook asserts that King and his ilk were prophetic agitators of conflict, confrontation, and ultimately, liberation.[63] On the one hand, black destiny was inconsistent with biblical, political, and racial analyses; on the other, though, black destiny was a presupposition of individual freedom and human equality.

Two conclusions emerge from an analysis of these selected nonfiction texts. First, when we position the messages of these texts within a racial (in)justice context, we can see the various ways in which the authors exploit the multiple constructs of national, racial, and religious destinies to persuade their audiences (both primary and secondary) toward primarily divergent viewpoints. Thus, the rhetoric of destiny represents a critical and prevalent tool for perpetuating the ideologies of various camps at work during the civil rights movement. However, when we consider what each of these authors suggests about the power of the individual in shaping his or her own destiny, a second conclusion surfaces. Through their attempts to negotiate religion, morality, history, and the future of the nation (and her people), Baldwin, Wallace, King, and Kennedy have four distinct thoughts about individual destiny. Baldwin ultimately rejects religion and society's control over his fate and vows to be master of his own. Wallace implies that the fate of all men has already been determined by God and, as such, we cannot and should not attempt to alter it (thus disempowering the individual). King sees the individual's life as a tool, one that must be put to work to advance God's plan; so, while we have control over our destinies, we should make decisions in accordance with what God would want for all humanity. And finally, Kennedy puts forward the notion that our individual destinies are connected to each other throughout history (and across the globe) and as such must not be squandered. Like King, Kennedy believes that the goal of the individual's destiny should be one of service, although Kennedy insists that they should be of service to our fellow men.

The messages of Baldwin, King, Wallace, and Kennedy represent the nuanced perspectives indicative of the US civil rights movement. Intentionally employing destiny as a rhetorical device, these legacies of the movement both evince and advance what have become distinctly American intersections of race, politics, and religion.

Approaches to Teaching Selected Nonfiction Texts

Discussion/Exam Questions

1 Write your own extended definition of *destiny*. Include an explanation of what *destiny* means to you personally and, with textual evidence from Baldwin, King, Wallace, or Kennedy, juxtapose your definition to his.
2 Why does religion (or religious beliefs) play such a significant role in the texts and oratory of the civil rights movement? Do you think religion plays more or less of a role in contemporary political rhetoric?
3 In your own words, describe the different viewpoints each of the selected authors/speakers had on racial equality and the future of the US.
4 Which author/speaker employs the most powerful rhetorical style? Support your response with evidence.

Research and Writing Projects

1 Watch actual footage of King's and Wallace's speeches. Note and analyze the potential effects of delivery (by the speaker) and reception (by the audience). Focus your attention on body language, tone, volume, and rhythm.
2 Locate and review at least two of Baldwin's, Kennedy's, King's, or Wallace's speeches, interviews, or writings. Write a collaborative essay analyzing the author/speaker's rhetorical style, referring directly to your primary source material.

3 Locate three to five civil rights movement-era artifacts using different mediums: essays, speeches, songs, poems, artwork, etc. Use PowerPoint, Prezi, or some other program to prepare a visual presentation of these artifacts and the "story" they tell about the movement.
4 Review the stories, poetry, and other documents available through the Civil Rights Movement Veterans project (crmvet.org) and construct your own response to the civil rights movement (through song, poem, essay, narrative, or video) based on what you learn from the stories of those who lived the experience.
5 Research the life of Baldwin, King, Wallace, or Kennedy and write a biographical essay focusing on the aspect of his life you find most significant. Include at least five secondary sources.

Notes

1 Gary Olson, "Working with Difference: Critical Race Studies and the Teaching of Composition," in *Composition Studies in the New Millennium: Rereading the Past Rewriting the Future*, ed. Lynn Z. Bloom, Donald A. Daiker, and Edward M. White (Carbondale: Southern Illinois University Press, 2003), 210.
2 Richard Delgado and Jean Stefancic, *Critical Race Theory: The Cutting Edge* (Philadelphia: Temple University Press, 2000), xiv.
3 Howard Thurman, "Black Spirituality and Critical Race Theory in Higher Education," *The Journal of Negro Education* 79.3 (2010), 357.
4 Romans 8:16–17 (Authorized Version).
5 Romans 8:29.
6 Douglas Davis, "Christianity," in *Human Nature and Destiny*, ed. Jean Holm and John Bowker (London: Pinter Publishers, 1994), 63.
7 Romano Guardini, *Freedom, Grace, and Destiny: Three Chapters on the Interpretation of Existence*, trans. John Murray (New York: Pantheon Books, 1961), 213.
8 Ibid.
9 Emil Brunner, *Faith, Hope, and Love* (Philadelphia: Westminster Press, 1956), 51.
10 Rollo May, *Freedom and Destiny* (New York: Norton, 1981), 84.
11 Sacvan Bercovitch, *The American Jeremiad* (Madison: University of Wisconsin Press, 1978), xiv.
12 Ibid., 176.
13 Jim Cullen, *The American Dream: A Short History of an Idea that Shaped a Nation* (New York: Oxford University Press, 2003), 47–48.
14 Michele Mitchell, *Righteous Propagation: African Americans and the Politics of Racial Destiny after Reconstruction* (Chapel Hill: University of North Carolina Press, 2004), 8.
15 Ibid., 9.
16 Ibid.
17 Andrew M. Manis, "With and Without Honor: The Prophetic Legacy of Martin Luther King Jr. and American Response," *The Cresset* 71.4 (2008), 17.
18 Wilson Jeremiah Moses, *Black Messiahs and Uncle Toms: Social and Literary Manipulations of a Religious Myth* (University Park: Pennsylvania State University Press, 1993), 31.
19 Cullen, *The American Dream*, 56.
20 James Baldwin, *The Fire Next Time* (New York: Vintage International, 1993), 25.
21 Ibid., 36.
22 Edith R. Sanders, "The Hamitic Hypothesis: Its Origin and Functions in Time Perspective," *Journal of African History* 10.4 (1969), 523.
23 Baldwin, *The Fire Next Time*, 31.
24 Ibid., 26.
25 Ibid., 19.
26 Ibid., 48.
27 Ibid., 49.
28 Ibid., 51–52.
29 Ibid., 105.
30 George Wallace, "The Inaugural Address of Governor George C. Wallace," 14 January 1963. Governor, Administrative files 1958–1968, Government Records Collections, Alabama Department of Archives and History, Montgomery, Ala.
31 Emphasis added.

32 Ibid.
33 Ibid.
34 Dan T. Carter, *From George Wallace to Newt Gingrich: Race in the Conservative Counterrevolution, 1963–1994* (Baton Rouge: Louisiana State University Press, 1992), 14.
35 Ibid.
36 Theodore G. Bilbo, *Take Your Choice: Separation or Mongrelization* (Poplarville: Dream House Publication Co., 1946), 2.
37 Martin Luther King, Jr., *Stride toward Freedom* (San Francisco: Harper, 1958), 36.
38 Moses, *Black Messiahs and Uncle Toms*, 180.
39 Robert Westbrook, "MLK's Manifesto: 'Letter from Birmingham Jail at 50,'" *The Christian Century*, April 8, 2013.
40 Edward Berry, "Doing Time: King's 'Letter from Birmingham Jail,'" *Rhetoric & Public Affairs* 8.1 (2005), 112.
41 Ibid.
42 Martin Luther King, Jr., "Letter from Birmingham Jail," in *50 Essays: A Portable Anthology*, ed. Samuel Cohen (Boston: Bedford St. Martin's, 2014), 211.
43 Ibid., 211–212.
44 Ibid., 212.
45 Ibid., 217.
46 Ibid.
47 Ibid.
48 Ibid., 218.
49 Martin Luther King, Jr., "I Have a Dream," *americanrhetoric.com*, last modified February 7, 2017.
50 Drew D. Hansen, *The Dream: Martin Luther King, Jr., and the Speech that Inspired a Nation* (New York: HarperCollins, 2003), 123.
51 Andrew M. Manis, *Southern Civil Religions in Conflict: Civil Rights and the Culture Wars* (Macon: Mercer University Press, 2002), 82.
52 Hansen, *The Dream*, 104.
53 King, Jr., "I Have a Dream."
54 Ibid.
55 Hansen, *The Dream*, 148–149.
56 See Yashuhiro Katagiri, "'Let the Word Go Forth': John F. Kennedy's Presidential Rhetoric on Civil Rights during the South's Second Reconstruction," *The Japanese Journal of American Studies* 17 (2006).
57 Ibid., 266.
58 John F. Kennedy, "Undelivered Remarks for Dallas Citizens Council, Trade Mart, Dallas, Texas, 22 November, 1963," *jfklibrary.org*.
59 Ibid.
60 Ibid.
61 See Meredith Grace Pascale, "Determining a Legacy: John F. Kennedy's Civil Rights Record" (master's thesis, Binghamton University, 2009).
62 Guardini, *Freedom, Grace, and Destiny*, 176.
63 Westbrook, "MLK's Manifesto," 22.

5

BACK TO BIRMINGHAM

Three Poets Remember the Sixteenth Street Church Bombing

StarShield Lortie and Laura Dubek

On June 17, 2015, a young white man sat quietly among black church members at Mother Emanuel AME Church in Charleston, South Carolina. For an hour, he participated in Bible study. Then, after spewing a racist rant, he opened fire with a handgun and killed nine people. This hate crime secured for Dylann Roof a place in an American history characterized by unimaginable acts of violence against black people. It also eerily echoed violence in another Southern city fifty-two years earlier. Much like the 2014 images of Ferguson, Missouri police officers tear-gassing protesters mirror the iconic 1963 photos of Alabama Safety Commissioner Eugene "Bull" Connor turning fire hoses and dogs on black children, the Charleston AME Church shooting took Americans, once again, back to Birmingham. On September 15, 1963, just eighteen days after the historic March on Washington, a bomb, set by four known segregationists and members of the Ku Klux Klan, took the lives of four black girls preparing for Sunday school: Addie Mae Collins, Cynthia Wesley, Carole Robertson, and Denise McNair. The connection between the church bombing in 1963 Birmingham and the church shooting in 2015 Charleston reminds us that the rallying cry of the civil rights movement—*we shall overcome*—is best thought of as a process rather than a goal. Understanding civil rights activity as an ongoing commitment underscores both the power and the responsibility each of us has to affect positive change. Poetry about the Sixteenth Street Church bombing in Birmingham can play a pivotal role in this change-making process.

Civil rights movement literature has, until fairly recently, received little scholarly attention. In her introduction to the *Cambridge Companion to American Civil Rights Literature* (2015), Julie Armstrong notes that "civil rights historiography [has] privileged analysis of political and social issues over the cultural and intellectual."[1] By focusing on literature, which, Armstrong asserts, has the power to create "an imaginative space where the interaction between reader and text results in transformation,"[2] the essays included in the *Cambridge Companion* not only map the contours of a more complex and rich cultural history, they also draw attention to the responsibility of the reader in the ongoing struggle for freedom and justice for all. Citing Audre Lorde's essay "The Transformation of Silence into Language and Action," Armstrong calls readers to raise their own voices in response to literary texts about the civil rights movement. Ideally, these readers will be moved in precisely the way John Lewis describes in his 2012 memoir *Across That Bridge: A Vision for Change and the Future of America*:

> The most important lesson I have learned in the fifty years I have spent working toward the building of a better world is that the true work of social transformation starts within. It begins inside your own heart and mind.[3]

Poems about the Sixteenth Street Church bombing can prompt such transformation by appealing, in various ways, to readers' hearts and minds.

In terms of the potential for individual transformation, poetry and song are perhaps the most potent genres of civil rights literature. After the mass shooting at Mother Emanuel, at the memorial service for the pastor, Reverend Clementa Pinckney, President Obama delivered the eulogy and surprised his audience—in the College of Charleston TD Arena and on TV—by lifting his voice in song. Obama's stirring rendition of "Amazing Grace" spoke to both the grief and the history of that moment.[4] His performance probably took some listeners back to pulpits in other churches where those left behind mourned those who had been targeted because of the color of their skin. As both recorded history and fertile ground for intellectual inquiry and reflection, civil rights movement poetry has been, according to Jeffrey Coleman, another casualty of Jim Crow: "The primary cause of the rupture between [communities and academia] would appear to be social segregation, which also produced segregation in the arts."[5] The primary consequence of such critical neglect is that we have yet to "[comprehend] fully the aesthetic and historical poignancy of the genre."[6] Coleman addressed this gap by editing the anthology *Words of Protest, Words of Freedom: Poetry of the American Civil Rights Movement and Era* (2012), thereby providing scholars with a rich resource of primary source material. In his contribution to the *Cambridge Companion*, he calls for civil rights movement poetry's "critical framing and rightful place in the ever-expanding canon of American letters."[7]

Poetry written about the Sixteenth Street Church bombing reminds us of the persistent need to overcome by bringing us back to a city whose nickname, Bombingham, testifies to the fact that from its beginnings, the US has been in a perpetual state of war with its own citizens. Despite our country's tendency toward a collective forgetting, the 1963 battle of Birmingham continues to be a mainstay of popular culture. Directly after the tragedy, Dudley Randall penned perhaps the most famous poem about the bombing, "The Ballad of Birmingham," and jazz musician John Coltrane paid tribute to the four girls in "Alabama," one of the tracks on *Live at Birdland*, released the following year. Folk singer Joan Baez memorialized the tragedy in her haunting rendition of Richard Farina's "Birmingham Sunday," also in 1964. More recent responses to this battle include Christopher Paul Curtis's 1995 young adult novel *The Watsons Go to Birmingham—1963* (made into a TV movie by Tonya Lewis Lee in 2013), Spike Lee's 1997 documentary *4 Little Girls* (the theme song of which is Baez's "Birmingham Sunday"), and Anthony Grooms's 2001 novel *Bombingham*. Grooms draws attention to another young life lost on the day of the Sixteenth Street Church bombing: while riding on the handlebars of a bicycle, thirteen-year-old Virgil Ware was shot by a white boy; in the novel, the protagonist's best friend Lamar is shot in just the same way.[8] By juxtaposing the adult male protagonist's experiences in Vietnam with his childhood in Birmingham, Grooms does more than ask readers to consider Addie Mae, Cynthia, Carole, Denise, and Virgil as casualties of domestic warfare—he calls attention to the trauma suffered by the survivors. The sculpture unveiled on the fiftieth anniversary of the church bombing acknowledges that trauma by including Addie Mae's sister Sarah, the only living witness to the explosion in the church basement girls' restroom. Like the fictional characters in *The Watsons Go to Birmingham—1963* and *Bombingham*, Sarah Collins struggled in the aftermath of the bombing, with permanent wounds to her body (she lost an eye) and even deeper wounds to her spirit (Figure 5.1).

In this chapter, we examine three poems about the Sixteenth Street Church bombing, each published within ten years of the tragedy, when its memory would still have been vivid in the US popular imagination. The poets—Michael Harper, Langston Hughes, and Alice Walker—are well known and widely anthologized, although readers may not be familiar with their civil rights movement poetry. The poems we have selected, like all the poetry collected in Coleman's *Words of Protest, Words of Freedom*, present opportunities for the transformation that Armstrong asserts is the result when a reader actively interacts with a literary text. Read together and

FIGURE 5.1 "Four Spirits" in Kelly Ingram Park, with the Sixteenth Street Baptist Church in the background. Sculptor Elizabeth MacQueen recognized Addie Mae's sister Sarah with a small medallion on the side of the bench. The sculpture's title comes from Sena Jeter Naslund's 2001 novel of the same name.
Photo courtesy of Chuck Offenburger.

properly contextualized, these poems take us back in order to move us forward, thereby expressing faith in Birmingham's other epithet, the City of Perpetual Promise.

"Can't Find What You Can't See": Michael Harper's "American History"

In a 1995 interview with Bill Moyers, Harper insists that the poet's job "is to tell the truth no matter what," and his purpose is "to put the criticism and the movement in the work, to make the tears go off in the reader."[9] Those tears are a prerequisite for modality, which he explains in terms of relationship: "modality is…about energy, energy irreducible and true only unto itself… the western orientation of division…is a way of misunderstanding what modality is: *modality is always about unity.*"[10] Profoundly influenced by musicians, Harper spent his life teaching and writing poetry.[11] In "American History," he connects the Sixteenth Street Church bombing in Birmingham to slavery, asking readers to resist the lie of American progress and face the truth of our violent past and present.

"American History" consists of a single stanza of nine, two- to six-word lines, the poem's brevity contrasting sharply with its title and thereby calling attention to the constructed and contested nature of both terms—"American" and "History." Scant punctuation, line breaks, and wording work together to build tension and emphasize the gaps in our historical knowledge and understanding. The first two lines of the poem, "Those four black girls blown up / in that Alabama church," end on contrasting images, leaving the reader to resolve a central conceit—"blown up" and "church."[12] Despite strong associations with safety, sanctuary, and the sacred, churches—particularly black churches in the American South—have a history of getting blown up. Furthermore, "that Alabama church" represents a potent site of memory. Building on the definition of *lieux de memoire* by French historian Pierre Nora, Armstrong notes that sites of memory "stand at the crossroads of personal and collective memory"; they are important to reading civil rights literature because they "often form counter-narratives to official or mainstream histories [so] interacting with them involves thinking critically about one's relationship to a particular past."[13] While the Sixteenth Street Church bombing has a place in the narrative of the civil rights movement, what happened on that day (and why) receives much less (if any) attention in the larger story we tell ourselves about our country. Harper's "American History" forces a confrontation with and a revision of that story.

By connecting the Sixteenth Street Church to eighteenth-century slave ships, Harper draws on multiple sites of memory for his history lesson and in the process puts the criticism *and the movement* in his work:

> Those four black girls blown up
> in that Alabama church
> remind me of five hundred
> middle passage blacks,
> in a net, under water
> in Charleston harbor
> so *redcoats* wouldn't find them.[14]

A major port in the transatlantic slave trade, Charleston was also the site of a devastating defeat for the colonists in the Revolutionary War, the city surrendering to the British on May 12, 1780. The italicizing of the word *redcoats* underscores white slaveholders' attitudes toward what they considered their cargo, implicating white colonists in the bloody business of subjugation and tyranny—the very thing they were purportedly fighting against. Having transported hundreds of black people (per ship) in unimaginable and horrific conditions, potential slaveholders were more willing to lose an investment than acknowledge and protect the human lives they bought and sold as commodities. Treating black people as commodities instead of living, sentient beings necessitated legal as well as moral justification, hence the creation of a multifaceted ideology of white supremacy. By putting the Sixteenth Street Church bombing in this wider context, Harper's "American History" effectively explains current racial violence in terms of an ideology adapting to its time and circumstance.[15]

"American History" ends with a question that rephrases the opening question of our national anthem: "Can't find what you can't see / can you?" Notice the shift from *redcoats* to *you*. In this short poem, Harper prompts reflection on (white) America's fight for freedom: intent on freeing itself from a tyrannical ruler, the "new world" fought for its right to self-govern while at the same time retaining the "inalienable" right to deny life and liberty to others. Essentially, Harper suggests that we remain (willfully) blind to the fact that American history is the story of white supremacy. And in this story, the four little girls who lost their lives in 1963—*the bombs bursting in air* as well as in the basements of black churches—represent the resistance. Addie Mae, Cynthia, Carole, and Denise are casualties, like the bodies of the slaves "in a net / under water," in a fight for freedom and equality that continues with no end in sight.

"Songs upon the Breeze": Langston Hughes's "Birmingham Sunday"

Hughes left readers with a rich body of work in multiple genres; he also influenced generations of artists and thinkers, including Martin Luther King, Jr. In *Origins of the Dream: Hughes's Poetry and King's Rhetoric* (2015), Jason Miller argues for a wider historical context for reading arguably the most famous African American poet by putting him in conversation with the African American preacher famous for challenging his country to live up to its promises:

> The repeated appearances of Hughes's poetry in King's rhetoric reminds us that Hughes made lasting contributions to the century's two most significant African American initiatives. In very different ways, Hughes's poetry is just as important to the civil rights movement as it is to the Harlem Renaissance….By transforming Hughes's poetry, King was able to inspire, unify, and organize people to work toward making lasting changes in American society…King validated Hughes's words more than any other poet's, because both of them wanted America to achieve what it claimed to believe.[16]

The influence of Hughes's work on King speaks to the power of his poetry to connect individuals to their humanity as well as to their national identity and moral responsibilities. Reading these two writers' work together also brings crucial attention to socio-economic class as a key factor in the struggle for freedom. In her Pulitzer Prize-winning *Carry Me Home: Birmingham, Alabama, the Climactic Battle of the Civil Rights Revolution* (2001), Diane McWhorter identifies President Franklin D. Roosevelt's New Deal as the catalyst for the war that raged in her hometown in 1963. This war had been going on for centuries: "The conflict that made Birmingham America's Armageddon in 1963 was the 'class warfare' that had always threatened the confidence of a young nation founded on the preposterous principle of equality."[17] *Carry Me Home* opens with the Sixteenth Street Church bombing. McWhorter then traces this act of violence back to an alliance between Birmingham's moneyed class (the Big Mules) and the politicians, police, and white residents who served and protected the ruling class' interests, often by using and/or responding to racist rhetoric and action. A combination of memoir and investigative journalism, McWhorter's work historicizes white resistance to integration, offering a more complex understanding of a struggle for black freedom that she boldly (and properly) calls "a continuation of the Civil War."[18] King clearly understood the economic underpinnings of white racism, shifting his focus, after the passage of the Civil Rights Act in 1964 and the Civil Rights Voting Act in 1965, to fighting the war against poverty.

Hughes's "Birmingham Sunday" sings the America that Harper describes in "American History." The poem begins with and keeps circling back to the young martyrs: "Four little girls / Who went to Sunday School that day / And never came back home at all / But left instead / Their blood upon the wall."[19] The reader essentially becomes a witness to the gruesomeness of racially motivated violence and the tragic consequences of segregation, the "wall" both a physical and metaphorical manifestation of the daily indignities of living black in white America. Hughes then traces the source of the blast to China, a country known for its own wall(s):

> With splattered flesh
> And bloodied Sunday dresses
> Torn to shreds by dynamite
> That China made aeons ago –
> Did not know
> That what China made
> Before China was ever Red at all
> Would redden with their blood
> This Birmingham-on-Sunday wall.[20]

The references to China place the violence of and motivation for the church bombing in a much broader context of world history and politics. The four little girls could not have known that China invented gunpowder for use in fireworks, nor could the girls have been aware of the evolution of the use of gunpowder in weapons, all hundreds of years before the Chinese government became part of the communist régime. In "Birmingham Sunday," Hughes casts the four little girls as both young warriors and innocent casualties of a war against oppression stretching back centuries and occurring around the globe.

In the second and third stanzas, Hughes looks forward to a revolution: "Four tiny girls / Who left their blood upon that wall, / In little graves today await / The dynamite that might ignite / The fuse of centuries of Dragon Kings."[21] Chinese mythological figures similar to the Greek God Poseidon, Dragon Kings rule over the ocean (water) and the weather, invoking massive destruction and change. The innocent girls caught in the crossfire of the battle of Birmingham thus wait for the moment when, presumably, the people (workers) unite to fight for their rights. Like Harper, Hughes puts the criticism in the work, pointing out the hypocrisy of white Americans: "Whose tomorrow sings a hymn / The missionaries never taught Chinese / In Christian Sunday School / To implement the Golden Rule." In King-like fashion, Hughes has faith that a change is gonna come: "Four little girls / Might be awakened someday soon / By songs upon the breeze / As yet unfelt among magnolia trees."[22] Notably, the poet known for his "weary blues" asserts that the girls will be remembered in *song*, their spirits fueling passion for the (Southern) resistance.

"What Did We Know?": Alice Walker's "Winking at a Funeral"

Walker's literary legacy rests on her fierce advocacy in the global struggle against sexism and racism, particularly for black women within their own communities, as well as her unflagging belief in the potential for individual and societal change. Widely recognized for her fiction, and in particular for the Pulitzer Prize-winning *The Color Purple* (1980), Walker also published several volumes of poetry. In *Transforming Words/Revolutionizing Verses: Four Poets of the American Civil Rights Movement*, Coleman summarizes the critical response to Walker's poetry: scholars consider her work in this genre "a mere stepping stone to [her] more 'important' or 'serious' creation of fiction."[23] The critical disparagement and subsequent neglect of Walker's poetry may reflect, in part, her perceived lack of an overt political focus. In her poem about the Sixteenth Street Church bombing, for example, Walker does not mention the four little girls; she does not memorialize the tragic event so much as affirm the experiences and feelings of the young survivors.

The second movement in an eight-movement poem titled *In These Dissenting Times* and published in *Revolutionary Petunias & Other Poems* (1973), "Winking at a Funeral" begins by remembering the carefree nature of growing up in the safety and joy of one's church. In *While the World Watched: A Birmingham Bombing Survivor Comes of Age During the Civil Rights Movement* (2011), Carolyn Maull McKinstry describes how her young life revolved around her church: at the Sixteenth Street Baptist Church, Carolyn attended classes, socialized with her friends (including her best friend Cynthia Wesley), worked in the office, read the announcements, and worshipped. The only place her strict father would allow her to go unescorted was the Sixteenth Street Church because "getting hurt just wasn't something you thought about happening at church."[24] Walker's poem captures the innocence of Carolyn's childhood:

> Those were the days
> Of winking at a
> Funeral
> Romance blossomed
> In the pews
> Love signaled
> Through the
> Hymns
> What did we know?[25]

In her memoir, McKinstry takes pains to point out what she did *not* know: despite living in a city whose white residents responded to integration with dynamite, she grew up with very little knowledge or experience of racism. The warm embrace of her church, her community, and her family protected her from all but the vaguest notions of what it really meant to be black in white America. All that changed on the day of the bombing:

> Not many young people can pinpoint the exact date, time, and place they grew up and became an adult. I can. It was September 15, 1963, 10:22 a.m., at the Sixteenth Street Baptist Church in Birmingham, Alabama. My life changed forever after that day. Not only did I lose four friends, but I also lost my innocence and naiveté about people and about the world in general. The loving trust I had in the goodness of humanity was gone.[26]

Divided into two stanzas, Walker's poem speaks directly to Carolyn's experience. The bombing had so profound an effect on Carolyn that she forever divided her life into BB (before the bombing) and AB (after the bombing).

In the second stanza, Walker asks two more questions that, in turn, raise questions about her audience and intent: "Who smelled the flowers / Slowly fading? / Knew the arsonist / Of the church?" The first question draws attention to the inevitable transition to adulthood that the bombing precipitated. For McKinstry, the fading of her youth had profound consequences:

> I began to see the world as a deadly and hostile place, where no one, not even my father or my brothers or my church, could protect me. And for the first time in my life, I felt all alone.[27]

Once vibrant and happy children, Carolyn and her brother Kirk became quiet and withdrawn. Particularly heartbreaking in McKinstry's account is that no one reached out to them:

> In the time immediately after the church bombing, no one spoke of the tragedy or of the girls who died. Not the afternoon of the bombing. Not that night. Not the next day or

the next month or the next year. After the funeral, no one mentioned again the four dead girls—my friends. Not my parents, not my teachers, not my pastor, not my Sunday school teachers, not my church members, not my friends. No one.[28]

After the bombing, the church elders sealed the girls' restroom with a wall. With no visible reminder and no words acknowledging the event or its painful effects, "it was almost as if it never happened."[29] For her memoir, McKinstry broke nearly fifty years of silence "to write down in permanent ink my eyewitness account of just what happened while the world watched… lest *I* forget. Lest we *all* forget."[30]

Walker's final question about knowing "the arsonist" speaks to the conspiratorial nature of the act of "winking at a funeral." While winking may signal innocent flirtation in the face of death, something a young person might feel far removed from, it also indicates being "in the know." Who "knew" the arsonist raises the question of culpability. The day after the bombing, Charles Morgan, Jr., a white Birmingham attorney, felt compelled to speak out about what he knew: "Every person in this community who has in any way contributed during the past several years to the popularity of hatred is at least as guilty, or more so, than the demented fool who threw that bomb." In a speech that must have been as satisfying as it was risky, Morgan insisted that "[w]e all did it."[31] The idea of a mass conspiracy, with active and passive conspirators at various stages of consciousness, all responsible for this crime (as well as all the bombings for at least a decade) suggests the enormity of the enemy. In his eulogy for three of the murdered girls, King joins Morgan in distinguishing between "the demented fool" who set the bomb and the conditions that allowed and encouraged the hatred to go unchecked. King insists that in their deaths, the girls "say to us that we must be concerned not merely about who murdered them, but about the system, the way of life, the philosophy which produced the murderers."[32]

Like Harper and Hughes, Walker puts the criticism and the movement in her poem about the Sixteenth Street Church bombing, drawing attention to what King calls "the system" but in a more subtle way. The personal is indeed political in "Winking at a Funeral." And, in characteristic fashion for Walker, the political must begin with the person(al): the question the poem poses but does not ask directly is now that you *do* know, what will you do?

An Unforgettable Day in Our Nation

In the aftermath of the 2015 mass shooting at Mother Emanuel Church in Charleston, many Americans focused their attention on the contentious issue of the Confederate flag: does it represent heritage or hate? In his eulogy for Reverend Pinckney, Obama commended South Carolina Governor Nikki Haley for removing the flag from her state's capitol. In subsequent years, several states have removed various Confederate monuments, this process accelerating after the murder of Heather Heyer during a Unite the Right rally of white nationalists in Charlottesville, Virginia on August 12, 2017.[33] While symbolic, and arguably long overdue, the actual impact of removing monuments is often exaggerated and the reaction, swift and furious, too often downplayed. In Alabama, for example, the legislature voted in 2017 to restrict the removal of "historically significant" monuments just two years after the Governor, following Haley's example, had removed the Confederate flag from the state capitol in Montgomery. The virulent nature of these debates speaks to the enormity of the stakes: whose version of history gets remembered—and how—has enormous, and sometimes deadly, consequences.

In the consensus narrative of the civil rights movement, the bombing of the Sixteenth Street Church in Birmingham shocked and shamed America(ns), galvanized supporters, and pressured politicians into passing civil rights legislation; in other words, it is a tragic chapter in a story with a triumphant ending. Indeed, King predicted such an ending in nearly every speech he gave, and in *Why We Can't Wait* (1968), he manipulated the timeline to place the bombing *before* the March on Washington. In King's narrative of the movement, the focus is thus on legislative victories, not violent backlash—on the faith of the freedom fighters, not the resilience of the racist rebels. In Obama's eulogy for Reverend Pinckney, he too connected the murders to a larger American story of a slow, painful yet steady march toward a more perfect union. Building on his theme of grace, Obama declared that taking down the Confederate flag was both "an expression of God's grace" and "one step in an honest accounting of America's history." In her retrospective, Carolyn McKinstry demonstrates this same impulse. Like McWhorter, who declares 1963 to be a "national turning point" when two events (the children's marches in Kelly Ingram Park that brought out Bull Connor's fire hoses and the Sixteenth Street Church bombing) "brought about the end of apartheid in America," McKinstry looks back at 1963 Birmingham with a desire to tell the truth but also the need to make meaning out of a senseless act of racially motivated violence.[34] She thus underscores the changes that immediately followed the murders of her friends. Expressing a "deep sense of outrage and grief" that the *Saturday Evening Post* presented as reflecting "the national temper," President Kennedy sent five hundred armed soldiers to Birmingham as well as a team of FBI investigators.[35] Twelve days after the bombing, *Time* magazine put Governor Wallace's face on its cover with the caption: *Alabama: Civil Rights Battlefield*. And the local news media cast the murdered girls as martyrs, commentary in the black *Birmingham World* predicting, "[t]his will be an unforgettable day in our nation, in world history, in the new rebellion of which the Confederate flag seems to symbolize."[36]

In September 1963, all eyes did seem to be on Birmingham, the City of Perpetual Promise with a deeply disturbing affinity for dynamite. This intense national attention inspired the title for McKinstry's memoir:

> Little did I know that the loss of those girls was, ironically, the real beginning of hope for blacks and whites in Birmingham. Their blood—the 'blood of the innocents'—had spilled on the hands of Birmingham's people. And now, finally, the whole world was watching.[37]

But at the time, and for several decades after, what McKinstry heard and felt was a deafening and devastating *silence*. Americans, in Birmingham and in Charleston, in Ferguson and Charlottesville, have a seemingly unlimited capacity for living quite comfortably with blood on their hands or, as Obama put it in his eulogy, "slip[ping] into a comfortable silence."

The transformative power of literature rests on its ability to break that silence. Not surprisingly, ceremonies marking the fiftieth anniversary of the Sixteenth Street Church bombing featured literary performances: Christina M. Ham's play *Four Little Girls: Birmingham 1963*, a reading by Sena Jeter Naslund from her novel *Four Spirits*, speeches by civil rights advocates, songs, and prayers. The Hallmark Channel aired *The Watsons Go to Birmingham—1963*, and Birmingham's Alabama Theater premiered *4 Little Girls*. Viewers of Lee's documentary might have recognized Chris McNair (Denise McNair's father) among the crowd at the unveiling of MacQueen's sculpture memorializing the tragic events of fifty years before. When asked about the potential impact of the sculpture, McNair said, "I don't know what it'll achieve, but I'm pleased with it."[38] What sculptures, sermons, novels, films, plays, and poems about the civil rights movement do is give us the opportunity to bear witness and to renew our commitment to civil rights activity—to the process of overcoming that each generation must accept as its challenge as well as its moral responsibility.

Teaching Approaches to Civil Rights Movement Poetry

Discussion Questions

1. Why do you think a poet would write about the Sixteenth Street Church bombing? What would be the poet's catalyst (the situation or problem to be addressed) and purpose? Who is the audience for such poetry?
2. Do you think poetry, as a literary genre, has a qualitatively different effect on a reader than other genres? How is poetry about the Sixteenth Street Church bombing different from a documentary, a photograph, or a song about the tragedy? How is it different from a stage production, fiction film, or novel?
3. How would your understanding of history be different if poetry were taught alongside standard textbooks, documentaries, and nonfiction such as King's "Letter from Birmingham Jail"? Do you think literary texts should be included in courses other than English?
4. Each of the poems discussed in this chapter was written a half-century ago. Do you think they are best understood as products of their time, or are they "timeless"? In what ways do you think the poems speak to readers for whom the civil rights movement is a chapter in a history textbook?

Research and Writing Projects

1. Rewrite King's "Letter from Birmingham Jail" as a poem. Then rewrite any of the poems about the Sixteenth Street Church bombing as a letter to the editor or speech. What happens when you switch genres?
2. Select at least three poems on the same theme from Jeffrey Coleman's *Words of Protest, Words of Freedom*. With reference to the poet's use of literary devices (imagery, juxtaposition, repetition, etc.), discuss how each poet puts the criticism and the movement in their work. Identify what truth(s) the poets are telling.
3. Find a detailed timeline of the civil rights movement from a credible source. Choose a historical figure, geographic location, or event on the timeline other than the Sixteenth Street Church bombing. Prepare a multimodal presentation that tells the story of your chosen focus, using a variety of sources, including poetry.
4. Browse the websites of your local, county, and state historical societies for information about monuments, memorials, and commemorations. What historical figures and events get remembered—and how? Create a slideshow of such remembrances, with captions, to tell a story about the history and values of your town or state.

Notes

1. Julie Buckner Armstrong, "Introduction," in *The Cambridge Companion to American Civil Rights Literature*, ed. Julie Buckner Armstrong (New York: Cambridge University Press, 2015), 4.
2. Ibid., 6.
3. John Lewis, *Across That Bridge: A Vision for Change and the Future of America* (New York: Hachette Books, 2012), 27.
4. An avowed white supremacist, Roof deliberately targeted Mother Emanuel because of its rich black history.
5. Jeffrey Lamar Coleman, "Civil Rights Movement Poetry," in *The Cambridge Companion to American Civil Rights Literature*, ed. Julie Buckner Armstrong (New York: Cambridge University Press, 2015), 144.
6. Ibid., 153.
7. Ibid., 144.

8 A sixth victim, 16-year-old Johnny Robinson, Jr., was shot in the back by a Birmingham police officer on that fateful day.
9 "The Heart of Things: Adrienne Rich, Michael Harper and Victor Hernández Cruz," *billmoyers.com*, July 28, 1995.
10 Abraham Chapman, "An Interview with Michael S. Harper," *Arts in Society: The Arts in the Post-Industrial Society* 11.3 (1974), 465.
11 In 1970, Harper published his first book of poetry, *Dear John, Dear Coltrane*, addressed to the famous jazz musician.
12 Michael S. Harper, "American History," in *Words of Protest, Words of Freedom: Poetry of the American Civil Rights Movement and Era*, ed. Jeffrey Lamar Coleman (Durham: Duke University Press, 2012), 61.
13 Armstrong, "Introduction," 5.
14 Harper, "American History," 61.
15 Michelle Alexander, author of *The New Jim Crow* (2010), and Ava DuVernay, director of the award-winning documentary *13th* (2016), would both cite mass incarceration as the most egregious modern example of white supremacy adapting to perceived gains by black people in the post-civil rights movement era.
16 Jason W. Miller, *Origins of the Dream: Hughes's Poetry and King's Rhetoric* (Gainesville: University Press of Florida, 2015), 11.
17 Diane McWhorter, *Carry Me Home: Birmingham, Alabama, the Cinematic Battle of the Civil Rights Revolution* (New York: Simon & Schuster, 2001), 17.
18 Ibid., 15.
19 Langston Hughes, "Birmingham Sunday," in *Words of Protest, Words of Freedom: Poetry of the American Civil Rights Movement and Era*, ed. Jeffrey Lamar Coleman (Durham: Duke University Press, 2012), 63.
20 Ibid.
21 Ibid.
22 Ibid.
23 Jeffrey Lamar Coleman, "Transforming Words/Revolutionizing Verses: Four Poets of the American Civil Rights Movement" (PhD dissertation, University of New Mexico, 1997), 131.
24 Carolyn Maull McKinstry, *While the World Watched: A Birmingham Bombing Survivor Comes of Age During the Civil Rights Movement* (Carol Stream: Tyndale House, 2011), 28.
25 Alice Walker, *Revolutionary Petunias & Other Poems* (New York: Harcourt, 1973), 4.
26 McKinstry, *While the World Watched*, 24.
27 Ibid.
28 Ibid., 79.
29 Ibid.
30 Ibid., x.
31 Roy Reed, "Charles Morgan Jr., 78, Dies: Leading Civil Rights Lawyer," *New York Times*, January 9, 2009.
32 Martin Luther King, Jr., "Eulogy for the Young Victims of the Sixteenth Street Baptist Church Bombing," in *A Call to Conscience: The Landmark Speeches of Martin Luther King*, ed. Clayborne Carson and Kris Shepard (New York: IPM, 2001), 96.
33 A years-long debate took place at our institution in Tennessee over renaming the ROTC building, currently named after Nathan Bedford Forrest, Confederate Civil War General and first Grand Wizard of the Ku Klux Klan. A recommendation to remove the name currently awaits legislative approval.
34 McWhorter, *Carry Me Home*, 15.
35 George McMillan, "The Birmingham Church Bomber," *Saturday Evening Post*, June 1964, 15.
36 "Killers of the Innocents—Commentary," *Birmingham World* (Birmingham), September 18, 1963.
37 McKinstry, *While the World Watched*, 62.
38 Tom Gordon, "Four Spirits unveiled across from Sixteenth Street Baptist Church," *Weld: Birmingham's Newspaper* (Birmingham), September 14, 2013.

6

"PASS IT ON!"

Legacy and the Freedom Struggle in Toni Morrison's *Song of Solomon*

Laura Dubek

> Oh, I wish I could fly
> Like a bird up in the sky
> And then wake up one morning
> To find out for myself, oh
> You don't even have to die
>
> Listen, I'd fly if I could fly, you see
> To the sun and then down
> To the deep blue sea
> Then I'd sing, yes
> I'd sing about freedom
>
>   Solomon Burke
>   "I Wish I Knew"[1]

Toni Morrison has written often about the relationship between her writing and black music. In "Rootedness: The Ancestor as Foundation," the novelist explains that

> [f]or a long time, the art form that was healing for Black people was music. That music is no longer *exclusively* ours…Other people sing it and play it…So another form has to take its place, and it seems to me that the novel is needed by African-Americans now in a way that it was not needed before.[2]

While Morrison does not specify when black music became mainstream, Craig Werner locates that shift in the mid-1960s: in *A Change Is Gonna Come: Music, Race and the Soul of America*, he tracks a key change from Mahalia Jackson's soulful gospel performance at the 1963 March on Washington to Diana Ross's unprecedented commercial "crossover" success in the final years of that decade.[3] Nina Simone provides backup for Werner's claim in her autobiography *I Put a Spell on You*, effectively connecting this key change to shifts in political vision. Simone identifies 1963 as a pivotal year in the civil rights movement, a time when activists felt compelled to choose between two very different ways forward—the integration and passive resistance model advocated by Martin Luther King, Jr. and his Southern Christian Leadership Conference (SCLC) and the black power vision promoted by Stokely Carmichael and other young militants increasingly at odds with SCLC as well as members of their own group, the Student Nonviolent Coordinating Committee (SNCC).[4] It is into this space—a crossroads in the freedom struggle—that Morrison's *Song of Solomon* enters, and it does so by referencing slavery and Jim Crow, linking characters to historical figures in the civil rights movement, and conjuring up the spirit of a gospel singer named Solomon Burke.

A Pulitzer Prize-winner and Nobel laureate, Morrison has occupied a wider circle of influence than Burke, a soul singer with gospel roots who never achieved the name recognition of Otis Redding, James Brown, or Aretha Franklin. Called the King of Rock and Soul in the 1960s, Burke grew up in his grandmother's church where, at the age of seven, he would begin preaching. At fourteen, he was singing in a gospel quartet, and at fifteen, he signed his first contract with Apollo Records. His music merges the spiritual with the secular, his albums provoking the same kind of emotional response that his sermons at Solomon's Temple inspired. A charismatic figure and native of Philadelphia, Burke lived most of his life near Danville, Pennsylvania and Shalimar, Virginia—the homes of the ancestors of *Song of Solomon*'s protagonist, Milkman Dead. Burke's godfather was Father Divine, mentioned in the novel's opening scene when Mercy Hospital personnel go outside to find out why a crowd has gathered and a black woman is singing: "[s]ome of them thought briefly that this was probably some form of worship. Philadelphia, where Father Divine reigned, wasn't all that far away."[5] And in a parallel that simply cannot be a coincidence, Burke, just like Milkman's great-grandfather Solomon, had twenty-one children.

Burke's spirit permeates Morrison's novel, from the title to the final scene at Solomon's Leap. When Milkman journeys south, he confronts the name Solomon everywhere:

> Everybody in this town is named Solomon, he thought wearily. Solomon's General Store, Luther Solomon (no relation), Solomon's Leap, and now the children were singing '*Solomon* don't leave me' instead of '*Sugarman*.' Even the name of the town sounded like Solomon: Shalimar, which Mr. Solomon and everybody else pronounced *Shalleemone*.[6]

The unusual pronunciation of Shalimar suggests the presence of another singer. An active participant in the civil rights movement, Simone recorded "I Wish I Knew (How It Would Feel to Be Free)" in 1967. The following year, Burke recorded the same song for Atlantic Records—but with a difference. Whereas Simone sings, "Well I wish I could be / like a bird in the sky / How sweet it would be / If I found I could fly," Burke sings, "Oh, I wish I could fly / Like a bird up in the sky / And then wake up one morning / To find out for myself, oh / You don't even have to die."[7] Simone's wistful lyrics, easily interpreted as a metaphor for freedom, are thus extended in Burke's version to include a "you" who does not have "to die." In *Song of Solomon*, Milkman yearns to fly, the narrator telling us that "when the little boy discovered, at four, the same thing Mr. Smith had learned earlier—that only birds and airplanes could fly—he lost all interest in himself."[8] The key to Milkman's regaining this interest in himself is more than just the discovery of his great-grandfather Solomon's flight: it is the acceptance that he carries within himself Solomon's spirit (the "you" who does not have "to die") as well as the spirits of *all* the dead whose names bear witness to the lives they lived in a country that denied them civil rights.

In the preface to *The Civil Rights Reader: American Literature from Jim Crow to Reconstruction* (2009), Julie Armstrong and Amy Schmidt argue that the "simple yet compelling" standard narrative of the civil rights movement has, in the last decade, been challenged by civil rights scholars and activists because of what that narrative leaves out:

> In terms of leadership, focusing on a handful of high-profile, nationally recognized figures fails to recognize the hard work of everyday people who made change happen in ways small and large…In terms of chronology, focusing on the 1954 to 1968 years leaves out everything that came before or happened after.[9]

The "expanded historical vision" informing the selections included in this anthology is fully realized in *Song of Solomon* as Morrison echoes and responds to Burke's call. Indeed, his 1968 version of "I Wish I Knew" underscores the need for an immediate and particular response: "Let me hear you say / I'd sing, yes, I'd sing, come on / Sing, children, sing about love now / Sing, sing, sing about peace / Sing, sing, sing about the joy / Sing, sing, sing, ohh…" Burke's call for the children to "sing" links him to Pilate's father Jake, who comes to his daughter several times after his death, each time saying the same thing—*sing*. It also links him to Pilate's mother, whose name is Sing (Byrd), and to Pilate herself, who, in her last breath, tells Milkman to "Sing…Sing a little somethin for me."[10] The freedom song that Morrison sings in her civil rights novel uses naming to allude to the civil rights movement both directly and indirectly, thereby engaging not only with conventional definitions of the movement, particularly models of leadership provided by King and Malcolm X, but also prompting a reconsideration of those definitions, suggesting that we move beyond restrictive dates and geography, and instead consider the freedom struggle in terms of legacy and responsibility.

Many Thousands Gone: 350 Years of Freedom Struggle

The narrative arc of *Song of Solomon* stretches back to slavery, with Solomon's flight from the cotton fields, and to the Emancipation Proclamation, with Solomon's son Jake and his wife Sing's journey north to what would become their farm, "Lincoln's Heaven." By framing the novel's opening scene—Robert Smith's suicidal leap off the roof of Mercy Hospital in 1931 Detroit—with local history and geography, Morrison begins with the assertion that the promise of freedom for black Americans has gone unfulfilled. The narrator tells us that in 1896, the only colored doctor moved to the city. This means that Dr. Foster, the protagonist's maternal grandfather, moved to Mains Avenue the year the Supreme Court issued its "separate but equal" ruling in *Plessy v. Ferguson*. To the consternation of the city legislators, Dr. Foster's patients begin calling Mains Avenue "Doctor Street," and as time passes and more blacks move to the street, letters begin arriving at the post office addressed to Doctor Street. The politicians then set out to reestablish what they consider to be proper distinctions and boundaries:

> Some of the city legislators, whose concern for appropriate names and the maintenance of the city's landmarks was the principal part of their political life, saw to it that "Doctor Street" was never used in any official capacity. And since they knew that only Southside residents kept it up, they had notices posted in the stores, barbershops, and restaurants in that part of the city saying that the avenue running northerly and southerly from Shore Road fronting the lake to the junction of routes 6 between Rutherford Avenue and Broadway, had always been and would always be known as Mains Avenue and not Doctor Street.[11]

In response to these official notices, the black residents begin calling the street "Not Doctor Street" and the hospital at its northern end, "No Mercy Hospital." Later in the novel, we learn that Dr. Foster's arrival in this segregated Northern city coincides with the birth of Pilate, Solomon's granddaughter and perhaps the most fascinating character in Morrison's oeuvre. Pilate's birth is an "unnatural" event that occurs *after* her mother Sing's death and leaves her with no navel, an aberration that marks her not just as different but as a threat to various communities that rebuke and scorn her. Among her prized possessions is a fourth-grade geography textbook. Her interest in geography reminds the reader not just of the segregated nature of American life in the mid-twentieth century but also of the distance some black folks had traveled from their past. Like August Wilson's *Piano Lesson*, set in 1936 Pittsburgh, *Song of Solomon* suggests that the great migration to the (unfulfilled) promised land of the urban North separated blacks from an essential source of strength: the belief in the presence and power of the ancestors.

While black resistance to white power—both before and after *Plessy v. Ferguson*—took many different forms, the civil rights movement represents the most concerted effort to challenge segregation in the twentieth century. In *Song of Solomon*, Morrison refers to this struggle in direct and indirect ways. The men in Tommy's barbershop huddle around the radio, hearing the news of Emmett Till's murder in Sunflower County, Mississippi. Guitar reacts to the bombing of the Sixteenth Street Baptist Church in Birmingham, which resulted in the deaths of four black girls. And either the narrator or a character mentions President Truman, the Commission on Civil Rights, the sit-ins, Bilbo country, Governor Orval Faubus, Elijah, and "that red-headed Negro named X."[12] Indirect references include Freddie's story of his mother dying from fright at the sight of a white bull, an image that calls to mind Bull Connor, the infamous Birmingham police chief who turned fire hoses and dogs on black children in 1963. Also, Dr. Foster's daughter Ruth is repeatedly called the "rose-petal" lady, a veiled reference to Rosa Parks, the forty-two-year-old seamstress who initiated the Montgomery bus boycott and is considered the mother of the civil rights movement. The first black woman allowed to give birth inside of (No) Mercy Hospital, the fictional "rose-petal" lady is the focus of one short but crucial passage and two lengthy ones. In the short passage, she nurses her son in a small room that the narrator tells us contains only two items: a dress form and a sewing machine. In both of the longer passages—the cemetery visit and her trip across town to confront Hagar—she rides a bus.

In a novel packed with unforgettable names—Pilate Dead, Milkman, Guitar, Railroad Tommy, Hospital Tommy, Empire State, First Corinthians, Circe, Sweet, and Sing—Robert Smith's is perhaps the most symbolic. A member of The Seven Days, a secret vigilante group that avenges the murders of blacks by killing whites in similar fashions, Smith dons blue wings and leaps off the roof of Mercy Hospital in the novel's opening scene. Smith may be an indirect reference not only to the many thousands gone but also to the murders of civil rights leaders, such as Robert Kennedy, the attorney general known for fighting organized crime for the Department of Justice. His assassination followed King's assassination by two months in 1968, the year historians mark as the end of the modern civil rights movement. In the novel's opening pages, the narrator points out that Smith works for the North Carolina Insurance Company, going door-to-door collecting $1.68 a month from Southside residents. The narrator reminds us of this date—1968—throughout the novel, telling us, for example, that in 1963, when the novel's final scene takes place, Pilate is sixty-eight years old. We are also constantly reminded that Pilate's father Jake was shot, "blown 5 feet in the air," while sitting on a fence in Danville, Pennsylvania. In 1963, Robert Kennedy's brother, Jack Kennedy, was shot while sitting on the back seat of a convertible in Dallas, Texas. One could argue, then, that *Song of Solomon* encompasses nearly 350 years of civil right history—from 1619, when the first slave ships arrived in Virginia, to 1968, when two well-known dreamers, one black and the other white, were shot dead. These dreamers, and the dream they had for an America that lived up to its promise(s), live on in Morrison's protagonist, Milkman.

A Change Is Gonna Come: Milkman's Dreams from His Fathers

Critics continue to draw attention to *Song of Solomon*'s male protagonist as a distinct departure from Morrison's other works. She identified the challenge of writing her third novel as "manag[ing] what was for me a radical shift in imagination from a female locus to a male one." So, she chose a journey "with the accomplishment of flight, the triumphant end of a trip through earth, to its surface, on into water, and finally into air. All very saga-like. Old-school heroic, but with other meanings."[13] Critics have used different frameworks to discuss Milkman's heroism. In her introduction to Oxford's *Toni Morrison's Song of Solomon: A Casebook*,

Jan Furman uses Joseph Campbell's work to put Milkman's journey in a universal context: "His is a timeless human tale based on the premise that every purposeful endeavor is a search for vitality."[14] In contrast, Gerry Brenner uses Otto Rank's monomyth to delineate all the ways in which Morrison's protagonist does, in fact, satisfy the requirements of a classic hero before boldly declaring Milkman a miserable failure.[15] His "heroism" takes on new meanings when considered within the context of the civil rights movement, with its charismatic male leaders as well as all the unsung heroes (male *and* female) who went to mass meetings in Montgomery, went to jail in Birmingham, went missing in Mississippi, and went to Washington to demand jobs and freedom. Reading Milkman within this historical context highlights his role as a change agent, as an unlikely hero whose "triumphant end" is but the promise of a contract that those of us witnessing his flight must execute. Like his great-grandfather Solomon, what's more important than what Milkman *does* is what he leaves behind.

The shame surrounding the protagonist's nickname—folks call him Milkman because his mother breastfed him long after he could walk—has obscured his connection to Martin Luther King: MLKman. Like other names in the novel, this one is both instructive and ironic; after all, Milkman spends almost the entire novel caring about no one but himself. He only begins to define himself in relation to others after a hunting trip with black men who gather at King Walker's defunct gas station in Shalimar.[16] Writing in 1982, Dorothy Lee discusses the "dual effect" of names in *Song of Solomon*, pointing out that they "widen the reader's perspective to mythical connotations and simultaneously provide ironic commentary on the historical plight of the American black."[17] Such commentary can be detected in Morrison's decision to associate Milkman with dreaming. In 1963, the year Milkman takes off from Solomon's Leap, King delivered his famous "I Have a Dream" speech, telling his audience, "And as we walk, we must make the pledge that we shall always march ahead. We cannot turn back."[18] He was referring, of course, to challenging segregation and working toward the goal of an integrated society. As the first black baby born in (No) Mercy Hospital, Milkman symbolizes that integrated society. Listen carefully, however, and you will hear a drumbeat of caution in Morrison's novel: in marching ahead, we must *continually* "turn back."

Although for most of the novel, Milkman neither marches forward nor turns back, he definitely represents a change that's gonna come. In a pivotal scene at the Dead family dinner table, Milkman takes a step toward claiming his manhood when he responds to his father's fist hitting his mother's face by throwing the older man into the radiator. Shortly after, Milkman goes to his bedroom and looks at his reflection in the mirror:

> Taken apart, it looked all right. Even better than all right. But it lacked coherence, a coming together of the features into a total self. It was all very tentative, the way he looked, like a man peeping around a corner of someplace he is not supposed to be, trying to make up his mind whether to go forward or to turn back. The decision he made would be extremely important, but the way in which he made the decision would be careless, haphazard, and uninformed.[19]

After hearing his father's explanation for why he physically assaulted his wife, Milkman takes to the streets. Deep in his troubled thoughts, he nonetheless notices two things: everyone is walking in a different direction than he is, and nobody, "[n]ot a soul," is walking on the other side of the street. The narrator points out that this observation does not lead to further reflection: "Milkman walked on, still headed toward Southside, never once wondering why he himself did not cross over to the other side of the street, where no one was walking at all."[20] Later, in a conversation with Guitar, Milkman will refer to this moment as a dream, as "one of those waking dreams he was subject to whenever indecisiveness was confronted with reality."[21]

If we read Morrison's protagonist within the context of the civil rights movement and its male leadership, we see what the novel's mirror scene suggests—that what is "tentative" in the way Milkman *looks* is the limited way in which he sees problems and so imagines solutions. On June 12, 1963, Richard Heffner's PBS television show *Open Mind* tried to imagine a solution to "Race Relations in Crisis." Heffner invited four men to discuss what was happening in the streets of Southern cities like Birmingham and Northern cities like Detroit: Wyatt T. Walker, executive director of SCLC; James Farmer, leader of CORE, Congress of Racial Equality; Malcolm X, national spokesman for the Nation of Islam; and Alan Morrison, New York editor of *Ebony Magazine*. Chosen because they represented different ways of addressing what W.E.B. Du Bois, in 1903, had called "the problem of the twentieth century," these men agreed that the solution to racial inequality in America would probably not come from the courts. Even Malcolm X, much less sanguine about the future for blacks in America, argued that the fight must occur in the streets. *Song of Solomon* offers a subtle critique of such political views—views that "looked all right" when "taken apart" but "lacked coherence." The novel suggests that while marching in the streets to gain access to voting booths, restaurants, restrooms, and universities such as Ole Miss (all places where blacks were "not supposed to be") is necessary, such protests will not be the primary means by which we overcome.

To be an effective change agent, Milkman must "cross over" to the other side "where no one was walking at all."[22] He will then become a "total self," which should be understood as a "coming together" *not* of different races or of multiple perspectives on the problem of racism but of different dimensions of space and time. Late in the novel, he begins to understand reality in a profoundly new way. After leaving Susan Byrd's home in Shalimar, he thinks about his ancestors and how Pilate had told him that her dead father visits her and always says *sing*:

> Jesus! Here he was walking around in the middle of the twentieth century trying to explain what a ghost had done. But why not? He thought. One fact was certain: Pilate did not have a navel. Since that was true, anything could be, and why not ghosts as well?

Immediately after accepting that anything could be true, Milkman checks his wrist and realizes that Grace Long, Susan's friend and a seemingly insignificant minor character (who teaches at the Normal school), has pilfered his watch: "'Damn,' he murmured. 'I'm losing everything.'"[23] Indeed, he is losing his grounding in Western notions of time and space, a loss that will allow him to connect with the sustaining power of his ancestors and to fly "To the sun and then down / To the deep blue sea."

Unlike his historical counterpart, Milkman has absolutely no sense of his role as the keeper of any "dream," no sense of the "extreme importance" of his decisions, not even to himself. Morrison, however, makes her protagonist's role clear well before he meets (amazing) Grace in Shalimar. Milkman's journey south begins in Danville, Pennsylvania, at the home of Reverend Cooper, who exclaims, "I know your people!"[24] Milkman spends several evenings talking to Cooper and his friends about his father's material success in the North. In turn, the old men tell Milkman stories about his grandfather's legendary prowess and prosperity. The narrator underscores the reciprocal nature of Milkman's relationship with these men: "Looking at Milkman in those nighttime talks, they yearned for something. Some word from him that would rekindle the dream and stop the death they were dying."[25] Milkman's dream is to find the gold that his father is convinced remains in a cave near the house where Circe provided shelter for Macon and Pilate after their father died. But rekindling the old men's dream and stopping the "death they were dying" will have nothing to do with gold. An obsession with material wealth and power—gold, ivory, rum, tobacco, sugar, cotton, spices, and slaves—is what caused all the dying. What is needed now is "some word."

In the myth of the flying African, *Song of Solomon*'s most central framework, a young witch doctor utters a "strange word," and all the slaves working in the cotton fields drop their hoes and fly home. The grandson of the first colored doctor to move to Mains Avenue, Milkman's fascination with flight finds expression in his dreams. His last dream, which he has just before deciphering the children's song about his family history, indicates that he is starting to understand that his eyes are on the wrong prize:

> It was a warm dreamy sleep all about flying, about sailing high over the earth. But not with arms outstretched like airplane wings, nor shot forward like Superman in a horizontal dive, but floating, cruising, in the relaxed position of a man lying on a couch reading a newspaper. Part of his flight was over the dark sea, but it didn't frighten him because he knew he could not fall. He was alone in the sky, but somebody was applauding him, watching him and applauding. He couldn't see who it was.[26]

Milkman's flight recalls his great-grandfather Solomon's flight from the plantation but with significant differences. While neither man needs an airplane to "cut across the sky," Solomon flies *away*, he goes *home*, he leaves everybody *behind*. Grounded in the everyday events recorded in the newspaper, Milkman belongs to the country of his birth, even as the laws of his country deny him civil rights based on the color of his skin.

The sacrifices made, the blood spilled, to make that belonging a reality is the lesson imparted by Reverend Cooper and his cohort in Danville. Using Milkman "as the ignition that gunned their memories," these men shout in a manner that recalls the call-and-response of Burke's gospel performances:

> We live here. On this planet, in this nation, in this country right here. *N*owhere else! We got a home in this rock, don't you see! Nobody starving in my home; nobody crying in my home, and if I got a home you got one too! Grab it. Grab this land! Take it, hold it, my brothers, make it, my brothers, shake it, squeeze it, turn it, twist it, beat it, kick it, kiss it, whip it, stomp it, dig it, plow it, seed it, reap it, rent it, buy it, sell it, own it, build it, multiply it, and pass it on—can you hear me? Pass it on![27]

In the dream where he sails "over the dark sea," Milkman cannot see the ancestors, but he can hear and feel them. Milkman's responsibility is to merge the spiritual (the evidence of things unseen) with the secular, identifying not just with Reverend Cooper and the black men who knew his grandfather but with the many thousands gone, all the Africans lost during the Middle Passage and all the slaves who worked the land and suffered the lash. What will keep their dream from dying is the knowledge that everything they worked for is being passed on. Morrison expresses this desire in the epigraph to *Song of Solomon*: "The fathers may soar / And the children may know their names."

Milkman's ascent requires knowing his family history, knowledge he gains through immersion in the rural Southern culture of his ancestors. After his second conversation with Susan Byrd, when she acknowledges Sing's marriage to Jake, Milkman finally understands why Pilate carries her name in a brass box dangling from her ear: "When you know your name, you should hang on to it, for unless it is noted down and remembered, it will die when you do."[28] He hears the story, though not the name, of his paternal grandfather on his first trip to his aunt's house. Pilate tells Milkman and Guitar about her father's murder and also about seeing his ghost for the first time: "It was like looking at a face under water."[29] Pilate's father has joined the ancestors, the "somebod[ies]" whom Milkman will eventually feel and hear as he flies, in his dream, "over the dark sea." Morrison links Milkman with the ancestors by associating him with water throughout the novel. After learning the names of his grandparents, Milkman practically sprints to Sweet's house, shouting that he wants to swim: "Come on, let's go swimming. I'm dirty and I want waaaaater!" Sweet offers to give Milkman a bath, but he scoffs, "The sea! I have to swim in the sea. Don't give me no itty bitty teeny tiny tub, girl. I need the whole entire complete deep blue sea!"[30] As Milkman's "triumphant end" draws near, it is clear that he has gained an interest in himself and his people, but he still has much to learn. What he must do in order to fly is combine the shout with the moan, something he cannot do without help from Guitar and Pilate.

What Else but Love?: Guitar's Lesson

Morrison links Milkman's best friend, Guitar Bains, to Malcolm X, the black leader often considered the ideological opposite of King and generally associated, in the American public imagination, with hate. When Milkman is fourteen, Guitar will become his friend and protector, the older boy serving as the younger boy's link to the Southside, to the rhythms of working-class black life, to Mary's bar and Tommy's barbershop. These class differences mirror the different experiences and sensibilities of Malcolm X and King. Nurtured by the comforts and trappings of a middle-class sensibility, Milkman is as apathetic as Guitar is politically engaged, a point Guitar makes clear: "You're not a serious person, Milkman."[31] What Morrison makes clear, however, is that Guitar has as much to learn from the spoiled rich kid as Milkman does from the angry militant. After Milkman calls Guitar's activities with The Seven Days "crazy," he asks if there are any other "young dudes" in the secret society, explaining his question by pointing out that "young dudes are subject to change the rules."[32] When Guitar decides to kill Milkman, he is the one changing the rules: The Seven Days only murder white folks. But what Guitar does not realize is that he is signaling a shift of a very different sort when he leaves his "calling card" for Milkman in Shalimar. The owner of Solomon's General Store tells Milkman that his friend left him a message: "[Y]our day was sure coming or your day…something like that…your day is here. But I know it had a day in it. But I ain't sure if he said it was comin or was already here."[33] Indeed, Milkman's day is coming, and it is the promise of a new day for *both* men.

Morrison chose MLKman as her protagonist, but she writes with obvious affection for Guitar, who (like Morrison's own father, to whom the novel is dedicated) believes that white people are genetically inferior to black people: "The disease they have is in their blood, in the structure of their chromosomes," he tells Milkman.[34] We can hear Morrison's own voice in Guitar's response to Malcolm's rejection of his slave master's name:

> I don't give a shit what white people know or even think. Besides, I do accept it. It's part of who I am. Guitar is my name. Bains is the slave master's name. And I'm all of that. Slave names don't bother me; but slave status does.[35]

Angry and bitter, Guitar is also generous and kind. After Hagar's final, failed attempt to kill Milkman, Guitar finds her practically comatose and drives her home. On the way, he counsels her, "You think he belongs to you because you want to belong to him. Hagar don't. It's a bad word, 'belong.' Especially when you put it with somebody you love. Love shouldn't be like that." Guitar insists that love should not be binding: "You can't own a human being. You can't lose what you don't own."[36] Like his historical counterpart, Guitar suffered devastating losses in childhood, his father dying in a work-related accident and his mother leaving her children when the meager insurance money ran out. Even Milkman, who wants desperately to fly "solo," away from "real life" where "other people's nightmares flapped in his face and constrained him," recognizes that what's missing in Guitar's life is love.[37] Wholly committed to his work, unable to marry or have children, Guitar scoffs at this observation: *"what else but love?"* The answer to this question can be found in what we are told about Guitar's name: he got it not because he plays the guitar but because when he was little, he yearned for a guitar he saw in a store window, crying uncontrollably when he did not get it. Guitar's blues—the deep despair fueling his anger—thus finds expression in violence, violence that threatens to destroy him as it destroyed Smith. What Guitar needs is to follow his own counsel: "Wanna fly, you got to give up the shit that weighs you down."[38]

The increasingly strained friendship between Milkman and Guitar provides the novel with creative tension, allowing Morrison not just to expand the traditional timeline of the civil rights movement but to reconfigure it as a circle. Although Milkman sets off on his journey alone, Guitar is close behind, at first just following his friend and then stalking him with the intent to kill. At each point along the way, Milkman pieces together more of his family history, a story that takes place against a backdrop of commerce that began in 1619 when the first slave ships arrived in Virginia. The first step of Milkman's journey involves theft. When he and Guitar stand in the dark, ready to steal what they think is gold hanging in a green sack from Pilate's ceiling, they smell ginger, "this heavy spice-sweet smell that made you think of the East and striped tents and the *sha-sha-sha* of leg bracelets."[39] Although the direct source of this smell is the south river, the narrator points out that both men are breathing "air that could have come straight from a marketplace in Accra." To make the historical context of their theft even more clear, the narrator adds that "[e]ach thought it was the way freedom smelled, or justice, or luxury, or vengeance."[40] At Milkman's next destination, outside the now dilapidated house in Danville where Circe hid Macon and Pilate after their father was murdered (by the white owners of this house), he smells "a sweet spicy perfume. Like ginger root—pleasant, clean, seductive."[41] And finally, in Shalimar, as he approaches Susan Byrd's house, he confronts "the smell of gingerbread baking."[42]

Connect these three locations on a map—Detroit, Danville, and Shalimar—and they form a triangle similar in dimension to the transatlantic trading route. In addition to gold and to spices such as ginger, Morrison links these three locations with velvet (cotton), tobacco, and sugar. The most important link, and the commodity that defined America as well as what it meant to be an American, is the black body. For over fifty years, Pilate has carried with her a sack of bones. She calls these bones her "inheritance," only learning at the end of the novel that they belong not to the white man her brother murdered in the cave but to her father, the son of Solomon, who returns after his death to tell his daughter, "you can't leave a body behind." In the novel's final scene, Pilate and Milkman bury these bones in Shalimar, at the site of Solomon's mythic flight:

> They looked a long time for an area of earth among the rock faces large enough for the internment. When they found one, Pilate squatted down and opened the sack while Milkman dug. A deep sigh escaped from the sack and the wind turned chill. Ginger, a spicy sugared ginger smell, enveloped them.[43]

Seconds later, Pilate herself will sigh, Guitar's bullet having shot through her neck. "I wish I'd a knowed more people," she tells Milkman. "I would of loved 'em all. If I'd a knowed more, I would a loved more."[44] Pilate's words link her to three members of The Seven Days: Smith, whose suicide note ends with "I loved you all"; Henry Porter, who screams from the rooftop, "I love ya! I love ya all!"[45]; and Guitar, who tells Milkman, "My whole life is love."[46] In this final scene, Morrison holds all three of her primary characters in a tight embrace, reconfiguring the three points of the triangle as a circle while echoing the title of Burke's "I Wish I Knew." The novel itself comes full circle as Milkman sings a variation of the children's song: "'Sugargirl don't leave me here/ Buckra's arms to choke me/ Sugargirl don't leave me here/ Buckra's arms to yoke me.'" After Milkman lays Pilate's head down, two birds circle around them: "[o]ne dived into the new grave and scooped something shiny in its beak before it flew away."[47]

The "something shiny" is Sing's snuffbox, which her daughter had made into an earring to carry the slip of paper with the only word her father had ever written—her name.

Song of Solomon revises civil rights history by mapping a spiritual geography grounded in the circle; central to both West African and Native American traditions, the circle emphasizes process and the continuous flow of energy. Milkman first experiences this energy force on the hunt, when the men and dogs move in a circle and talk to one another:

> And the men agreed or told them to change direction or to come back. All those shrieks, those rapid tumbling barks, the long sustained yells, the tuba sounds, the drumbeat sounds, the low liquid *howm howm*, the reedy whistles, the thin eeeee's of a cornet, the unh unh unh bass chords…it was what there was before language. Before things were written down.[48]

The call-and-response of the hunt is repeated during the skinning of the bobcat, when Morrison not only intersperses snippets of an earlier conversation between Milkman and Guitar but also makes an indirect reference to Pilate, whose soft-boiled eggs have yolks "like wet velvet":

> *"It is about love. What else?"*
> They turned to Milkman. "You want the heart?" they asked him. Quickly, before any thought could paralyze him, Milkman plunged both hands into the rib cage. "Don't get the lungs, now. Get the heart."
> *"What else?"*
> He found it and pulled. The heart fell away from the chest as easily as yolk slips out of its shell.
> *"What else? What else? What else?"*[49]

What else besides love? Milkman's answer to this question echoes from the mountaintop where Pilate takes her last breath: *"Life life life life."*[50] Solomon and Ryna had twenty-one children, the last one Jake. Jake plowed and irrigated the land, grew peaches, raised hogs and wild-turkeys, and fished in his two acre-wide pond. Circe spent her (unnaturally) long life delivering babies and now breeds Weimaraners. Pilate made sure that the Dead family line did not end with her brother Macon, and before laying Pilate's head down, Milkman says something that suggests that this line will not end with him: "'There must be another one like you,' he whispered to her. 'There's got to be at least one more woman like you.'"[51]

Guitar's lesson, as important as Milkman's and as crucial to our understanding of civil rights history, is to consider what he is passing on. He tells Milkman that his work with The Seven Days makes it more likely that Milkman's "children can make other children."[52] Milkman questions this reasoning in a manner that recalls King's criticism of Malcolm X and, after his break with the Nation of Islam in 1964, Malcolm's questioning of himself: what is generative about anger, no matter how legitimate the grievance? The novel's ending suggests that Guitar may see things differently now. After all, the last thing the militant does is put his rifle down: "'My man,' he murmured to himself. 'My main man.'" By claiming Milkman as *his*, Guitar seems to revise his earlier stance on belonging as a "bad word." Morrison seconds Guitar's emotion in the description of Milkman's flight: "As fleet and bright as a lodestar he wheeled toward Guitar and it did not matter which one of them would give up his ghost in the killing arms of his brother."[53] A journey that began with two black men stealing a sack of bones has thus come full circle—encompassing the original theft and the violence done to black people beginning in 1619 and continuing for almost 350 years. When Milkman and Guitar steal what Pilate calls her inheritance, Morrison locates them in a specific moment in time: September 19, 1963.

This is the day in American history when twelve black men at Morgan State College in Baltimore, Maryland, founded Iota Phi Theta, a black fraternity. By 1968, Martin and Malcolm had both passed on. *Song of Solomon* honors what these two men left behind—a legacy that speaks to the power of and need for brotherhood.

There's Music in the Air: Pilate's Song

The history of the Dead family is encoded in a children's song about Milkman's great-grandfather Solomon, a slave who "whirled about and touched the sun": one day in the fields, "Solomon done fly, Solomon done gone / Solomon cut across the sky, Solomon gone home."[54] Pilate sings a variation of this children's song in the novel's opening scene as Smith makes his suicidal leap: "*O Sugarman done fly away / Sugarman done gone / Sugarman cut across the sky / Sugarman gone home.*"[55] Retold in Julius Lester's 1969 collection *Black Folktales*, the myth of the flying African begins this way:

> It happened long, long ago, when black people were taken from their homes in Africa and forced to come here to work as slaves. They were put on ships, and many died during the long voyage across the Atlantic Ocean. Those that survived stepped off the boats into a land they had never seen, a land they never knew existed, and they were put into the fields to work.[56]

The story then focuses on a pregnant woman and the son of an African witch doctor, both working in the hot sun under the watchful eye and sharp whip of a white overseer on a South Carolina plantation. The pregnant woman faints and then receives a lashing. When she faints a second time, the young witch doctor whispers something in her ear, and she whispers it to the next person and so on throughout the field. After more people faint and receive whippings, the witch doctor utters "a strange word," and all the slaves drop their hoes, spread their arms, and fly home to Africa.

In "Folklore and Community in *Song of Solomon*," published just three years after the novel, Susan Blake identifies Morrison's source for the myth of the flying African as *Drums and Shadows*, the Georgia Writers' Project collection of folklore from Georgia Coastal Blacks. This source lists twenty-seven variations of the myth, only two of which feature an individual, *not* a group, flying off. Because Blake (like so many critics who followed) sees Milkman's leap as a solo flight, she concludes that Morrison "has chosen the least common and least communal variants of the story and changed the tale's emphasis."[57] To read Morrison in this way, however, requires turning a deaf ear to the music in the air and at the core of this civil rights novel. It is, after all, "Pilate's song" that Milkman hears the children of Shalimar singing. In Morrison's version of the myth, the granddaughter of an African American slave, *not* the son of an African witch doctor, teaches others to fly and herself flies "[w]ithout ever leaving the ground."[58]

In Pilate, Morrison gives us a heroine who nobody can turn around. In a 1993 interview for *Paris Review*, Elissa Schappell asked Morrison if she ever had to tell one of her characters "to shut up." The novelist responds,

> Pilate, I did. Therefore she doesn't speak very much. She has this long conversation with the two boys, and every now and then she'll say something, but she doesn't have the dialogue the other people have. I had to do that, otherwise she was going to overwhelm everybody. She got terribly interesting…I had to take it back. It's *my* book; it's not called *Pilate*.[59]

Literary critics find Pilate as interesting as Morrison does. Gay Wilentz argues that through Pilate, "Morrison emphasizes the dead-end of both mainstream assimilation [Macon Dead II's way] and radical separatism [Guitar's way] by offering an alternative."[60] Joyce Wegs sings Pilate's praises, calling her and Jake "the two guiding figures and true role models in the novel"[61]; associated with singing *and* flying, Pilate is "a strong, admirable figure" who represents "a possible new beginning."[62] Reading Pilate within the context of the civil rights movement supports the view of her as an "alternative" in the same way that Ella Baker and Fannie Lou Hamer represented alternatives to the models of leadership provided by King and Malcolm X.

Pilate exemplifies a realistic "by any means necessary" politics of love. At fourteen years old, she threatens her brother Macon with a knife to keep him from stealing a white man's gold. The next time we see Pilate with a knife, she is threatening another man, her daughter Reba's lover-turned-abuser. Pilate uses violence (she knocks Milkman unconscious with a glass bottle), magic (she leaves a voodoo doll in Macon's office to keep him from trying to end Ruth's pregnancy), and minstrelsy (she plays to racist stereotypes to get Milkman and Guitar out of jail) to achieve her purpose, which is always to show "compassion for troubled people" and "concern for and about human relationships."[63] Most importantly, Pilate claims what is hers and loves it fiercely. At Hagar's funeral, after lifting her voice in song with her daughter Reba (Hagar's mother), Pilate looks the mourners in the eye, telling each of them, "That's my baby girl. My baby girl. My baby girl. My baby girl…And she was *loved*!"[64] A commanding presence in the mostly empty church, Pilate's call for "Mercy!" brings the mortician, not the minister, to her side. Both Pilate's appearance and her behavior call into question the efficacy of top-down, patriarchal civil rights organizations like King's Southern Christian Leadership Council.

Milkman's first encounter with his free-spirited Aunt Pilate includes lessons in how to make a perfect soft-boiled egg, how to remove blackberries from the branch, and how to overcome despair. The latter lesson involves the meaning of words and the healing power of song. When Hagar declares that she has, in fact, had some hungry days, Reba is alarmed until Pilate tells her that Hagar doesn't mean food:

> Realization swept slowly across Reba's face, but she didn't answer. Pilate began to hum as she returned to plucking the berries. After a moment, Reba joined her, and they hummed together in perfect harmony until Pilate took the lead: *O Sugarman don't leave me here / Cotton balls to choke me / O Sugarman don't leave me here / Buckra's arms to yoke me*.[65]

Pilate has been singing to overcome despair for most of her adult life. Her dead father visits her for the first time following Reba's birth, when Pilate is "extremely depressed and lonely"; Jake says, "Sing. Sing" and "Pilate understood all of what he told her. To sing, which she did beautifully, relieved her gloom immediately."[66] Milkman experiences a similar transformation in Danville when, standing outside the Butler house, "[n]ever, not since he knelt by his window sill wishing he could fly, had he felt so lonely."[67] His mood is lifted when he meets a witch (Circe), who tells him his grandmother's name—Sing.

Morrison's version of the myth of the flying African casts Pilate in the leading role, putting her at both the margin and the center of the beloved community. "People Who Could Fly" ends this way: "That was long ago, and no one now remembers what word it was that the young witch doctor knew that could make people fly."[68] No one except Pilate. When Milkman returns from Shalimar, he tells Pilate that her father was not telling her to "sing" but simply repeating his wife's name, a name he would not say after Sing died giving birth to Pilate. But why can't Pilate's father be repeating his wife's name and also be telling his daughter to lift her voice and sing? Indeed, by also repeating, "you can't just fly on off and leave a body," the son of Solomon is telling his daughter to remember, and thus to keep alive, all those "bodies," including her Native American mother, who have been left behind; to remember as the children in Shalimar remember; and to "sing about love now / Sing, sing, sing about peace / Sing, sing, sing about the joy / Sing, sing, sing, ohh…" Jake's refusal to speak his wife's name was a mistake, as wrong-headed as Sing's insistence that Jake keep the name "Macon Dead." Pilate explains her mother's reasoning to Milkman: "Mama liked it. Liked the name. Said it was new and would wipe out the past. Wipe it all out."[69] *Song of Solomon* insists that you cannot and should not wipe out the past. The son of Solomon returns after his death to correct his mistake and to make sure his daughter honors her ancestors.

Recognizing Pilate's responsibility underscores the communal aspect of *Song of Solomon* and so its relationship to a freedom movement that continues. Morrison ends her novel by stating the primary lesson learned by her male protagonist: "For now he knew what Shalimar knew: If you surrendered to the air, you could ride it."[70] Notice that *Shalimar*, not Solomon, is the source of Milkman's knowledge. In *Song of Solomon*, the African witch doctor is played by Circe, the midwife who Milkman repeatedly calls a witch. The pregnant woman is Sing (who births Pilate) and also Ruth (who births Milkman). The white overseer who wields the whip is played by the Butlers, who murder Jake, thereby serving the interests of white power. All the slaves in the field are played by Milkman and Guitar, the "brothers" whose fates are linked at the novel's end and who each, for very different reasons, whisper in other people's ears. The son of the African witch doctor who utters the "strange word" is played by Pilate, the granddaughter of Solomon and Ryna, the daughter of Jake and Sing, and the embodiment of African, Native American, and African American spiritual and cultural traditions that strengthen and sustain the beloved community. And the griot, the person keeping the dreams alive and urging the dreamers to "pass it on" is Morrison, with inspiration from Burke.

Teaching Approaches to Toni Morrison's *Song of Solomon*

Discussion Questions

1. In 2012, President Obama awarded Morrison the Medal of Freedom and said this: "I remember reading *Song of Solomon* when I was a kid and not just trying to figure out how to write, but also how to be and how to think." What lessons about writing do you think Obama learned from Morrison's novel? What lessons do you think he learned about "how to be" and "how to think"?
2. How do you explain the ending of *Song of Solomon*? What do you think happens to Guitar and Milkman, and why does Morrison say that "it did not matter which one of them would give up the ghost in the killing arms of his brother"?
3. How far back can you trace your family genealogy? Whose names do you know, and whose remain a mystery? For some people, genealogy is a hobby, but for Morrison, it's a matter of life and death. How do you explain the difference in perspectives?
4. How does the US remember the civil rights movement? What did that generation (1954–1968) of activists pass on to us, and how have we honored their legacy? Consider both memorials *and* current movements for social change such as #blacklivesmatter. What is at stake in our choice, as individuals and as a nation, to remember (or forget) this part of our history?

Research and Writing Projects

1. For the date of Smith's fictional flight off the roof of (No) Mercy Hospital, the opening scene of *Song of Solomon*, Morrison chose her own birthdate: February 18, 1931. Smith's flight prompts Ruth to go into labor, which means that Morrison and her male protagonist, Milkman, were born on the same day. Consider the novelist's biography and oeuvre in order to determine what this parallel might suggest about Morrison's audience and purpose for *Song of Solomon*.

2. Much work still needs to be done on women in the civil rights movement, a point made by Davis W. Houck and David E. Dixon, editors of *Women and the Civil Rights Movement* (2009). Their idea of "rhetorical leadership" can be usefully applied to Pilate, whose voice, whether she is speaking or singing, both mesmerizes and moves those who hear it. Prepare a presentation that describes and illustrates Pilate's leadership style, comparing it to real-life black women activists such as Ella Baker, Fannie Lou Hamer, Diane Nash, Rosa Parks, and/or Pauli Murray.
3. *Song of Solomon* is set in an unnamed city in Michigan, presumably Detroit. Research the civil rights history of this Northern city in order to challenge the idea that the conditions (political, economic, psycho-social) that necessitated the civil rights movement existed primarily, if not exclusively, in the South.
4. Consult both primary and secondary sources in order to describe the role music played in the civil rights movement. You can begin with Burke and Simone. In declaring that at some point black music was no longer "*exclusively*" ours," Morrison insists that the novel, as an art form, is now much more important in terms of "healing." How does *Song of Solomon* address the same or similar needs that black music during the civil rights movement did? In other words, what do you consider to be the "healing" properties of this novel?

Notes

1. "I Wish I Knew How It Would Feel to Be Free," composer Billy Taylor, lyricist Richard Lamb, published by Duane Music, Inc. and administered worldwide by 1630 Music Publishing Services, Inc., *1630music.com*.
2. Toni Morrison, *What Moves at the Margin: Selected Nonfiction*, ed. Carolyn C. Denard (Jackson: University of Mississippi Press, 2008), 58.
3. Craig Werner, *A Change Is Gonna Come: Music, Race, and the Soul of America* (New York: Penguin, 2002).
4. Nina Simone and Stephen Cleary, *I Put a Spell on You: The Autobiography of Nina Simone* (New York: Da Capo, 1993).
5. Toni Morrison, *Song of Solomon* (New York: Vintage, 1977), 6.
6. Ibid., 302.
7. Solomon Burke, vocal performance of "I Wish I Knew (How It Would Feel to Be Free)," by Billy Taylor and Dick Dallas, recorded in 1968, on *I Wish I Knew*, Atlantic 8185, 33 1/3 rpm.
8. Morrison, *Song of Solomon*, 9.
9. "Preface," in *The Civil Rights Reader: American Literature from Jim Crow to Reconstruction*, Julie Buckner Armstrong and Amy Schmidt, eds. (Athens: University of Georgia Press, 2009), xx.
10. Morrison, *Song of Solomon*, 336.
11. Ibid., 4.
12. Ibid., 160.
13. Ibid., xii.
14. Jan Furman, "Introduction," in *Toni Morrison's Song of Solomon: A Casebook*, ed. Jan Furman (Oxford: Oxford University Press, 2003), 5.
15. Gerry Brenner, "*Song of Solomon*: Rejecting Rank's Monomyth and Feminism," in *Toni Morrison's Song of Solomon: A Casebook*, ed. Jan Furman (Oxford: Oxford University Press, 2003).
16. From 1960 to 1964, Wyatt T. Walker served as King's Chief of Staff.
17. Dorothy H. Lee, "*Song of Solomon*: To Ride the Air," *Black American Literature Forum* 16.2 (1982), 66.
18. Martin Luther King, Jr., *I Have a Dream: Writings and Speeches That Changed the World*, ed. James M. Washington (New York: HarperCollins, 1986), 103.
19. Morrison, *Song of Solomon*, 70.
20. Ibid., 78.
21. Ibid., 179.
22. Ibid., 78.
23. Ibid., 294.
24. Ibid., 229.
25. Ibid., 236.
26. Ibid., 298.

27 Ibid., 235.
28 Ibid., 329.
29 Ibid., 43.
30 Ibid., 327.
31 Ibid., 102.
32 Ibid., 161.
33 Ibid., 262.
34 Ibid., 157.
35 Ibid., 160.
36 Ibid., 306.
37 Ibid., 220.
38 Ibid., 179.
39 Ibid., 184.
40 Ibid., 185.
41 Ibid., 239.
42 Ibid., 287.
43 Ibid., 335.
44 Ibid., 336.
45 Ibid., 26.
46 Ibid., 159.
47 Ibid., 336.
48 Ibid., 279.
49 Ibid., 282.
50 Ibid., 337.
51 Ibid.
52 Ibid., 160.
53 Ibid., 337.
54 Ibid., 303.
55 Ibid., 6.
56 Julius Lester, "People Who Could Fly," in *Toni Morrison's Song of Solomon: A Casebook*, ed. Jan Furman (Oxford: Oxford University Press, 2003), 21.
57 Susan L. Blake, "Folklore and Community in *Song of Solomon*," *MELUS* 7.3 (1980), 80.
58 Morrison, *Song of Solomon*, 336.
59 Elissa Schappell, "Toni Morrison: The Art of Fiction," in *Toni Morrison's Song of Solomon: A Casebook*, ed. Jan Furman (Oxford: Oxford University Press, 2003), 251.
60 Gay Wilentz, "Civilization Underneath: African Heritage as Cultural Discourse in Toni Morrison's *Song of Solomon*," in *Toni Morrison's Song of Solomon: A Casebook*, ed. Jan Furman (Oxford: Oxford University Press, 2003), 144–145.
61 Joyce M. Wegs, "Toni Morrison's *Song of Solomon*: A Blues Song," in *Toni Morrison's Song of Solomon: A Casebook*, ed. Jan Furman (Oxford: Oxford University Press, 2003), 178.
62 Ibid., 181.
63 Morrison, *Song of Solomon*, 149.
64 Ibid., 318.
65 Ibid., 49.
66 Ibid., 147.
67 Ibid., 239.
68 Lester, "People Who Could Fly," 23.
69 Morrison, *Song of Solomon*, 54.
70 Ibid., 337.

7

"LIVING PROOF OF SOMETHING SO TERRIBLE"

Pearl Cleage's *Bourbon at the Border* and the Politics of Civil Rights History and Memory

Julius B. Fleming, Jr.

> [C]ollective memory works selectively, imaginatively, and often perversely.
>
> Joseph Roach[1]

On February 27, 2013, US dignitaries, from senators to President Barack Obama, assembled in the rotunda of the US Capitol for the unveiling of a nine-foot bronze statue of Rosa Parks. House Speaker John Boehner opened the ceremony by calling attention to the gravitas of the moment: "Every now and then," he contended,

> we have got to step back and say to ourselves: *what a country*. This is one of those moments. Because yes, all men and women are created equal, but as we'll hear during this ceremony, some grow to be larger than life, and to be honored as such.[2]

Later in the program, Senate Republican Leader Mitch McConnell echoed these sentiments but layered on even more self-congratulatory rhetoric placing the US nation-state on a moral high ground:

> Rosa Parks may not have led us to victory against the British. She didn't give a single speech in the Senate or the House. Or blast off into space. Or point the way West in the western wilderness. Yet, with quiet courage, and unshakeable resolve, she did something no less important on a cold, Alabama, evening in 1955. She helped unite the spirit of America, which the founders so perfectly and courageously expressed…We have had the humility as a nation to recognize past mistakes, and we've had the strength to confront those mistakes, but it has always required people like Rosa Parks to help us get there. Because of the changes she helped set in motion, entire generations of Americans have been able to grow up in a nation where segregated buses only exist in museums, where children of every race are free to fulfill their God-given potential… and where this simple carpenter's daughter from Tuskegee is honored as a national hero. What a story. What a legacy. *What a country.*[3]

For McConnell, US democracy, mixed with a little individual grit, successfully hedges against inequalities that have long limited the claims Parks, and so many others, have been able to make upon the promises of US democracy. In his narrative, Parks emerges as a humble carpenter's daughter-cum-national hero, whose symbolic relationship to Christ—a carpenter's son—is most likely not without intent. The lawmaker weaves Parks' brave performances of civil rights activism into an impressive narrative of national progress—one that spans from US space travel to the "American Revolution." Extoling the US nation-state for confronting the "mistakes" of the past, the politician paints a portrait of the present in which all Americans can realize their "God-given potential," citing as evidence the ostensibly passé reality of segregated buses.

The society that McConnell imagines is an ideal model of democratic change that hardly accords, at least in such a matter-of-fact way, with the realities of racial inequality that continue to animate the present. Infused with what Laruen Berlant calls "cruel optimism," both lawmakers' effusive praise of the nation-state overestimates its historical commitments to racial parity while underplaying contemporary formations of racial inequality.[4] In this way, the idea of Parks occasions an opportunity to congratulate the US nation-state and to promote logics of neoliberal progress more so than to commemorate the legacy of an accomplished civil rights activist. Indeed, the lawmakers' speeches are linked by an optimistic and illuminating refrain: "What a country!"

I begin with this particular ceremony, and its specific constellation of remarks, because they index some of the varied and strategic ways in which those in power mobilize and appropriate the legacy of the modern civil rights movement.[5] As the US celebrates the fiftieth anniversaries of landmark civil rights events, and the lives of prominent activists, the movement's historical matter is routinely transformed into fodder for national grandstanding. To be sure, putting the movement's legacy in the service of fortifying ideals of US "greatness" has not been limited to the Republican Party. Take, for example, Obama's address not only for the Parks ceremony but also for the dedication of the Dr. Martin Luther King, Jr. memorial in 2011. Both of the president's speeches are laced with abundant praise of the US nation-state while unabashedly touting the nation's logic of individualism.[6]

Obama, however, makes significant observations about the present-day life of inequality and the ways in which it continues to thrive in a putatively post-racial moment. "[N]early 50 years after the March on Washington," he asserts, "our work, Dr. King's work, is not yet complete."[7] It would certainly be misleading to disregard the (relative) racial progress that has followed in the wake of the modern civil rights movement. As McConnell suggests, the eradication of (*de jure*) segregation on public buses stands out as a shining example. Yet scholars such as Imani Perry, Sharon Holland, and John Jackson, Jr. have furnished more complex analytics, which encourage and enable us to look beyond segregated buses, and other blatant sites of inequality, to critically analyze assemblages of racial injustice that are perhaps less obvious.[8] As the nation celebrates some of the movement's most watershed events and the courageous activists who reconfigured its social and political landscapes, we must contemplate the contemporary hues of inequality, the social constructedness of historical memory, and the social and political work that each performs in shaping the present as well as the future.

Bourbon at the Border, Pearl Cleage's 1995 play, troubles popular histories and memories of the civil rights movement. Originally commissioned by Alliance, *Bourbon* returns to the Mississippi Summer Project—better known as "Freedom Summer"—nearly thirty years after this experiment in US democracy formally ended. Against this historical backdrop, Cleage examines the temporality of racial injustice—the relationship, that is to say, between time and anti-black oppression. More specifically, she explores the transhistorical life of what Perry terms "the practices of racial inequality," foregrounding the ways in which these practices, and the havoc they wreak, move across historical time, not only in the form of social, legal, political, and economic inequities but also in the materiality of black human flesh that has been scarred by enactments of racial violence.[9] In this way, the playwright invites audiences to contemplate a less remarked upon dimension of the movement's legacy: the embodied traumas that continue to haunt activists who, as King put it, offered their "bodies as a means of laying [their] case before the conscience of the local and the national community."[10]

The Politics of Civil Rights History and Memory

Recollections of the past, histories, and memories are also often barometers of the present and omens for the future. In the US nation-state, this has been particularly true within the context of race. The construction of history and memory—and indeed our very conceptions of who has "history" and who has "memory"—has often reified and been cultivated upon the grounds of social power. Recollections of the modern civil rights movement are certainly no exception. As Renee Romano and Leigh Raiford have argued, the movement frequently becomes "evidence of the nation's ongoing quest to live up to its founding ideals of egalitarianism and justice."[11] Where the movement has not been marshaled to celebrate the inherent "good" of the US nation-state, it has often been deployed, quite ironically, to reverse social and political "gains" that were achieved during the movement. In this way, strategic productions of civil rights histories and memories, especially within legal and political discourses, often aim to safeguard hierarchies of social power, thereby coming to function as "tool[s] of…fostering and fomenting hegemony."[12]

Recollections of the movement have not, however, been limited to law and formal politics or even to monuments and state commemorations. They have surfaced in music, cartoons, commercial advertisements, comics, and a host of other media. In 2010, for example, hip-hop artist Blitz the Ambassador commemorated Martin Luther King, Jr. Day by releasing a lyrical rap homage to Emmett Till. Entitled "Emmett (S)till," the rapper's sonic rendering of elegiac history and memory limns one of the movement's most formidable and galvanizing moments. With a title that signals the continuity of anti-black violence through the temporal semiotics of the word "still," Ambassador links Till's tragedy to the present, suggesting the possibility of a tragic return that hinges upon a knowledge of history: "We know not our history, we doomed to repeat it."[13]

Within this vast field of cultural production, African American literature has long been—and continues to be—central to the cultural work of producing civil rights history and memory. As Geneviève Farbe and Robert O'Meally remind us, "the writing—narrating—of history has not been the exclusive concern of historians…[but] has also been the province of artists and writers."[14] From Toni Morrison, Ernest Gaines, and Ntozake Shange to Julius Lester, Thulani Davis, and Katori Hall, contemporary black writers have crafted innovative literary works that trouble conventional histories and memories of the movement, whether challenging patriarchal tenets of charismatic black leadership or portraying risqué sexual desires that circulated during the movement.[15] But whereas monuments that honor the likes of Parks and King have garnered substantial national recognition, African American literature that returns to the movement has received less attention. As Brian Norman points out, this has been especially true for those works that engage "contemporary racial issues."[16]

What the Parks commemoration elucidates is that whether histories and memories of the movement are crafted in formal theaters or staged in the rotunda of the US Capitol, they are all invented acts that are linked to larger structures of power. Undoubtedly, the aesthetic form of *Bourbon* indexes the play's fictionality and evinces the imaginative labor upon which its very essence depends. But imagination also plays a key, if camouflaged, role in those genres of remembering the movement that might appear to be more intimately connected to reality. Indeed, much like Cleage and the performers in *Bourbon*, Obama, Boehner, and McConnell all rely upon scripts, bodies, and imagination to produce their own subjective versions of civil rights history and memory. Their speech acts, in short, are both performed and performative. Unlike many of their narratives, however, Cleage refrains from advancing triumphalist accounts of national progress, opting instead to craft stories of the movement that the US nation-state is prone and eager to forget.

Disappearing and Reappearing

Opening in 1997 at Alliance Theater in Atlanta, Georgia, *Bourbon at the Border* ran from April 30 to June 15. In a note that accompanies the script, Cleage states that Freedom Summer was the brainchild of three major civil rights organizations: the Student Nonviolent Coordinating Committee (SNCC), the Congress of Racial Equality (CORE), and the National Association for the Advancement of Colored People (NAACP). Navigating the treacherous terrain of one of Dixie's most stalwart bastions of inequality, these organizations worked tirelessly to improve black Mississippians' social, political, and ontological realities. "Their experiences that summer," Cleage writes,

> including the murders of Summer Project workers James Chancy [sic], Andrew Goodman and Michael Schwerner, as well as the violence against many others whose names are unknown to us—exposed the level of American racial warfare in a way that was as dramatic as it was undeniable.[17]

Cleage's allusion to warfare and her concern for those activists whose names are perhaps "unknown to us" index the broader centrality of violence and "unknown" histories to her dramatic vision and "political aesthetics."[18]

A daughter of civil rights activists, Cleage is no stranger to the movement. As works such as her play *A Song for Coretta* (2008) and her novel *Till You Hear from Me* (2010) reveal, the Atlanta-based playwright has often utilized imaginative literature to engage and recalibrate discourses surrounding African American civil rights activism. Throughout these and other works, she has shown a keen interest in the experiences of black women as well as of everyday activists. This preoccupation with the marginalized, or what Cleage calls the "unknown," also drives the plot of *Bourbon*. Thus, while the murders of Chaney, Goodman, and Schwerner have achieved nearly iconic status in recollections of the movement, Cleage is more interested in the disappearances of the "unknown" because theirs, she shows, has not been limited to abduction and death but has also entailed a troubling disappearance from history and memory. Hence, rather than foreground this familiar cadre of casualties, Cleage employs techniques of what Nicole Fleetwood calls "non-iconicity" to excavate recollections of the movement that are not as frequently articulated.

The black visual icon often contributes to what Fleetwood calls a "grand narrative of overcoming that solidifies American exceptionalism."[19] A "non-iconic" image, she posits, "cannot stand-in for historical process in the way that the photograph of Rosa Parks on the bus has come to do."[20] By foregrounding the non-iconic, *Bourbon* not only challenges rhetorics of US exceptionalism—such as those that pervade the Parks and King ceremonies—but it also critiques the uneven distribution of value that society maps onto the fatal disappearances of those activists who have been accorded iconic status. The problem with this gesture has not only to do with habits of forgetting the fatal disappearances of the "unknown" but also with the tendency to ignore, as Cathy Caruth puts it, the "disappearances of those who returned: the living testimony of the disappeared who actually reappear in the new democracy"—especially, I would add, when those who return have not been transformed into one of society's celebrated icons.[21] A dramatized microhistory of Freedom Summer, *Bourbon* foregrounds the experiences of two non-iconic activists. May and Charles ("Charlie") Thompson "disappeared" and "reappeared" in the "new democracy." Thirty years after Freedom Summer, each is haunted by the traumas of their violent encounters with "American racial warfare."

In this two-act, romantic tragicomedy, Cleage uses May and Charlie's volatile but deeply sincere marriage to explore how past enactments of racial violence reverberate in the present, socially and politically but also physically and psychologically. Set in 1995, *Bourbon* takes place over the course of two and a half weeks. The play's dramatic present is set entirely in May and Charlie's Detroit, Michigan apartment. In the opening scene, May waits anxiously for Charlie, who has been "gone almost all summer," to return.[22] As the audience soon learns, he has spent the summer at a psychiatric institution. His absence forces May not only to work in a cafeteria to supplement the income she receives as a union representative but also to wrestle with a glaring emotional void.

When the audience meets May, she is bubbling with anticipation, obsessively tidying an already-immaculate apartment. But May's nervous excitement begins to wane when Rosa St. John—May's bold, feisty, widowed-but-dating friend—stops by for a visit. Recalling the fierce women characters throughout Alice Childress's literary corpus, particularly in plays such as *Florence* (1949) and *Trouble in Mind* (1955), Rosa lives on the edge, defies social conventions, and hardly waits for an invitation before offering her opinion. Whereas May is bursting at the seams with anticipation, Rosa views Charlie's return through a less-optimistic lens. She recommends, in fact, that she and Tyrone, her significantly younger boyfriend, be present when Charlie arrives, just to "make sure that he's.... okay."[23] Reaching for any shard of hope, May cites Charlie's discharge as sufficient evidence that he will, indeed, be "okay." "They sent him home last time, too," Rosa retorts, "and said he was fine. Next thing you know he's back up on the roof."[24] Hurt by the biting reality of Rosa's remarks, May retaliates by inviting her friend to leave. "You don't have to put me out, honey. I'll give you my opinion all day and all night, but once you make your choice, I'm on your side. Whichever way it comes out."[25] As the two friends move past this awkward moment—though they return often in the wake of Rosa's razor-sharp commentary—their dialogue provides more details about the roots of Charlie's mental illness.

According to May, Charlie routinely enters and exits bouts of depression, which are regulated by medications and occasional stints at psychiatric institutions. However, in Rosa's estimation, his ailment exceeds depression. "A lot of people get depressed from time to time," she contends. "But Charlie is the first black person I ever knew who went all the way crazy."[26] Soon after, May retrieves an envelope that had occupied her attention earlier that day. Its contents include a range of ephemera from the modern civil rights movement or what Rosa calls "that sixties thing."[27] As the friends journey back into history, they discover photographs of May and Charlie's time in the movement and eventually stumble upon a "yellowed" clipping with a headline that reads: "Three civil rights Workers Missing, Feared Dead"—a clear nod to the disappearances and subsequent murders of Chaney, Goodman, and Schwerner.[28] The physical proximity of the photographs that capture May and Charlie's role in the movement to the seemingly more official "clipping" is a significant aesthetic choice. Taken together, these theatrical props form a symbolic pastiche of civil rights history in which the couple's experiences collide, both figuratively and materially, with the more notorious, photojournalistic account of the movement. This encounter with May's personal archive sets the stage for a much more illuminating conversation about Charlie's mental illness and its relationship to Freedom Summer.

Like scores of college students across the country, May and Charlie joined a movement that was changing the tide of US democracy in the 1960s. In fact, May had enrolled at Howard University with the hope of becoming a civil rights activist. Her goal came to fruition after crossing paths with Charlie, the young student activist who would ultimately become her husband and fellow soldier in Freedom Summer. According to May, Charlie was the main one talking people into going to Mississippi…talking about how it wouldn't be fair for [blacks] to let those white kids fight our battles for us…[Blacks] would be the sorriest people on the face of this earth if we let a bunch of white kids go down there to register all those black folks to vote.[29]

Attempting to evoke laughter from the crowd assembled for Charlie's fiery speech, May interjected with a rather facetious query: "[F]air to who"? "[F]air to the memory of our ancestors' bones," Charlie retorted, bringing to mind Stokely Carmichael's legacy of civil rights activism on the campus of Howard. Hoping to atone for her snide remarks, May agrees to have coffee with the young activist, who lingers in recruiting mode as he attempts to build a movement. Despite these solicitations, May remains steadfast in her resistance to spending the summer "trudging around Mississippi trying to register some scared Negroes to vote."[30] That summer, however, she found herself "on the bus to Sunflower County [Mississippi]."[31]

At this juncture of the play's dramatic present, May's histories and memories of the movement are noticeably scant. Outside of stories about the Hemphills, the poor but "neat as a pin" black family with whom she lived in Mississippi—stories that recall Du Bois's early travels throughout the US South—May's most salient memory is having been chased by a mob down one of those "Mississippi backroads [that] were pitch-black at night."[32] "I was taking those curves at sixty miles an hour," she asserts in an almost reveling tone. But as she begins to recall the terror and gravity of this vicious pursuit, the tenor of her memory shifts into a more somber register. "Once we hit town," she says, "they just turned off. I was shaking so bad when we finally got back to where we were staying, it was a shame."[33]

May's shaking body assumes a nearly tropological quality throughout the play, signifying Cleage's broader investments in the relationship between temporality and racial injustice, namely the ways in which black bodies remember "past" instantiations of "American racial warfare." If May's embodied terror exceeds the temporal boundaries of the primal traumatic event, and carries memories and knowledge of this event into the present, then more than fifty years after Freedom Summer, we can turn to other black bodies that were traumatized during this historical moment to map more complex histories and memories of the modern civil rights movement and to theorize how practices of racial inequality continue to haunt the present. In *Jim Crow Wisdom: Memory and Identity in Black America Since 1940*, Jonathan Holloway argues that black bodies are key sites of "archival memory" and are, therefore, essential to contemporary recollections of black being (and being black) in the US nation-state. "If any one aphorism can characterize the experiences of black people in this country," he contends, "it might be that the white-authored national narrative deliberately contradicts the histories our bodies know."[34] The black body is thus an archive in its own right. It both remembers and facilitates the production of histories and memories that occasionally destabilize conventional epistemologies and narratives of the past.

Consider, for example, Fannie Lou Hamer's body, which continued to remember the violence, the kidney damage, and the vision impairment she suffered at the hands of white police in a rural Mississippi jail in 1963. In the wake of the modern civil rights movement, traces of this violent encounter did not abruptly vanish. They were etched into the material landscape of Hamer's body, manifesting as external "scars" upon the flesh and internal "scars" upon a bodily organ. These traumatic "practices of inequality" found their way into the present, into a "post-civil rights" era—not through law, politics, or social custom per se but rather through the materiality of Hamer's black body. This particular mode of embodied memory takes center stage throughout *Bourbon*. By framing black flesh as a material vector that links the past to the present, the play invites a reconceptualization of those metrics that often govern the ways in which we trace the transhistorical character of racial inequality. Put another way, in addition to court cases, voter registration laws, and redistricting tactics, Cleage suggests that the black body is a tenable and necessary framework for tracking the perpetuities of racial injustice.

If bodies are central to remembering histories of the "unknown" and to portraying repressed "histories our bodies know," drama is an especially suitable genre for Cleage's aesthetic and political projects. As the playwright suggests, performances of racial violence that sought to suppress "Freedom Summer" were, in a word, "dramatic." So too were the various modalities of embodied action that civil rights activists employed while riding buses, marching down streets, arguing in courtrooms, and sitting courageously at segregated lunch counters. Thus, it is certainly fitting that Cleage turns to drama and embodied performance to engage a phase of the black freedom struggle so rife with occasions of performing bodies.

By transmuting these logics of embodied performance to the contemporary theatrical stage and thereby pushing beyond conventional genres of civil rights history and memory, Cleage calls attention to the relationship between what Diana Taylor calls "the archive and the repertoire." According to Taylor, the archive consists of "supposedly enduring materials," much like the clippings and photographs that May and Rosa find in the envelope. The repertoire, on the other hand, refers to a "so-called" ephemeral set of "embodied practice" and "knowledge." It "enacts embodied memor[ies]," such as performances, gestures, orality, movement, and dance.[35] If Holloway identifies the black body as a site of archival memory, Taylor urges a more careful accounting of the "practices" in which material bodies engage. For her, these modalities of embodied performance are central to uncovering historical pasts, to "making visible the crimes committed" in previous historical moments, and to transmit[ting] "traumatic memory."[36] In *Bourbon*, Cleage elucidates the ways in which the repertoire works toward these ends. But she suggests, however, that the value of black bodies in performance is not limited to a live event, but also encompasses returns to these live moments that are enabled in and through the space of memory.

Throughout *Bourbon*, both May and Charlie's transmission of "traumatic memory" unfolds in a detective-like plot. As the play progresses, fragments of their personal memory slowly appear, building to a climactic moment that unveils the roots of their embodied traumas. In Act I, May limits her traumatic memories of the movement to abrupt, reserved descriptions, such as "[Charlie] got hurt in Mississippi a long time ago."[37] When Charlie returns home, he is similarly selective in deciding which memories of Freedom Summer he shares as well as the ways in which he frames and articulates these memories. During a conversation with Tyrone, for example, Charlie situates his traumatic encounters during Freedom Summer within a warlike narrative of male bravado.

After Tyrone, a Vietnam veteran, recalls the traumatic experience of shrapnel "slic[ing] [his] arm open like a grape," he shares a joke that eventually invites Charlie to take his own journey into a traumatic past. "May said you messed up your leg in Mississippi. What the hell happened? You weren't down there winkin' at them white girls, were you?"[38] "Not me, brother," Charlie responds. "I was registering people to vote. I ran into a deputy sheriff who didn't appreciate it…Broke my leg in three places, threw me in a hole and waited two days before they called somebody to set it."[39] Their next exchange is telling:

TYRONE: Damn, man, that's ugly. You might as well have been in 'Nam, but at least when they hit us, we could hit 'em back!
CHARLIE: Sometimes, it seems like it was all one big war, you know? Some over here and some over there, but one thing guaranteed—you weren't coming out the same way you went in.
TYRONE: Mississippi got the meanest crackers God ever made. I know if it's any meaner, I don't wanna see 'em.

CHARLIE: When they threw me in that hole, they looked at me and said, "We're going to be fair about this, nigger. You gonna leave your mind down there or your nuts. You can decide." *(A beat.)* So whenever a muthafucker calls me crazy, I say, goddamn right![40]

This dialogue reveals striking similarities between the two radically different theaters of war in which Tyrone and Charlie fought in the 1960s. While both wars leave physical traces of violence on the veterans' bodies, Charlie points out the psychological injury that was part and parcel of his Freedom Summer experience. Directly attributing his mental illness to the traumatic acts of anti-black violence he suffered in Mississippi, Charlie illuminates the ways in which his mind, as well as his body, was vulnerable to the whims of "American racial warfare." More still, the injuries that resulted from these traumatic violences continue to manifest in the present, amounting to a form of post-traumatic stress disorder (PTSD) that was not triggered by the Vietnam War—which made this condition popular in the US cultural imaginary—but rather by Freedom Summer: a war, as Charlie suggests, in its own right.

In Act II, the audience discovers that Charlie has strategically withheld the primal traumatic event that provoked his struggles with mental illness. And while May is deeply invested in helping Charlie to cope with his traumatic memories of Freedom Summer, she reveals that she was also physically and psychologically traumatized and that it was her own traumatic encounter with white supremacist sexual violence that spiraled Charlie into a fraught psychological state. Much like Charlie, May has repressed these particular memories, but during a conversation with Rosa, they begin to surface, adding more context to the physical and psychological injuries she and Charlie sustained during the movement. Confiding in Rosa, May recalls an arduous and unsuccessful day of voter registration during Freedom Summer. With wounded spirits, she and Charlie paused on the side of a road, disappointed in the black Mississippians who had "r[u]n in the house and slammed the door."[41] During their brief respite, May and Charlie reflect on their work, anticipate sharing memories of the movement with their children, and begin to kiss. A white sheriff and two deputies interrupt this intimate moment and eventually haul the couple off to jail, locking them in a basement. Aware of her rights, May constantly demands permission to call their lawyer. Angered by what they perceive as utter impudence, the officers present Charlie with a stark ultimatum: he could beat May for "having such a smart mouth" or "watch while they finished what he had started by the side of the road."[42] Attempting to use rationality and compromise to convince a rather irrational mob, Charlie pleads with the officers to release them, claiming that he will not press charges. The officers find Charlie's attempts laughable, asking him flippantly if he had seen any FBI agents around before suggesting that he must "want [them] to show him how it's done."[43]

Torn between the violent demands of Jim Crowism and his love for May, Charlie capitulates to the officers' desires and begins to beat May with a belt one of the deputies had supplied. "They stood right there and made him hit me harder and harder," May remembers.

> I started screaming so they'd let him stop, but they wouldn't. They just laughed and said, 'Go on, nigger. We'll tell you when to quit.' So they made him beat me half to death and then that one who had told me to take my clothes off pulled my dress over my face and did it anyway. They all did it anyway. Right in front of Charlie.[44]

May's recounting of these traumatic events exposes the danger of sexual trauma that threatened the minds and bodies of movement activists, challenging our understanding of the threatening nature of civil rights activity. According to Danielle McGuire, "analyses of rape and sexualized violence play little or no role in most histories of the civil rights movement, which present it as a struggle between black and white men." She continues, "If we understand the role rape and sexual violence played in African Americans' daily lives and within the larger freedom struggle, we have to reinterpret, if not rewrite, the history of the civil rights movement."[45] Through the transmission of May's traumatic memories, Cleage utilizes drama to reinterpret and rewrite histories of the modern civil rights movement, not only by engaging rape but also by acknowledging the centrality of black women's experiences to histories and memories of the movement. She does so over and against the tendency to foreground what Erica Edwards calls black male "charisma."[46]

Being forced to witness May's rape traumatizes Charlie in ways that are decidedly apparent throughout the play. It is perhaps tempting, then, to elide May's own response to this traumatic encounter, and to over identify with the ways that this event shapes Charlie's quotidian realities. May's decision to cope with her trauma by keeping memories of it at bay certainly fuels this proclivity. Rosa plays a key role in this regard, probing and pushing May beyond the limits of her comfort zone:

ROSA: You always talk about what happened to Charlie. What about what happened to you, May?
MAY: I survived it. He didn't.
ROSA: That doesn't make it right.
MAY: Nothing makes it right.
ROSA: I'm sorry.
MAY: *(Suddenly angry.)* You're sorry? Sorry for what? Sorry Charlie's so messed up? Sorry they hurt me so bad I could never have his babies? Sorry they took our whole lives from us in one mean Mississippi Summer?[47]

As this dialogue makes clear, May's body has also continued to remember the egregious violences of Freedom Summer. Her inability to reproduce is an everyday manifestation of a past traumatic event that unfolded during the modern civil rights movement. In this way, her body—much like Charlie's, like Fannie Lou Hamer's, and so many others' who participated in the movement—continues to remember its traumatic encounters with "American racial warfare" over thirty years after Freedom Summer.

Hierarchies of gender identity play a key role in fostering May's silence, thereby determining whose histories and memories of the movement survive into the present, even among the "unknown." Although May finally musters the confidence to give voice to her own traumatic experiences in the movement, she continues to emphasize their effects on Charlie, from *his* traumatic experience of witnessing *her* rape to *her* inability to "have *his* babies."[48] According to Nell Irvin Painter, "women often wish to suppress unfortunate occurrences in order to demonstrate that they succeeded in transcending oppression…which they interpret also as a service to their race." *Bourbon* joins literary works such as Jean Toomer's *Cane* (1923)—particularly his vignette "Blood Burning Moon"—that expose the ways in which patriarchal authority gets enacted and contested at the sight of black female bodies. Black men, Painter suggests, often perceive "attacks on the bodies of black women as an insult to black men, as though the mistreatment of women served as a proxy in a struggle between black and white men."[49]

Painter's insights elucidate the gendered relations of power that inform the suppression of black women's narratives of sexual trauma. As Painter, Toni Morrison, and others have argued, this albatross has historically weighed heavily on the shoulders of black women writers. Often perceiving the details of their sexual traumas as injuries "too terrible to relate," black women authors have sometimes purged their narratives of traumatic sexual assaults. May experiences firsthand the risks of divulging incidents of sexual violence. In the wake of her horrific rape, even May's family—who told her how "dumb" she was for "going [to Mississippi] in the first place"—shuns her, essentially blaming May for this unfortunate violation of her own body. For them, May was "living proof of something so terrible nobody wanted to think about it."[50] In a quite different register, however, Cleage invites her audiences to "think about" the unthinkable—to, as Morrison puts it, "rip that veil drawn over 'proceedings too terrible to relate.'"[51] For Morrison, such an aesthetic and political gesture provides access to the "unwritten interiors" of black life and to this we might add, to the histories of the "unknown."[52]

This metaphor of excavating "unwritten interiors" helps to make sense of Cleage's broader efforts throughout *Bourbon* to voice "unknown" histories and memories of the movement. May's and Charlie's "unwritten interiors" are both physical and psychological, ranging from "unwritten" histories of mental illnesses that manifested during Freedom Summer to "unwritten" histories of sexual assault that targeted black women's genitalia during the movement. Whether manifesting as depression or as a physical inability to reproduce, these traumas continually show up in the present, marking a transhistorical relation of racial violence that Cleage places at the center of contemporary histories and memories of the modern civil rights movement. Moreover, the playwright invites us to include this mode of perpetuity within critical discourses that track how racial injustice moves across time and space, finding its way into the contemporary moment. So, while the reparative work of "healing" must unfold within legal and socio-political realms, it should also include those traumatized black bodies that are "living proof of something so terrible."

Historical Memory and Racial Critique

At a time when histories and memories of the modern civil rights movement are mobilized to exaggerate the US nation-state's historical commitments to racial equality and when advocates of inequality routinely transmute history and memory into a mode of enacting power, Cleage turns to drama to expand and recalibrate popular recollections of the movement which often obscure how "practices of racial inequality" animate the present. In addition to engaging traumatic embodied memories, Cleage offers a compelling example of what Tavia Nyong'o calls a "genealogy of the contemporary," calling attention to the ways that the contemporary is "intertwined with the exclusion of minoritarian and gendered voices from its unfolding question."[53] According to Nyong'o, "an aesthetic 'redress' of history can never simply restore missing voices but must continuously strive to think the genealogy of a contemporaneity characterized by its relations of exclusion. It must work to shape a black representative space in memory."[54] In *Bourbon*, audiences find a balance among restoring "missing" voices, creating a black representative space in memory, and thinking the contemporary moment through its "relations of exclusion."

Rather than limit memory to occasions of psychic return, Cleage also transmutes objects and geographical spaces into sites of historical memory and racial critique of the contemporary. In this vein, May and Charlie's small apartment looks out upon the Ambassador Bridge, which connects Detroit, Michigan, and Ontario, Canada. These symbolic geographies of racial terror and freedom evoke something of the historical precarity of black life in the US nation-state. If Canada, for enslaved Africans, represented a land of hope and freedom, it is imbued with similar meanings throughout *Bourbon*, particularly for May and Charlie. For them, Canada is a refuge from the US nation-state, which, in their opinion, constrains possibilities for black being. Rather than a misplaced or ahistorical symbol, the bridge, and the geographies that it links, signify the continued vitality of racial hierarchies nearly a century and a half after the legal abolishment of slavery. While May and Charlie's experiential realities in twentieth-century Detroit do not compare to the horrors of US slavery, they are rooted in practices of racial inequality that, much like slavery, devalue blackness and black bodies. If Detroit once represented a geographical site of hope and freedom for black migrants who, during the "Great Migration," were desperate to escape the US South and its practices of Jim Crowism, Cleage portrays the city in which she grew up in a radically different light—a city whose contemporary social customs are yet marred by traces of anti-blackness.

Cleage's return to Freedom Summer is far from the triumphalist narratives that animate those versions of the movement that the US nation-state prefers. In fact, when the play ends, the audience learns that Charlie has taken the advice of Clay, the protagonist of Amiri Baraka's *Dutchman* (1964), who offers murder as a panacea for racial inequality and anti-black violence. After returning home, Charlie journeys down the path of becoming a serial killer, seeking revenge for the traumas that he and May endured during Freedom Summer. After finding several whites murdered throughout the city, the Detroit police, who are ostensibly working tirelessly to solve the crimes because the victims are white, link Charlie to the evidence from the crime scenes. As the play reaches its denouement, the police knock furiously at May and Charlie's apartment door, signaling an impending arrest. While this ending might signify a certain foreclosure of Charlie's future, it also invites audiences to contemplate how the modern civil rights movement and its traumatic occasions of anti-black violence lead Charlie down the path of murder, leaving him constantly dreaming, like his enslaved ancestors, of taking flight to Canada in an ostensibly post-racial twentieth-century moment. Thus, not only do the couple's bodies carry resonances of anti-black violence into the present, their contemporary encounters with racial hierarchies should give much-needed pause to those who appropriate civil rights history and memory in order to promote problematic and self-interested personal and national agendas. When the stories that *Bourbon at the Border* tells take their rightful place among popular accounts of civil rights histories and memories, we can celebrate the movement's legacy with a clearer sense of the work that lies ahead and with a greater awareness of those strands of the past that are struggling to find voice amidst the clamor of national triumph.

Approaches to Teaching Pearl Cleage's *Bourbon at the Border*

Discussion Questions

1. What is the significance of Cleage's title? What do the play's portrayals of "bourbon" and "borders" suggest about the civil rights movement—about black life in the wake of the movement?
2. How does the play confront regional mythologies that frame the US South as the essence of racial oppression while touting the US North as the bastion of racial equality?
3. What is the role of memory throughout the play? Why do Cleage's characters routinely turn to silence? What do we make of their tendencies to repress recollections of the past?
4. What does *Bourbon at the Border* teach its audiences about gender and sexuality in the civil rights movement?
5. Why are Americans so prone and *eager* to forget historical narratives that are not triumphalist, that do not culminate with neat "victories"? What are the risks of telling stories that do not advance narratives of American progress and exceptionalism—stories of a nation that makes but finally corrects its mistakes?

Research and Writing Projects

1. Activists such as Fannie Lou Hamer and Robert Moses were instrumental to Freedom Summer. Focusing on one of these activists, research their contributions to this particular segment of the movement as well as their broader significance to this historical moment. Based on your research, write a brief play (7–9 minutes) that dramatizes your findings.

2 What was Freedom Summer or the Mississippi Summer Project? Why was voting such a critical arena of civil rights activism on the heels of the Emancipation Proclamation? Prepare a presentation that (1) details the history of Freedom Summer and (2) outlines how this specific phase of the movement builds on a much longer history of fighting for black suffrage.
3 The civil rights movement is consistently described—by the press and scholars alike—as a "theater of activism." But far less has been said about how playwrights used theater to imagine the movement and to advance its goals. What other black-authored plays were produced during and about the classical phase of the civil rights movement (1954–1965)? Compare one of these works to those accounts that dominated popular media (particularly television and newspapers) during the movement. How does the play's engagement with the movement align with, or depart from, the stories and images that pervaded conventional media? Was the play reviewed? If so, what do the reviews tell you about how audiences might have responded to the play, to this other theater of civil rights activism?
4 In recent years, Detroit, Michigan, has faced a number of highly publicized challenges—from historic loss of jobs to a housing crisis of catastrophic proportions. In effect, Detroit has become a cautionary tale of the American city. What once was a thriving site of possibility for black migrants from the US South now exists as a much more precarious place. At the same time, Detroit has long had a deep history of racial violence and inequality. With these dynamics in mind, prepare a short presentation that examines the history of black people and black experience in Detroit, paying particular attention to the "Great Migration." Why did black migrants leave the South? What did they find in Detroit? What do the conditions of present-day Detroit say about "black progress" decades after the civil rights movement?
5 Search for information on PTSD in your school or local library. What are the origins of this psychiatric disorder? What is its relationship to war? Considering frequent allusions to the civil rights movement as a "battlefield" or a "theater of war," reflect on whether the lingering psychological traumas of civil rights activism can be usefully conceived as PTSD. With the rise of the Black Lives Matter Movement and heightened awareness of police violence, how might PTSD help to make sense of the trauma that continues to haunt those who participate in social movements?

Notes

1 Joseph Roach, *Cities of the Dead: Circum-Atlantic Performance* (New York: Columbia University Press, 1996).
2 "President Obama Dedicates a Statue Honoring Rosa Parks," YouTube video, 54:29, from remarks delivered on February 27, 2013, posted by "The Obama White House," February 17, 2013. Emphasis added.
3 Ibid.
4 Lauren Berlant, *Cruel Optimism* (Durham: Duke University Press, 2011), 24. Berlant defines "cruel optimism" as a "relation of attachment to compromised conditions of possibility." She is interested in the quotidian nature of violence and the ways in which these conditions often become "ordinary" such that a problematic optimism can thrive over and against the shocking reality of these violences.
5 My understanding of "appropriation," within this particular nexus of history, memory, race, and politics, borrows from E. Patrick Johnson's conception of the term in *Appropriating Blackness: Performance and the Politics of Authenticity* (Durham: Duke University Press, 2003).
6 Obama asserts, for example, "That is why Dr. King was so quintessentially American—because for all the hardships we've endured, for all our sometimes tragic history, ours is a story of optimism and achievement and constant striving that is unique upon this earth." In a similar tenor, he says of Parks,

> This morning, we celebrate a seamstress, slight in stature but mighty in courage. She defied the odds, and she defied injustice. She lived a life of activism, but also a life of dignity and grace. And in a single moment, with the simplest of gestures, she helped change America—and change the world.

He calls King, "a little-known pastor, new to town and only 26 years old."

7 "President Obama Dedicates"; "President Obama Delivers Remarks at the Martin Luther King, Jr. Memorial Dedication," YouTube video, 20:22, from remarks delivered October 16, 2011, posted by "The Obama White House," October 16, 2011.
8 See John Jackson, Jr., *Racial Paranoia: The Unintended Consequences of Political Correctness* (New York: Basic, 2008); Imani Perry, *More Beautiful and More Terrible: The Embrace and Transcendence of Racial Inequality in the United States* (New York: New York University Press, 2011); and Sharon P. Holland, *The Erotic Life of Racism* (Durham: Duke University Press, 2012).
9 Perry, *More Beautiful and More Terrible*, 3.
10 Martin Luther King, Jr., "Letter from Birmingham Jail," *africa.upenn.edu*.
11 Leigh Raiford and Renee C. Romano, "The Struggle over Memory," in *The Civil Rights Movement in American Memory*, ed. Renee C. Romano and Leigh Raiford (Athens: University of Georgia Press, 2006), xvii.
12 Ibid. For critical discourses that explore the ways in which the "New Right" and "Neo Conservatives" often mobilize the legacy of the modern civil rights movement to roll back the social and political gains at the movement's core, see Mary L. Dudziak, *Cold War Civil Rights: Race and the Image of American Democracy* (Princeton: Princeton University Press, 2000); Nikhil P. Singh, *Black Is a Country: Race and the Unfinished Struggle for Democracy* (Cambridge: Harvard University Press, 2005); and Jacquelyn Dowd Hall, "The Long Civil Rights Movement and the Political Uses of the Past," *Journal of American History* 91.4 (2005), 1233–1263.
13 Blitz the Ambassador, "Emmett (S)till," *bandcamp.com*, audio file, 3:57, January 18, 2010.
14 Geneviève Fabre and Robert O'Meally, "Introduction," in *History and Memory in African-American Culture*, ed. Geneviève Fabre and Robert O'Meally (New York: Oxford University Press, 1994), 6.
15 See Ernest Gaines, *The Autobiography of Miss Jane Pittman* (New York: Dial, 1971); Ntozake Shange, *Betsey Brown: A Novel* (New York: St. Martin's, 1985); Katori Hall, *The Mountaintop* (London: Methuen Drama, 2011); and Toni Morrison, *Paradise* (New York: Plume, 1997), *Love* (New York: Knopf, 2003), and *Remember: The Journey to School Integration* (Boston: Houghton Mifflin, 2004).
16 Brian Norman, *Jim Crow in Post-Civil Rights American Literature* (Athens: University of Georgia Press, 2010), 3.
17 Pearl Cleage, *Bourbon at the Border* (New York: Dramatists Play Service, 1997), 3.
18 Ivy G. Wilson coins the term "political aesthetics" to make sense of the intimate relationship between politics and various forms of artistic production.
19 Nicole Fleetwood, *Troubling Vision: Performance, Visuality, and Blackness* (Chicago: University of Chicago Press, 2011), 33.
20 Ibid.
21 Cathy Caruth, *Literature in the Ashes of History* (Baltimore: Johns Hopkins University Press, 2013), 56.
22 Cleage, *Bourbon at the Border*, 9.
23 Ibid.
24 Ibid.
25 Ibid.
26 Ibid., 13.
27 Ibid.
28 Ibid., 14.
29 Ibid., 13.
30 Ibid., 14.
31 Ibid.
32 Ibid., 15.
33 Ibid.
34 Jonathan S. Holloway, *Jim Crow Wisdom: Memory and Identity in Black America since 1940* (Chapel Hill: University of North Carolina Press, 2013), 67.
35 Diana Taylor, *The Archive and the Repertoire: Performing Cultural Memory in the Americas* (Durham: Duke University Press, 2003), 19–20.
36 Ibid., 165.
37 Cleage, *Bourbon at the Border*, 16.
38 Ibid., 33.
39 Ibid.
40 Ibid.
41 Ibid., 56.
42 Ibid., 57.
43 Ibid.
44 Ibid.

45 Danielle L. McGuire, *At the Dark End of the Street: Black Women, Rape, and Resistance—A New History of the Civil Rights Movement from Rosa Parks to the Rise of Black Power* (New York: Vintage, 2010), xx.
46 See Erica R. Edwards, *Charisma and the Fictions of Black Leadership* (Minneapolis: University of Minnesota Press, 2012).
47 Cleage, *Bourbon at the Border*, 59.
48 Ibid. Emphasis added.
49 Nell Irvin Painter, *Southern History Across the Color Line* (Chapel Hill: University of North Caroline Press, 2002), 129.
50 Cleage, *Bourbon at the Border*, 57.
51 Toni Morrison, "The Site of Memory," in *Inventing the Truth: The Art and Craft of Memoir*, ed. William Zinsser (New York: Houghton Mifflin, 1995), 91.
52 Ibid., 92.
53 Tavia Nyong'o, *The Amalgamation Waltz: Race, Performance, and the Ruses of Memory* (Minneapolis: University of Minnesota Press, 2009), 144.
54 Ibid.

8

"A LIVING THEATER" FOR HUMAN RIGHTS

Jill Freedman's *Old News* and Visual Legacies of the 1968 Poor People's Campaign

Katharina Fackler

> The power of photographs is not only their ability to depict events but to bring human scale to those experiences…images act not only as repositories of memory but also as stimulants and beacons for remembering.
>
> Lonnie G. Bunch III[1]

The most iconic photographs of the civil rights movement feature black protesters being attacked by white police officers, a compelling yet simplified visual narrative that focuses our attention on the struggle for *de jure* racial equality. In this sanitized public image, the socio-economic dimensions of the civil rights movement have too often been ignored, the complex issues of poverty and class removed from the picture. The vision of Martin Luther King, Jr. and the Southern Christian Leadership Conference (SCLC), however, focused not only on dreams of black and white children sitting at the same table but also, metaphorically speaking, on the food on that table. This understanding of the links between race and class led activists in the 1960s to question a political and socio-economic system that perpetuated a costly war in Vietnam while tolerating abject poverty on the home front. King and SCLC brought attention to the root of the nation's problem with their staging of the 1968 Poor People's Campaign (PPC). Jill Freedman's stunning photographs of the PPC, presented in her photobook *Old News: Resurrection City* (1970), challenge what scholars such as Leigh Raiford, in *Imprisoned in a Luminous Glare* (2011), call the consensus narrative of the civil rights movement by visualizing socio-economic inequality and thus broadening our understanding of a movement that was always about human rights.

Movement historians insist that human rights and economic justice lay at the heart and center of King and SCLC's agenda. As the 1960s progressed, African Americans' increasing disillusionment with the limited impact of both the Civil Rights Act (1964) and the Voting Rights Act (1965) on their daily lives, as well as the violent race riots in urban areas, caused King and SCLC to address more openly the problem of socio-economic inequality in the US.[2] The PPC, a nonviolent campaign expanding on the tradition of the civil rights marches, brought forth a class-based coalition among various African American groups, Appalachian whites, Mexican Americans, Puerto Ricans, and American Indians. Nearly three thousand campaigners moved into Resurrection City, a shantytown on the Washington Mall, participating in protests that lasted from May 12 to June 24 and climaxed in a mass rally on

Solidarity Day, June 19. This campaign should be considered SCLC's central effort to dramatize its concern about poverty and the basic pattern of (unequal) material distribution in the US, an effort with a clear precedent in the collective resistance of black sharecroppers in Fayette County, Tennessee, who built Freedom Tent City in 1959 to protest evictions made in retaliation to their attempting to register to vote. The PPC and its encampment on the Washington, DC Mall in Resurrection City is itself a precedent for the current work of Reverend William Barber, who, in 2017, stepped down from his role leading the National Association for the Advancement of Colored People (NAACP) in North Carolina to launch a new poor people's campaign. In his public announcement, he referenced King directly: "Dr. King said in 1968 we needed a moral revolution of values, and we say we need a moral revival."[3]

The PPC has mostly been remembered as the unsuccessful last chapter of the civil rights movement, which proved its nonviolent strategies to be outdated. Indeed, until very recently, the PPC has been memorialized as *the* civil rights campaign that did not leave a legacy. Historians have mostly based their evaluation on the perceived lack of political successes and favorable media coverage at the time, describing it as "almost a perfect failure…poorly timed, poorly organized, and poorly led"[4] and "contribut[ing] to the overall demise of the Civil Rights Movement."[5] For diverse reasons, it is not surprising that this campaign did not achieve the same public acclaim as the 1963 March on Washington. After another wave of riots had shaken major US cities in the wake of King's assassination on April 4, 1968,[6] many white middle-class Americans were afraid that the campaign would spark even more violent race riots. They were also reluctant to take the blame for racial discrimination, feeling that blacks, with whom the campaign was often exclusively associated in the press, were asking too much after the milestones of the Civil and Voting Rights Acts. The media mostly portrayed the campaign in a negative light, stressing "conflict, disunity, and an ever-present threat of chaos and violence," obscuring the multiethnic nature of the campaign, its demands, and its protest actions.[7] Robert T. Chase has argued that the campaign's primary goal and focus—the idea of a multiethnic class insurrection and a restructuring of the socio-economic and political structure of the country—led to the loss of its Northern white liberal support base and thus to the ultimate demise of the campaign. But while the PPC may not have been a popular success with middle-class white liberal audiences and media, it most certainly did successfully adapt and expand core ideas and tactics of the civil rights movement, opening up spaces for a larger social movement and a more inclusive, radical social vision.

While alternative visual narratives of the PPC make this radical social vision clear, they rarely made their way into the press. The most dominant visual formula reinforcing the negative interpretation is what might be usefully called "riot iconography"; established during the violent race riots in urban centers and transferred to the PPC, it presented the campaigners as an uncontrollable, impersonal black mob living in filth and mud, lacking adequate leadership and therefore posing a threat to order and state power. Alternative intermedial—visual and literary—narratives, told in photobooks like SCLC's *The Poor People's Campaign: A Photographic Journal* (1968), subvert the implications and presuppositions of the riot iconography, offering a visual and verbal rhetoric that promotes a richer, more complex understanding and memorialization not only of the PPC but also of the civil rights movement. The most prominent of these is *Old News* by Freedman, a white freelance photographer from New York City who describes her experiences as a campaign participant in a subjective first-person account. *Old News* develops a visual and verbal narrative that builds on, adapts, and expands the earlier, successful iconography of the civil rights movement to visually enact what Aaron Bryant calls King's "most daring dream"—an interracial protest by the poor for economic equality and a decent life for all.[8]

Protest as Performance

Visual Culture Studies, Performance Studies, and Memory Studies offer theories that challenge our understanding of the PPC as either a success or a failure. Dance scholar Susan Leigh Foster has suggested that classic theories of political protest "dismiss the body" in neglecting its function "as an articulate signifying agent" as they "either conceptualiz[e] protest as a practice that erupts out of a bodily anger over which there is no control, or…envision…it as a practice that uses the body only as an efficacious instrument that can assist in maximizing efficiency."[9] The first approach leads to an understanding of protest as "mob performance"—a concept that succinctly describes many contemporary responses to the PPC. The second approach entails a narrow assessment of protest actions as either a success or a failure—a theoretical framework that has dominated most historical accounts of the PPC. To complement classic theories of political protest, Foster proposes considering protest actions not as fixed products with definite outcomes but as performances that use the "body as a vast reservoir of signs and symbols."[10] Besides asking, "What did they achieve?", she suggests the following questions for the investigation of the symbolic, political, cultural, and social meanings created by protest choreographies:

- What are these bodies doing?
- What and how do their motions signify?
- What choreography, whether spontaneous or pre-determined, do they enact?
- What kind of significance and impact does the collection of bodies make in the midst of its social surround?
- How does the choreography theorize corporeal, individual, and social identity?
- How does it construct ethnicity, gender, class, and sexuality?
- What do they share that allows them to move with one another?
- What kinds of connections can be traced between their daily routines and the special moments of their protest?[11]

Seen as performance, protest actions are much more than just another way to reach a political goal. They invite people to use "the materiality of their bodies" to claim public spaces and visibility, and "to perform…their respective political agendas,"[12] expressing views that otherwise remain unheard. Protest choreographies often invite people to bond and mutually support one another, to share common experiences, and to "choreograph…an imagined alternative."[13] Many of these functions of protest are independent of or only loosely connected with its publicly perceived success or failure. Rather, they represent a form of individual or communal empowerment as the protesting bodies "*perform* agency."[14] These facets of the protest choreography were particularly important in the case of the PPC as the political demands of the campaign were kept consciously vague for a long time. In order to point out the fundamental "revolution of values" and basic alterations of the socio-economic system that they considered necessary for the eradication of poverty, PPC leaders refused to name goals that would have appeared "manageable" for Washington administrators—a tactic that frustrated many journalists.[15] Instead, the organizers aimed to bring the persistence of dire poverty in the US to public attention to pressure the government into action. The PPC provided a nonviolent outlet for the frustration that many people were feeling, giving them a sense of agency and a platform to express their protest against the status quo.

Organizers frequently presented the PPC as riot prevention and a form of self-help.[16] Amy Nathan Wright, for example, sees some of the campaign's major achievements in bringing people together, allowing them a pleasurable escape from their oppressing everyday lives, helping them understand that they were not alone, and encouraging them to establish bonds with people in a similar situation and thus improving their skills in administration and petitioning on the local level.[17] Adam Fairclough summarizes King's priorities for the PPC as follows:

> On the matter of demands, King discounted the importance of having comprehensive and detailed proposals. Poor people were not going to be 'fired up' by a long list of demands, and proposals like a negative income tax were too complex…If SCLC dramatized the basic problem, the rest would follow.[18]

"Performing" or "staging" poverty in this sense does not mean that the protesters feigned nonexistent destitution. Rather, it implies that certain choreographic techniques were consciously employed to display poverty to the public. The two key elements of this choreography were the meaningful physical presence of poor people in the capitol, who, in marches and diverse protest actions, displayed and performed their disagreement with social inequality in the US, and of a shantytown on the most sacred space of American civil religion—the Washington Mall.

Yet, as a performance, the protest action is by nature ephemeral, and the audience that can experience it directly is very limited. For any protest to be widely perceived and understood, it has to rely on technologies of reproduction. Photography, a performative medium in itself, can capture physical performances of bodies, retaining, disseminating, amplifying, and memorializing a specific perspective on protest actions.[19] Davi Johnson thus argues that photographs "destabilize" the "line between presence and absence."[20] As has often been argued, the persuasive power of photographs of civil rights protests was indispensable in achieving the shift from a political to a moral rhetoric in the public discourse about civil rights. Indeed, photographs were a part of SCLC's strategies to such a degree that some scholars have called the organization's protest actions "image events."[21] Vicki Goldberg describes the strong emotional, intersubjective effect of the iconic Birmingham photographs:

> By May 1963 it was impossible to be unaware of southern racism, but these images seemed to raise the temperature of inhumanity several degrees. The irresistible force of the water and the bestial dogs turned on young people by officers of the law struck Americans as savage and cruel. Racism had been an abstract idea, an *ism* like socialism or unionism. The photographs gave this abstraction a visible image, which was easier to hate than an idea.[22]

The photographs' rhetorical potential was multiplied by the awareness that people around the world were seeing them, shaping the image of the US on a Cold War globe.[23]

A comparison of visual representations of the PPC by different actors affirms the truism that photographs never purely document a situation but always create selectively framed interpretations of actual events. While few press photographs have represented the PPC in a way that would win the viewers' sympathy or support, Freedman's *Old News* presents a compelling alternative to dominant visual interpretations. Her photobook avoids the visual rhetoric that merged poverty, blackness, and rioting into one negative stereotype and instead harnesses iconographies of powerful and widely circulated photographs of major civil rights campaigns to anchor the PPC in the visual and ideological repertoire of nonviolent protest actions. Most importantly, *Old News* expands the visual legacy of the civil rights movement in ways that perform the crucial work of intersectionality—integrating issues of poverty, race, and global economic justice to remind us that the struggle did not end with the Voting Rights Act or King's death. The movement continued, with successes and setbacks, to make social problems visible, to lend agency to and promote bonding among disempowered members of society.

Appropriating the Visual Repertoire of the Civil Rights Movement

A self-taught photographer from New York City, Freedman lived in Resurrection City for six weeks, "immersing herself in her subjects."[24] While it remains unclear whether she saw herself as "poor" at the time, she clearly identified with the campaigners and their goals, using the first-person plural "we" when talking about the protesters. She sold six of her pictures to *Life* magazine, where they appeared on June 28, 1968.[25] In 1971, her photographs of the PPC were published as a book with Grossman Publishers under the title *Old News: Resurrection City*. In the preface, she positions herself as a participant-observer of the PPC:

> I had to see what was happening, to record it and be part of it…So I went and had one of the times of my life, and this is my trip. And I never realized how much it had become a part of me until I was writing this and saying we and us and feeling homesick.[26]

Her work is thus not framed as an authoritative, historiographic account but rather as a subjective, first-person form of life writing about the events by a participant. The photobook presents an interpretation of the actual protest performance, designed and choreographed from the perspective of a participant. While photojournalists did not stay in Resurrection City and necessarily were forced to cover the campaign from an outside perspective, sometimes hindered by self-proclaimed "marshals,"[27] *Old News* positions the first-person voice as a subjective participant rather than a supposedly objective outside observer. As a form of life writing, Freedman's photobook allows the viewer a glance at life in Resurrection City through the eyes of a first-person narrator. She conveys her campaign experience in rough chronological order from the point when the protesters arrived in Washington, DC to the time when the shantytown was torn down.

Old News employs a wide range of visual strategies to create a counter-narrative to press accounts that stressed violence, disorder, and defeat as the main themes of the campaign. Most significantly, it participates in the iconographic repertoire of the most iconic and popular photographs of the civil rights movement and "its respective ideological implications and presuppositions."[28] The photobook persuasively visualizes the campaign's performance of the choreography of nonviolent action, using iconographies in which participants, many of whom are black, perform their criticism of the status quo through their meaningful physical presence in culturally and politically significant locations. It also makes use of the sentimental visual formulas of police violence on passive, victimized protesters. These iconographies locate the campaign in the visual repertoire of the most central methods and ideologies of the civil rights movement, countering perceptions of the campaign as a germ for violence by framing it as inherently nonviolent, as an outlet for discontent and anger that avoided further riots, and as a means of legitimate participation in public politics. The focus on the *process* rather than the *product* of campaigning reframes the visual legacy of the campaign (Figure 8.1).

The cover page of *Old News*, featured again on the last page of the photobook, frames the entire narrative, inscribing the campaign into the visual and ideological archive of nonviolent protest actions, such as the civil rights marches on Washington and the lunch counter sit-ins. It shows a black woman sitting on the bottom of the stairs leading up to the US Capitol, which had by 1968 become a favored spot for Americans to protest against the policies of their government.[29] The low frontal angle, making the viewer look up to the participant, stresses her conscious physical presence in a highly symbolical space. She is over-towered by the rotunda, which represents the powerful US government whose representatives (police officers) are placed as tiny figures roughly above her shoulders. Through its framing and

FIGURE 8.1 Cover photograph of *Old News: Resurrection City*.
Photo courtesy of Jill Freedman.

perspective, the photograph thus creates a vision of a highly stratified socio-economic system, which disempowers and oppresses the poor, who are all too often black and/or female. While the woman in the photograph clearly does not emanate the sense of hope that characterized many photographs of the March on Washington, she is presented as performing one of the central protest choreographies of the civil rights movement in that she uses her mere physical presence to publicly perform her dissent with US policies. Her action appears comparable to the lunch counter sit-ins and Rosa Parks' famous protest in that this woman, in the words of Pia Wiegmink, "effectively stages her body in public to protest against…inequality. The moment this body becomes visible, seen in public, her cause—i.e. the political motivation—also comes to the fore."[30] Photographs of the sit-ins, for example, those by Fred Blackwell and

Danny Lyon,[31] show protesters consciously and purposely placing their bodies in the segregated space of the lunch counter to perform their protest against Jim Crow as well as their "imagined alternative" of a world without segregation. Through this woman's visible presence at the US Capitol as a member of the PPC, the photograph stages her body as performing the campaign's choreography. In placing her body in the space most central to patriotic US self-representation, the woman pictured on the cover inscribes the shameful persistence of poverty into national narratives otherwise marked by nationalist Cold War ideas of (white) power and superiority.

This visualization of a peaceful but nevertheless powerful protest performance counters associations of the campaigners with black power and urban riots. The photographs that dominated coverage of the urban riots were shot from a distance, which precluded the recognition of facial features and thus intersubjective identification. Vickie Goldberg notes that cameras, which had been positioned on the side of civil rights protesters in the first half of the 1960s, "had taken refuge behind the police lines and were picturing the fury of black mobs by the end of the decade."[32] These pictures showed young black male bodies moving rapidly and violently, inciting fears of an aggressive, impersonal, uncontrollable mob that is about to destroy America's inner cities.[33] Freedman moved the camera back among the dissenters. In contrast to the rioters, the woman on the cover's body is presented as static, in a waiting position, facing the viewer frontally and looking into the camera, encouraging intersubjective engagement rather than fear.

Photographs of people marching pervade the photobook. A far cry from the immense human masses that peopled images of the 1963 March on Washington, Freedman's photographs nevertheless repeatedly take up marching iconographies that, from a slightly slanted frontal angle, portray this protest performance as a positively connoted communal claim to space, agency, and visibility. The shots on pages 9 and 10, for example, are taken at eye level, where "the point of view is one of equality and there is no power difference involved."[34] Frontal angles imply that "the image producer (and hence, willy-nilly, the viewer) is 'involved' with the represented participants."[35] The short distance between the viewer and the marchers increases this effect as it allows a direct glance at the faces of individual protesters. The activity of marching was an indispensable element of SCLC's choreography of nonviolent protest as it was not only an impressive way to demonstrate visible, physical presence and agency in a public space but also had powerful psychological effects on marchers. Summarizing King's address "See You in Washington," Fairclough describes King's understanding of marching:

> Demonstrations would give the poor a sense of dignity and destiny. They would unite existing allies and create new ones. 'Out there on the line,' moreover, 'black folk and white folk get together in a strange way.' Above all, SCLC had to keep alive a feeling of hope. Hope was the kingdom of God, 'an inner power within you,' driving people to strive for their ideals. Hope was 'the courage to be'; it was a refusal to be stopped or to give up.[36]

Given their powerful meanings and potential effects, it is not surprising that negative press articles about the PPC tended to avoid photographs of protesters engaged in marching. In contrast, Freedman's photobook puts the marching iconography front and center. Depicting orderly lines moving purposefully into a certain direction, she visualizes how venturing out into public space and making themselves heard lent a sense of agency and community to the represented participants (Figure 8.2).

FIGURE 8.2 Untitled. *Old News: Resurrection City* 9.
Photo courtesy of Jill Freedman.

Many photographs in *Old News* participate in the iconographic networks of the civil rights movement by appropriating a sentimental visual formula of violent officer vs. passive and innocent protester that was widely distributed in the white Northern press. Martin Berger observes that

> [w]ith great regularity, iconic [civil rights] photographs show white actors exercising power over blacks—dignified black schoolchildren silently suffering the jeers of unruly mobs, well-mannered black students at lunch counters weathering the abuse of mirthful white crowds, and stoic protestors buckling under the assaults of water jets and police dogs.[37]

Famous examples include Bill Hudson's and Charles Moore's photographs of demonstrators being attacked by police dogs and high-pressure water hoses in Birmingham.[38] Johnson describes these photographs as endowed with a "sense of extreme visual polarity…featuring a clear dichotomy between villain and victim, and inviting unequivocal moral judgment from viewers."[39] While this iconography, which played into mass media's sensationalism, was instrumental in arousing strong feelings and action against segregation, its dominance is also highly problematic. Berger argues that the iconography of black-on-white violence severely limited the perceived agency of African American protesters and thus the scope of social change these photographs invited their viewers to imagine.[40] These visual formulas thus render invisible "the expansive expressions of black political desire" that marked the twentieth century.[41] *Old News* appropriates but does not limit itself to the sentimental visual formula depicting the victimized protesters violently oppressed by police officers, which had often been skillfully and consciously choreographed by the leaders of nonviolent protest actions.[42] To this end, the photobook frequently juxtaposes peaceful protesters and armed, (potentially) aggressive police officers with an

"A Living Theater" for Human Rights   **117**

FIGURE 8.3 "Might vs. Right." *Old News: Resurrection City* 14.
Photo courtesy of Jill Freedman.

unequivocal power imbalance. Two photographs will serve as examples for the ways in which this formula is adapted in *Old News* (Figure 8.3).

"Might vs. Right" fills an entire page of the photobook. Shot from behind an officer's back and from a low, frontal angle, this dramatic photograph focuses on a group of protesters, most saliently a middle-aged black couple. The man wears a clerical collar, holds a book in his right hand, and has protectively put his left arm around the woman. They thus come across as typical members of the often religiously driven, peaceful civil rights protests, their static poses asserting their visual, spatial presence rather than a penchant for violence. Their visual conformity with US family and gender ideals increases their perceived respectability. A group of young black men, just as static, stand behind the couple. A close-up of the officer's back takes up more than half of the composition, the entire left side of the photograph, and the officer holds a billy club, which roughly separates the picture's lower and upper half. Whereas the angle allows a direct view of the protesters' faces, the mass of the officer's body remains obscure. This elaborate and highly stylized composition skillfully uses scale to juxtapose the imposing, threatening, and dark body of the officer with the much smaller figures of the protesters, evoking a sense of their powerlessness at the hands of the officer. The body of the officer represents an anonymous, powerful, and potentially aggressive system that relegates certain innocents to the margins of society in a violent and discriminating manner (Figure 8.4).

"Busted During Demonstration" presents a slight variation on this theme that increases the agency of the police officer. Wearing sunglasses that recall Hudson's iconic Birmingham photograph,[43] a white male officer in uniform gestures to a woman to move on with his left arm while his right arm holds out a billy club. His gestures, his determined facial expression and posture, as well as the figure of the young man in the background, who is reluctantly being guided away by an officer (presumably to jail), leave no doubt about what will happen if the woman,

FIGURE 8.4 "Busted During Demonstration." *Old News: Resurrection City* 55. Photo courtesy of Jill Freedman.

who, tucked away toward the right margin of the photograph, does not follow suit. The composition places the viewer behind the woman, the viewer thus aligned with her in opposition to the officer. The officer's uniform and the straight lines created by his body and the baton evoke the strict rules of a social system that forcefully marginalizes some of its members. The iconography presents the protesters not as a threat but as oppressed by a violent, racist, and patriarchal social system, inviting sympathy for their cause. While this image employs a sentimental visual formula established by iconic civil rights photographs, the word *Cherokee* written on the woman's coat directs the viewer's attention toward the broader agenda and constituency of the PPC. Lost in the dominant narrative of the civil rights movement is the fact that representatives of the PPC demanded, among other things, land and fishing rights for American Indians.[44] By integrating the struggle for Native rights into the signature formula of civil right photography, "Busted" visually aligns the struggles of African Americans and Native Americans against white oppression. Its visual rhetoric thus challenges the parameters of the civil rights movement as starting with *Brown v. Board*, the murder of Emmett Till, and the Montgomery bus boycott in the mid-1950s, embedding the PPC into a long freedom struggle for the economic rights of all ethnicities in the US that began when white settlers first set foot onto the continent.

From Civil Rights to Human Rights: Expanding Visual Legacies

While Freedman appropriates iconographic patterns that had been established by widely circulated photographs to anchor her account of the PPC in the visual and ideological legacy of the nonviolent struggles for civil rights, her photographs also expand and adapt the visual legacy of the civil rights movement to include the issue of economic human rights. They effectively perform what King identified as the central goal of the campaign's protest choreography: the "dramatization of the poverty problem."[45] The three central features of this choreography include a bodily performance of poverty through clothing, the construction of a shantytown on the Washington Mall, and interethnic bonding along class lines.

A second glance at the cover (and closing) photograph thus reveals iconographic elements, besides the woman's facial expression, that distinguish her from typical participants of the March on Washington. With her salient bare feet, a staple signifier in poverty photography as well as in protest actions, she forms a contrast not only to the visible prosperity and power of the US Capitol but also to earlier civil rights protesters. For the famous civil rights marches, such as the Birmingham campaign, the 1963 March on Washington, or the 1965 Selma to Montgomery March, protesters usually wore their best clothes to emphasize their respectability and thus, implicitly, the legitimacy of their demands as US citizens. John Lewis describes how he dressed up for sit-ins and consciously selected attire and occupations that would signify middle-class respectability:

> It was like going to church, I guess. You would put on your church-going clothes, Sunday clothes, and we took books and papers and did our homework at the lunch counter, just quiet and trying to be as dignified as possible.[46]

The protesters' fine clothes visually aligned them with the white middle class, thereby downplaying class differences.

These strategies presented a post-war version of what Evelyn Brooks Higginbotham calls the "politics of respectability," African Americans' strategic adherence "to the dominant society's norms of manners and morals."[47] In the context of the post-war civil rights movement, many protesters strategically deployed techniques of black respectability to refute deeply entrenched stereotypes that, by de-humanizing African Americans, sought to legitimate diverse forms of racial violence and exploitation.[48] In other words, many post-war civil rights protesters used the politics of respectability to make a larger audience understand that they too deserved the basic citizenship rights that seemed to be granted naturally to the white middle class but were systematically denied to blacks. As I have shown elsewhere, many iconic photographs of the civil rights movement of the 1950s and early 1960s are marked by a "visual grammar of respectability" that asserted traditional gender roles; self-control; and middle-class manners, morals, and attire.

The agenda of the PPC required a reversal of these sartorial tactics. As it aimed to bring forth, perform, and visualize class difference, "poor" clothing was an integral part of its choreography. Commenting on the difference between the 1963 March on Washington and the PPC, Luther Jackson, an official of the NAACP, remarked that

> you can almost tell by the clothes. Five years ago the thing was almost solidly middle-class, and even the poor dressed in their Sunday best. Yet the country has failed to change, and there is disenchantment which affects them in so many ways.[49]

Shoeless feet, in particular, represent a symbolic iconography that is almost formulaically associated with the public rhetoric and visualization of poverty. King famously countered the bootstrap metaphor often used by proponents of the ideology of self-help by stating that "[i]t's all right to tell a man to lift himself by his own bootstraps, but it is a cruel jest to say to a bootless man that he ought to lift himself by his own bootstraps."[50] The many photographs of bare feet in Freedman's photobook persuasively visualize poverty and so powerfully support King's argument. The woman on the cover photograph thus represents what the PPC's Public Relations Committee wanted to see in the media when it set as one of its goals to "[g]et Foreign Documentary Film makers to film poverty in the shadow of the capitol."[51] By representing protesting bodies that, often ostentatiously and playfully, claim visual signifiers of poverty and

FIGURE 8.5 "To us all. We are all we have." *Old News: Resurrection City.*
Photo courtesy of Jill Freedman.

lower-class status, Freedman expands and enriches the visual legacy of the civil rights movement (Figure 8.5).

The protesters used dramatic and—in the civil rights movement—unprecedented props to stage their criticism of the status quo, the most prominent being the shantytown Resurrection City on the Washington Mall. The center of Freedman's narrative, its unique iconography reappears throughout the book, creating and framing the space in which this visual narrative evolves. Freedman's photographs of the shantytown appropriate, combine, and interweave various iconographic "conventions, traditions, and repertoires," creating a complex photographic narrative that visualizes the dire living conditions of the poor and at the same time depicts their creative strategies of empowerment.[52] They thereby construct an image of poverty that neither victimizes nor exoticizes the poor. The very first page of the photobook, which precedes even the preface, persuasively visualizes this theme. "To us all" shows a picture of two shacks typical for Resurrection City. Made from raw wood, beside a muddy dirt road, these temporary shelters present a striking contrast to the suburban homes advertised as the epitome of the American dream and way of life by the Cold War media. Reduced to the mere basics of a roof over one's head, resembling tents rather than cozy homes, lacking bathrooms and modern amenities, they powerfully visualize the poor living conditions of the "other America," as Michael Harrington called it, debunking myths of general affluence through capitalism. They also link the PPC with the visual repertoire of older class-based movements, such as the Bonus Army March, which also drew on the multivalent symbolic meaning of the shacks as markers of poverty and resistance.[53] The strategy and iconography of the encampment, disputed among SCLC leaders, most saliently differentiated the PPC from earlier civil rights campaigns, powerfully visualizing poverty in the US Capitol.

Nevertheless, these shacks do not evoke a sense of defeat. The slogans written onto them—"peace" and "we shall overcome"—locate their inhabitants in the counterculture to the pro-Vietnam War, white backlash US mainstream and at the same time announce a sturdy resistance to the depressing conditions that surround them. "To us all" suggests that the poor have claimed public space to turn it into commons neither private nor public but open to the poor. The visual proximity and similarity of the shacks symbolically depicts the closeness of their inhabitants, who are bonding communally against the odds. A little entrance room to one of the shacks with an open door forms the center of the composition, inviting the viewer to enter the shack and thus the commons created by its inhabitants. The photograph thus has the potential to create what Nicholas Mirzoeff has called "the visual commons," a "sensation [that] occurs when we see, in the sense of coming to understand, a photograph *of* the commons that emanates *from* the commons and is not simply about the commons."[54] The caption, "To us all. We are all we have," emphasizes the importance of communal bonding for both the subjects and the viewers in going beyond the materialism of a consumer society in order to retain a vital sense of humanity.

A panoramic shot of the shacks on the Mall, the largest picture in the book that takes up the entire spread on pages 15 and 16, continues this multivalent visual rhetoric. Only the lower third of the composition represents the settlement, named by a sign "Soul City New York," from a distance. A patch of grass and a fence separate it from the viewer. The upper two-thirds of the composition are taken up by the sky, formed by the trees and the shacks into a V-shape that points toward the shacks. Compared to the grass, the trees, and the sky, the shacks seem very small, their makeshift style adding to the impression of powerlessness and deprivation. At the same time, the dominance of natural elements links the picture with the iconographic repertoire of romantic nature images and photographs of the frontier era. The camp looks peaceful, quaint, and bucolic, countering the press narrative of "the one-time 'city of hope' that, as the story went, had devolved into a dirty and debilitated gang-infested ghetto."[55] Nothing reveals the presence of a big city or of an oppressive class system. Pictured just by itself, Resurrection City resembles early frontier settlements, which imply a life full of deprivations but are also associated with core American ideals of self-reliance, independence, freedom, hope, and progress. The poor are thus represented not as paupers with moral and intellectual flaws dependent on welfare but as sturdy individuals braving harsh conditions.

The association with a frontier setting reveals a third function of Resurrection City as a space for the creation of an "imagined alternative" to reality,[56] a space where people would "come…to start a new life."[57] Writing about Resurrection City in his autobiography, Ralph D. Abernathy (who chose to stay in a motel) uses a nationalist city-upon-a-hill rhetoric that dates back to colonial times to link the campaign's imagined alternatives with the basic promises of the US:

> We would set up a model for the rest of the nation to emulate. Everyone would live together in peace and mutual respect…We would have people of all races, ethnic backgrounds, and religious beliefs. Since everyone would be poor, there would be no greed or envy. We would have a common dining room where everybody would eat together, and our business would be to go from government agency to government agency, representing the poor, speaking out for their interests, asking for several concrete things from our government, the richest in the world.[58]

While hardly ever mentioned in the press, the idea of Resurrection City as a better "imagined alternative" is one of the major assertions of Freedman's photobook. She verbally clarifies how what may look like substandard housing to the middle-class beholder actually was an improvement for many campaigners, stressing at the same time the moral superiority of the poor in comparison to those people who are members of the society that supposedly exploits the poor:

> Some of those people raised their whole standard of living just by moving in. For the first time in their lives, they knew their kids would eat every day. Not only that, they thought they were eating good. Soggy cabbage leaves and baloney sandwiches. Even the houses were better than what they'd come from. Electric lights, clean new wood, and—believe it!—enough beds for everyone. This mudhole was a paradise, that's how poor some of those people were. And it showed. In the wizened children and winos and junkies and schizos, casualties of the war for survival, their eyes broken as their shoes. And in the others, wearing their faces like medals. Tough, proud, dignified faces. I've seen poorer people commuting to Wall Street. Much poorer. But not as hungry.[59]

In *Old News*, Freedman captures many of these "[t]ough, proud, dignified faces." The most frequent iconography is a medium-distance portrait of individuals or small groups of people, living together in Resurrection City described as "pretty much just another city."[60] Although in this instance, Freedman distances herself from these people through the use of the third-person pronoun "they," her photographs always place the viewer on the same plain as the participants. They either show individuals bonding among one another or engaging with music or other creative activities, or the camera. They show the participants as dignified individuals "liv[ing] together in peace and mutual respect."[61] They also portray the act of bonding and communal campaigning as a pleasurable experience. In interaction with the reader, Freedman recreates the humor with which many campaigners communally faced the adverse conditions. Six photographs accompanied by verbal text are arranged to tell the story of a few women who, being refused access to the Capitol, find out that they will be let in individually to use the ladies' room and spontaneously stage "the first Washington Pee-in"[62] (Figure 8.6).

After the bucolic panorama shot of the self-contained Resurrection City on pages 15 and 16, Freedman introduces a picture of Resurrection City that criticizes the socio-economic system of the US. The similar, albeit smaller, photograph depicts a number of shacks surrounding a little open square, with a few individuals standing or sitting in front of their homes, engaged in conversations or warming their hands over a fire in a barrel. The idyllic camp scene, again framed by trees, is disrupted by the presence of the Washington Monument that looms large behind the shacks, indicating the presence of a powerful nation that can afford massive monuments but nevertheless tolerates—if not causes—the suffering of the poor. In an article for *Soul Force*, the official journal of SCLC, Gordon White explicates Resurrection City's function of providing a stage where the protesters consciously perform and make public social evils that otherwise go unnoticed:

> This is a man's attempt to display reality so that others may understand and attempt to correct the problems…Resurrection City is a living theater. It is our disciple of truth about the genocide, the racism, and other sicknesses of the American Society…But the problems are not in Resurrection City, because the city is only the theater and the actors portray how they and others live around our country.[63]

Consciously acting and "staging" Resurrection City in the center of national attention, the protesters, according to White, perform a constructive criticism of a political and socio-economic system whose shameful and deadly tolerance of poverty is interlinked with pervasive racism.

FIGURE 8.6 Untitled. *Old News: Resurrection City* 17.
Photo courtesy of Jill Freedman.

The most powerful strategy Freedman uses to expand on the dominant visual legacy of the civil rights movement is her portrayal of race, which is significant in two ways. First, she constructs a counter-narrative to the essentializing portrayal of African American participants, debunking late 1960s stereotypes that equate poverty with blackness and violence.[64] *Old News* instead portrays black protesters as diverse individuals, picturing young men in Black Panther outfits and banners endorsing Huey Newton and Bobby Seale (29, 117, 92, 117); supporters of John and Robert Kennedy (30, 40) of the National Welfare Rights Organization (35–36, 38, 49) and of King (65); and draft resisters and advocates of the peace movement (85–86). By visualizing the diversity of black experiences and political positions, Freedman counteracts essentializing views of black campaigners as violence-prone radicals eager to start another riot. Freedman's photographs depict all these people as individuals or small social units in eye-level close-ups. Most of them, looking directly into the camera, seem to be posing for the photograph, which not only lends them a sense of agency but also makes the portraits call for intersubjective exchange. The static poses and the clearly recognizable, friendly facial features invite the viewer to consider the depicted participants as dignified individuals, their performance of political affiliation a legitimate choice to be taken seriously and to engage with. Freedman's photographs thus present the campaign as integrating different African American political views into SCLC's nonviolent agenda, visualizing its continuing power and appeal. The photo in which the young men stand back behind the older couple is a case in point. The portrayal of African Americans as diverse, full-rounded, peaceful, and social individuals propagates a counter narrative that emphasizes the importance of the PPC for *avoiding* rather than creating further riots.

Second, Freeman portrays the campaign as a multiethnic endeavor, even as she omits the people lodged at Hawthorne School and at St. Augustine Episcopal Church, including most of the Mexican American and American Indian contingent. The representation of race in *Old*

News thus counters and corrects depictions in the news media, which portrayed the campaign as "just another chapter of the black freedom struggle, dominated by African Americans and their distinct priorities" and "in the process, ignored what made it truly militant: its multiracial quality."[65] Freedman expands on the visual legacy of the civil rights movement, in which the most iconic photographs juxtaposed black protesters with white segregationists—a portrayal that significantly simplifies the racial complexities of many civil rights campaigns. Her photographs lend visual presence for non-black protesters by, among others, purposefully arranging close-ups of individuals of different ethnicities. On page 95, Freedman juxtaposes similarly sized images: Dana, a white girl with bare feet; a Native American with traditional headgear and an "Indian Power" button; Alex, a topless young black man; and Ray, who could be representing the Mexican American contingent and is wearing a tag that says, "SCLC marshal." All of them are engaging with the camera and by mentioning their names—with the exception of the Native American—Freedman underscores their individuality. On the opposing page, a large portrait of a black woman leaning against one of the shacks and, again, looking straight into the camera, completes the set. This spread unequivocally visualizes the ethnic diversity—as well as the impressive presence of women—and the individuality of the protesters, who are nevertheless unified by their static pose, their straight look into the camera, and the page layout (Figure 8.7).

In other cases, individual photographs display scenes of interethnic bonding among the campaigners. On pages 101 and 102, black and white children are immersed in play, and on page 58, women of all ages and ethnicities form an organic line that is heading toward a row of police officers on the opposing page, who are equally mixed-race. On page 122, a multiethnic "Jewish Community Council" smiles into Freedman's camera. The most memorable visualization of ethnic bonding, "Hand Like a Shawl," performs a reversal of dominant stereotyping based on gender, age, and race. While the elderly white lady stares aggressively at the line of

FIGURE 8.7 "Hands Like a Shawl." *Old News: Resurrection City* 32.
Photo courtesy of Jill Freedman.

officers that the multiethnic group of protesters is passing, as if they were taking the salute, the young black men protectively put their arms around her, guiding her away from the scene of conflict. They seem to collectively return the gaze that seeks to relegate them to the margins of society. Furthermore, the composition juxtaposes the organic and colorful formation of bonding individuals, which invites the viewer to join, and the straight line of police officers holding their batons, which excludes the viewer. What separates these formations, however, is not skin color (as in earlier civil rights photographs) but rather, the claiming and criticizing of the problem of poverty in the US. Accordingly, one could read this photograph as a claim that the problem of the twentieth century is not—or not *only*—the color line, as Du Bois stated in 1903, but the class line.

Visions of Class Lines and Color Lines

Old News leaves the reader with the certainty that not all the hopes of the campaigners were fulfilled. Freedman ends her photobook with a song written by members of the Western Caravan and titled "This Is the Last Time." The lyrics are accompanied by a close-up shot of three trash-strewn steps and a battered sign reading "ALL Rights For ALL" and followed by the title photograph of the sullen, lonely lady on the stairs leading up to the Capitol. This does not discount, however, the photobook's optimistic assessment of the campaign as a lifetime event that brought together thousands of people of all races to carry the methods and ideologies of the civil rights movement into its next phase—the struggle against poverty. Adapting and appropriating highly successful visual formulas of the civil rights movement, ranging from the meaningful presence of marchers in symbolic public spaces to the sentimental iconography of police violence on protesters, Freedman's photographs expand the visual legacy of the civil rights movement to include visual elements of class struggle, such as the protesters' clothing, the shantytown Resurrection City, and class-based interethnic bonding. Its visualization of the PPC thus comes very close to the organizers' vision of the protest choreography. Whereas the campaign may not have eradicated poverty or even achieved a favorable media response, *Old News* articulates a positive visual interpretation, stressing the fact that it afforded many poor people not only a pleasurable escape from their oppressive everyday lives but also the chance to perform their protest against the status quo, to draw the eyes of the nation to their problems, and to establish lasting bonds with other poor people. Looking at the PPC through the lens of Freedman's photobook, we might agree with Robin Kelley's claim that "too often our standards for evaluating social movements pivot around whether or not they 'succeeded' in realizing their visions rather than on the merits or power of the vision themselves."[66]

Looking backward, *Old News* invites us to reconsider earlier civil rights photographs for visual markers that point to its focus on social and economic justice, making us realize, for example, that the signs branded during the 1963 March on Washington demanded not only *freedom* but also *jobs* for everybody. Looking forward, *Old News* reminds us of the unfinished work of the civil rights movement. Recent events in cities such as Ferguson, Baltimore, Baton Rouge, and Dallas, for example, confirm not only the timeliness and necessity but also the challenges of SCLC's vision of an all-out war against poverty. In the wake of the unrest in Ferguson, Missouri, after the shooting of Michael Brown by a white police officer, many commentators pointed toward the intersectionality of race and poverty. Kareem Abdul-Jabbar claimed that "we have to address the situation not just as another act of systemic racism, but as what else it is: class warfare."[67] What may have been "old news" for Freedman and the participants of the PPC seems to pose a very current challenge to US society: the color line remains inextricably linked with the class line, the ongoing struggle against inequality demanding alternative visions of the civil rights movement.

Approaches to Teaching Jill Freedman's *Old News*

Discussion Questions

1. Why do you think the Poor People's Campaign has not been as well remembered as its predecessors? For example, as recently as 2015, the 1965 Selma to Montgomery March was made into a Hollywood film starring David Oyelowo as King and featuring Oprah Winfrey and Common.
2. What are typical visual elements of iconic photographs of the civil rights movement? Consider the pictures typically shown on television on anniversaries of civil rights events or on Martin Luther King, Jr. Day and look at photographs by Charles Moore and Bill Hudson taken in Birmingham in 1963. Why do you think photojournalists selected images with these elements among the thousands of pictures taken at these events? What is the potential, and what are the limitations of this visual rhetoric?
3. Look at photographs of the Greensboro sit-ins and the 1963 March on Washington. How do these photographs visually stage the "protest performance"? How did protesters and photojournalists avoid visual markers of poverty or class hierarchies?
4. What photographs in Freedman's *Old News* remind you of the famous civil rights photographs? Why? What kinds of photographs are atypical for the civil rights movement? What are their implications?

Research and Writing Projects

1. Use the internet to compile a list and find photos of protest movements that address the issue of poverty or social inequality. How did the protesters go about staging their bodies in the public? In what ways are the photographs similar to or different from Freedman's representation of the US Poor People's Campaign?
2. Review all the photographs and texts in Freedman's *Old News: Resurrection City*. What image of poor people in the US is propagated? Compare and contrast with other (stereo)typical images of poor people either in visual culture (e.g. in the photographs of the Great Depression), in literature (e.g. by Stephen Crane, William Faulkner, and Eudora Welty), in TV shows (e.g. *The Wire*, *Here Comes Honey Boo Boo*, *Homeland*), or in political debates. How are the differences in the representation of poor people linked with the ideas and visual representation of the civil rights movement? Do you think the civil rights movement changed the way we see poor people or how poor people see themselves?
3. Search for articles on the civil rights movement in *Life* magazines from the 1950s and 1960s, accessible online at books.google.com. What kinds of photographs did *Life* use? How do the images relate to the verbal text? What kind of relationship between black and white bodies do the photographs suggest? Compare and contrast with Freedman's *Old News*.
4. Look at the photographs with the hashtag #blacklivesmatter on Twitter along with photographs of the twenty-first-century PPC led by Reverend Barber in the news. Fifty years have passed since the PPC. Do you see any of the visual legacies of the campaign reflected in these photographs? What is different?

Notes

1. Lonnie G. Bunch III, Founding Director of the National Museum of African American History and Culture on "More Than a Picture," the Museum's first Special Exhibition. *Charter Member News* 3.2 (Summer 2017).

2 Thomas F. Jackson, *From Civil Rights to Human Rights: Martin Luther King, Jr., and the Struggle for Economic Justice* (Philadelphia: University of Pennsylvania Press, 2007), 2.
3 Martha Waggoner, "Rev. William Barber to Launch Poor People's Campaign," *Equal Voice*, May 11, 2017.
4 Gerald D. McKnight, *The Last Crusade: Martin Luther King, Jr., the FBI, and the Poor People's Campaign* (Boulder: Westview, 1998), 107.
5 Robert T. Chase, "Class Resurrection: The Poor People's Campaign of 1968 and Resurrection City," *Essays in History* 40 (1998).
6 Mark Speltz's *North of Dixie: Civil Rights Photography beyond the South* (Los Angeles: J. Paul Getty Museum, 2016) brings together photographs and histories of civil rights struggles that took place outside of the South and that have often been forgotten in the public memory of the movement.
7 Gordon K. Mantler, "'The press did you in': The Poor People's Campaign and the Mass Media," *The Sixties, A Journal of History, Politics and Culture* 3.1 (2010), 35.
8 Aaron Bryant, "Most Daring Dream: Robert Houston Photography and the 1968 Poor People's Campaign," *Callaloo* 31.4 (2008), 1272.
9 Susan L. Foster, "Choreographies of Protest," *Theater Journal* 55.3 (2003), 396.
10 Ibid., 395.
11 Ibid., 397.
12 Pia Wiegmink, *Protest EnACTed: Activist Performance as Engaged Citizenship in Contemporary US America* (Heidelberg: Winter, 2011), 56.
13 Foster, "Choreographies of Protest," 412.
14 Wiegmink, *Protest EnACTed*, 58.
15 Chase, "Class Resurrection," n.p.
16 Mark Beach and Oralee Beach, "Open Letter to a Concerned Friend," n.d., SCLC Archives, Manuscript and Rare Book Library, Emory University, Atlanta, GA.
17 Amy N. Wright, "The 1968 Poor People's Campaign, Marks, Mississippi, and the Mule Train: Fighting Poverty Locally, Representing Poverty Nationally," in *Civil Rights History from the Ground Up: Local Struggles, a National Movement*, ed. Emilye Crosby (Athens: University of Georgia Press, 2011), 112, 123, 131–134.
18 Adam Fairclough, *To Redeem the Soul of America: The Southern Christian Leadership Conference and Martin Luther King, Jr.* (Athens: University of Georgia Press, 1987), 363.
19 Robert Hariman and John Louis Lucaites, *No Caption Needed: Iconic Photographs, Public Culture, and Liberal Democracy* (Chicago: University of Chicago Press, 2007), 31–32.
20 Davi Johnson, "Martin Luther King Jr.'s 1963 Birmingham Campaign as Image Event," *Rhetoric and Public Affairs* 10.1 (2007), 7.
21 Ibid., 1; Kevin M. DeLuca, *Image Politics: The New Rhetoric of Environmental Activism* (New York: Guilford, 1999), 3.
22 Vicki Goldberg, *The Power of Photography: How Photographs Changed Our Lives* (New York: Abbeville, 1991), 204.
23 Johnson, "Martin Luther King Jr.'s 1963 Birmingham Campaign as Image Event," 2.
24 Niko Koppel, "Through Weegee's Lens," *New York Times*, April 27, 2008.
25 See John Neary, "Resurrection City, D.C. And So the Poor People Came," *Life*, June 28, 1968.
26 Jill Freedman, *Old News: Resurrection City* (New York: Grossman, 1970), n.p.
27 Charles E. Fager, *Uncertain Resurrection* (Grand Rapids: Eerdmans, 1969), 42.
28 Udo J. Hebel, "'American' Pictures and (Trans-)National Iconographies," in *American Studies Today: New Research Agendas*, ed. Winfried Fluck, Sabine Sielke, and Erik Redling (Heidelberg: Winter, 2014), 408.
29 See Lucy G. Barber, *Marching on Washington: The Forging of an American Political Tradition* (Berkeley: University of California Press, 2002).
30 Wiegmink, *Protest EnACTed*, 56.
31 See Steven Kasher, *The Civil Rights Movement: A Photographic History, 1954–68* (New York: Abbeville, 1996), 67, 81.
32 Goldberg, *The Power of Photography*, 212.
33 See National Advisory Commission on Civil Disorders, *Report of the National Advisory Commission on Civil Disorders* (Washington, DC: Government Printing Office, 1968), 18, 32, 36, 41, 47–52, 59, 88, 94; Earl Caldwell, "87 Poor in Capital Held in Protests: Street Sit-In Halts Traffic-Police Hurl Tear Gas," *New York Times*, June 21, 1968.
34 Gunther Kress and Theo van Leeuwen, *Reading Images: The Grammar of Visual Design* (London: Routledge, 2005), 140.
35 Ibid., 136.

36 Fairclough, *To Redeem the Soul of America*, 364.
37 Martin A. Berger, *Seeing Through Race: A Reinterpretation of Civil Rights Photography* (Berkeley: University of California Press, 2011), 7.
38 Kasher, *The Civil Rights Movement*, 88, 104, 106–107.
39 Johnson, "Martin Luther King Jr.'s 1963 Birmingham Campaign as Image Event," 6.
40 Berger, *Seeing Through Race*, 7.
41 Leigh Raiford, *Imprisoned in a Luminous Glare: Photography and the African American Freedom Struggle* (Chapel Hill: University of North Carolina Press, 2011), 4.
42 Johnson, "Martin Luther King Jr.'s 1963 Birmingham Campaign as Image Event," 2–3.
43 See Kasher, *The Civil Rights Movement*, 88.
44 Mantler, "'The press did you in,'" 38; for a comprehensive analysis of the campaign's effects on Mexican American and African American coalition building, see Mantler's *Power to the Poor: Black-Brown Coalition and the Fight for Economic Justice* (Chapel Hill: University of North Carolina Press, 2013).
45 Qtd. in McKnight, *The Last Crusade*, 20.
46 Qtd. in Howell Raines, *My Soul Is Rested: Movement Days in the Deep South Remembered* (New York: Penguin, 1983), 99.
47 Evelyn B. Higginbotham, *Righteous Discontent: The Women's Movement in the Black Baptist Church, 1880–1920* (Cambridge: Harvard University Press, 1993), 187.
48 Marisa Chappell, Jenny Hutchinson, and Brian Ward, "'Dress modestly, neatly . . . as if you were going to church': Respectability, Class and Gender in the Montgomery Bus Boycott and the Early Civil Rights Movement," in *Gender and the Civil Rights Movement*, ed. Peter J. Ling and Sharon Monteith (New Brunswick: Rutgers University Press, 2004), 72–73.
49 Qtd. in Chase, "Class Resurrection," n.p.
50 Martin Luther King, Jr., "Remaining Awake through a Great Revolution," National Cathedral, Washington, DC. March 31, 1968. The Martin Luther King Research and Education Institute. Stanford University.
51 Public Relations Committee, "Brainstorming Session with Bernard Cherin," May 1–15, 1968, SCLC Archives, Manuscript and Rare Book Library, Emory University, Atlanta, GA.
52 Hebel, "'American' Pictures and (Trans-)National Iconographies," 414.
53 Barber, *Marching on Washington*, 81.
54 Nicholas Mirzoeff, "The Visual Commons: Counter-Power in Photography from Slavery to Occupy Wall Street," in *Image Operations: Visual Media and Political Conflict*, ed. Jens Eder and Charlotte Klonk (Manchester: Manchester University Press, 2016), 206.
55 Mantler, "'The press did you in,'" 35.
56 Foster, "Choreographies of Protest," 412.
57 Ralph Abernathy, *And the Walls Came Tumbling Down: An Autobiography* (New York: Harper and Row, 1989), 502.
58 Ibid.
59 Freedman, *Old News*, 31.
60 Ibid., 18.
61 Abernathy, *And the Walls Came Tumbling Down*, 502.
62 Freedman, *Old News*, 59–60.
63 Gordon White, "Soul Force Article Submissions, undated [1 of 2]," n.d., SCLC Archives, Manuscript and Rare Book Library, Emory University, Atlanta, GA.
64 Lisa A. Crooms, "Picturing Poverty (II): 1960s-Present," in *Poverty in the United States: An Encyclopedia of History, Politics, and Policy*, ed. Gwendolyn Mink and Alive O'Connor (Santa Barbara: ABC-CLIO, 2004), 544–547.
65 Mantler, "'The press did you in,'" 35–36.
66 Robin Kelley, *Freedom Dreams: The Black Radical Imagination* (Boston: Beacon, 2008), ix.
67 Kareem Abdul-Jabbar, "The Coming Race War Won't Be About Race," *Time*, August 17, 2014.

9

"GETTIN' READY TO RIDE INTO HISTORY"

Spike Lee's *Get on the Bus* and Sites of Memory

Jesse Williams, Jr.

> I don't think you can never be taught too much history. Today it seems like young people especially aren't taught enough of it and aren't interested in things that were happening before they were born. If you don't know who you are or where you came from, if you don't acknowledge your ancestral roots, then you really are asleep.
>
> Spike Lee[1]

Spike Lee's *Get on the Bus* (1996) testifies to the power of the traumatic history inherited by black men living in the US during the mid-1990s. Arriving in North American theaters on October 16, 1996, exactly one year after the Million Man March (MMM), the film dramatizes the fictional pilgrimage of black men from Los Angeles to Washington, DC to attend the march. Working from an original screenplay by Reggie "Rock" Bythewood, Lee goes to painstaking lengths to capture the *intra*racial diversity among the black men making the journey, foregrounding their various skin tones (and at one point even ethnic makeup), generational allegiances, sexual preferences, religious beliefs, political ideologies, and economic classes. In this sense, *Bus* constitutes the prototypical Spike Lee Joint, which follows the example of nonviolent direct action, such as the MMM, by functioning as a protest against the US motion picture industry for its tendency to construct and (re)affirm monolithic mythologies about black folk and black life. Because of the film's central storyline and the director's rendering of its characters, critics justifiably read *Bus* as an exploration of black masculinity at the end of the twentieth century. Despite its undeniable contemporariness, however, the film should be viewed using a much wider historical lens. In *Get on the Bus*, Lee forces a confrontation with history by telling the story from the perspective of black men who observe and experience mid-1990s US culture as deeply and traumatically informed by the past. By revisiting this past through the eyes of black characters while using the cinematic shorthand of the Hollywood civil rights movement film, the ever-transgressive Lee exposes both the subgenre itself and the myths it engenders as illustrative of and counterproductive to the nearly 400-year-long struggle for freedom.

The Million Man March/Day of Absence

On October 16, 1995, in a stunning display of nonviolent direct action, nearly one million black men gathered at the National Mall in DC for a "Holy Day of Atonement and Reconciliation."

According to its declaration, the MMM/Day of Absence (DOA) was called in May 1995 by the leader of the Nation of Islam (NOI), Minister Louis Farrakhan, in response to his perception of the state of black America in the mid-1990s.[2] The MMM/DOA mission statement stipulates that the gathering in part functioned as a wake-up call, casting black men as the problem as well as the solution:

> [S]ome of the most acute problems facing the Black community within are those posed by Black males who have not stood up…in the context of a real and principled brotherhood, those of us who have stood up, must challenge others to stand also.[3]

The MMM/DOA mission statement defines this challenge in terms of atonement, reconciliation, and responsibility:

> it is through being at one with the Creator, each other and creation, and reconciling our differences with each other, that we can stand up and together in unity, strength and dignity accept and bear the responsibility heaven and history have placed on us at this critical juncture in the life and struggle of our people.[4]

Mid-1990s US culture constitutes this critical juncture, a period defined by escalating racial tensions that Craig Watkins attributes to "the rising tide of social conservatism in American politics, marked in 1995 by the ascendancy of Newt Gingrich and the Republican-led 'Contract with America'" as well as the acquittal of OJ Simpson on charges of double murder—an acquittal handed down just twelve days before the march.[5] *Bus* explores the aforementioned critical juncture from a black male perspective, expanding and complicating our understanding of black leadership and activism by connecting the MMM in Washington, DC to key sites of memory from the modern civil rights movement (1954–1968).

In the aftermath of the Simpson verdict, the US news media seemingly intensified its often-antagonistic approach to covering black America and black Americans, which some commentators argue manifested as biased coverage of the MMM. Much ink has been spilled over Farrakhan's racially-inflammatory rhetoric, particularly his unquestioned anti-Semitism, which perhaps prompted the misguided, media-fueled assumption identified by Haki Madhubuti that "the Black community, specifically Black men, had to make a choice between the 'messenger and the message.'"[6] A representative of the MMM/DOA Executive Committee, Madhubuti characterizes this assumption as a "white lie that suggested if we joined hands with Minister Farrakhan… we would somehow relinquish all critical faculties and negate our ability to think or function independently or collectively at the local, national, and international levels."[7] The MMM/DOA mission statement emphasizes the lengths to which the National Organizing Committee functioned independent of Farrakhan's influence. Valuing collaboration and cooperation, the committee relied on "a broad spectrum of scholars, activists, and religious, political, business and civic leaders" participating in "numerous local organizing committees…to draw on a wide-ranging source of knowledge, experience and differing views," which culminated in national "meetings… marked by lengthy debates over critical issues and a series of fraternal and sororal disagreements as well as agreements."[8] Despite the judiciousness of the National Organizing Committee, however, the MMM/DOA became synonymous with the "Farrakhan march," probably due to the US news media's failure to adequately cover its buildup in favor of "the trial of the century."

Lee and Bythewood examine the Farrakhan factor in *Bus* through a minor character who explicitly refers to the MMM as the Farrakhan march. This remark occurs inside a dive bar in Memphis, Tennessee, and it consists of Lee riffing on the familiar narrative that the mid-1990s US news media was all too eager to promulgate: black politics coalesces under only one, usually male, authoritative voice. In his trademark in-your-face manner, Lee illustrates that Farrakhan speaks for only *some* blacks, contriving a conversation between father-son MMM pilgrims Evan Sr. (Thomas Jefferson Byrd) and Evan Jr. (DeAundre Bonds), and white bar patrons Mitch (Gary Lowery) and Rodney (Bob Orwig). Lee juxtaposes Mitch's tenuous understanding of black politics circa 1995 to the contentious understanding the estranged father and son have reached while traveling to the MMM. Mitch's assertion that "Farrakhan is the new black leader, like Martin Luther King was," elicits conflicting responses from Evan Jr. ("Yeah, you could say that") and Evan Sr. ("Uh, not really. But, he's one of our leaders"), thus underscoring the father's role in teaching his son history. In addition to functioning as Lee's acknowledgment of the criticism levied upon the MMM because of Farrakhan's role in it, Evan Sr.'s declaration that the minister stands as but one of several black leaders functions as Lee's corrective for common (mis)understandings of not only black politics but also black people.

By correcting the common media narrative concerning black political leadership, the aforementioned scene represents *Bus* in microcosm. Lee challenges the popular notion that black politics and black people, especially black men, represent a monolithic group by foregrounding the diversity among the black men who travel by bus from Los Angeles to DC for the MMM. Not surprisingly, his vision of mid-1990s black manhood has dominated discussions about the film: critics more or less agree that the director's foregrounding of *extra*racial factors among the bus riders counters the myth of essential black masculinity. Watkins observes that this focus obscures "the personality-driven frames of the [MMM] news coverage…to excavate the lives of those who made the march a genuinely newsworthy event—ordinary black men" and that Lee's focus on the diversity among these fictional ordinary black men exposes essential black manhood as "illegitimate and irreconcilable with the everyday realities of life."[9] Elvin Holt and William Jackson argue that by dramatizing these realities through such diverse black male characters, Lee "challeng[es] the prevailing negative representations of black men."[10] It is hard to exaggerate the stakes in this rhetorical battle. By the morning of the MMM, Simpson had been tried in a court of law for murdering his white ex-wife and her Jewish "friend," and found not guilty, becoming for many the real-life embodiment of such negative representations.

Some commentators perceived the MMM news coverage in light of the Simpson trial and the centuries-old cultural practice of scapegoating black males for the ills of US society. Ishmael Reed, for example, argues that in the mid-1990s, mainstream publications, such as the *New York Observer*, *New York Times*, *Village Voice*, *New Yorker*, *New Republic*, *Ms.*, *Atlantic Monthly*, and *Vanity Fair*, and programs on broadcast networks, such as NPR, CNBC, CNN, CBS, and C-Span, consistently designated black men "as the sacrificial lambs for male evil."[11] Reed characterizes this (im)balance as an epidemic, "an ongoing vindictive attack on black men by…neoconservative ideologues, who believe that black male behavior is the root of all social pathologies."[12] Richard Muhammad, the managing editor of the NOI's newspaper *Final Call*, argues that such media coverage

> is rooted in America's ideology of white supremacy…[which] promotes an arrogance and hostility that ignores, marginalizes and makes it nearly impossible to appreciate Black movements and Black leaders, which [in turn] makes independent Black information sources critical for our survival.[13]

This is the catalyst for Madhubuti and coeditor/co-executive council member Maulana Karenga in *Million Man March/Day of Absence* (1996), an anthology of MMM documents, speeches delivered at the event, photographs captured at the event, poetry and art inspired by the event, and commentary about the event. Inspired and informed by the MMM, Lee's *Bus* is as much a literary response to the march itself as it is to the history that made the march both possible and necessary.

Perhaps the need for black information sources also accounts for the conclusion of the MMA/DOA mission statement, which outlines post-march strategies in a section labeled "Continuing Practice and Projects." Of these continuing practices, the following most accounts for Lee's execution of *Bus* as well as its critics:

> continuing and reinforced efforts to reduce and eliminate negative media approaches to and portrayals of Black life and culture; to organize a sustained and effective support for positive models, messages, and works; to achieve adequate and dignified representation of Blacks in various media and in various positions in these media; and to challenge successful and notable African Americans in various media to support all these efforts.[14]

Although Lee would argue that his primary goal in filmmaking is *not* to create positive models, messages, and works, these post-MMM/DOA strategies characterize his career as a director, writer, producer, and celebrity, his films and public persona providing black audiences with non-stereotypical characters with which to identify. In the case of the MMM/DOA, media coverage of the event confirmed the myth of the 1990s black male as "deficient, irresponsible, lacking in moral and ethical character, [and] unable to speak truth to power," which itself builds on centuries-old mythologies of black male pathology.[15] Lee has long identified the US motion picture, television, and advertising industries as partners with the news media, and he speaks truth to power by taking to task the film, TV, and ad industries for their affirmation, proliferation, and sometimes construction of negative racial mythologies that too often go unanswered.

Lee speaks truth to power in *Bus* by fashioning the film's midpoint into an answer to what had become a national myth, which MMM organizers would argue necessitated the event: social circumstances for blacks were once dire, but the modern civil rights movement came, and now everything is better. Lee collapses the distance between 1995 and the civil rights era in dramatic fashion. On a starry night, with a full moon overhead, the charter carrying the marchers is pulled over by Tennessee state troopers in Knoxville. The lead trooper (Randy Quaid) boards the bus, blinding the driver, George (Charles S. Dutton), with his flashlight while justifying a clear case of racial profiling by stating that he and his partner stopped the bus because they have orders to "beef up surveillance…a lot of *boys* [emphasis added] been smuggling drugs through our state." Despite the respectful intervention of Gary (Roger Guenveur Smith), who presents his badge and calmly identifies himself as an officer with the Los Angeles Police Department, the lead trooper calls for his partner to commence executing a search. While the partner brings a German shepherd down the aisle, the lead trooper shines his flashlight into the face of every man on board. Holt and Jackson observe obvious civil rights references in this scene, noting that the soundtrack (The Impressions' "People Get Ready"), cinematography, and action (including white policemen and police dogs) recall freedom songs, Rosa Parks, and the Birmingham Children's Crusade of 1963.[16] However, by filming the troopers primarily from the back of the bus, hence from the viewpoint of the black men, Lee proves himself a revisionist, forcing a confrontation with history from the perspective of the lion rather than the hunter, thus suggesting a much more expansive history that reaches back before the US Supreme Court's decision in *Brown v. Board* (1954) and stretches forward into the late twentieth century.

400 Years a Slave: The Long Civil Rights Movement

Lee signals an expanded narrative of civil rights history in the film's opening title sequence. Set to Michael Jackson and Kenneth "Babyface" Edmonds' "Put Your Heart on the Line," the title sequence opens in close-up on the right eye of a black man, staying in close-up for a montage set against a black background that lasts the duration of the song and forms the nexus of African

American history. After resting on the man's open eye, the camera cuts to iron chains, then pans down to a shackle. A sequence of transitions reveals his shackled right wrist, iron chain links forming a gig line on his naked torso, which connects to a rusted, iron collar around his neck, and his wrist fettered to his shackled right ankle. At the beginning of the second verse, the camera cuts to the black man's right-side-up fists, panning up to reveal his wrists restrained in modern, law enforcement-style handcuffs. Subsequent transitions reveal metal chains linked to handcuffs resting in the hoop of an iron eyebolt. The song's bridge commences with the camera zooming out from extreme close-up, revealing both of the black man's ankles fettered in iron shackles. The subsequent cut brings us back to his open eyes, which he directs toward the camera. The final cut lingers on a metal present-day handcuff, slowly zooming into extreme close-up, the black background becoming an iris transition that introduces the diegesis of the film. In two minutes and forty seconds of screen time, Lee not only teaches an abridged version of black history, but he also suggests that not much has changed in 400 years: correctional control remains a clear and present danger for black men in the US.

The first scene within the diegesis of *Bus* makes visible these vestiges, the opening title sequence suggesting that centuries-old institutional racism persists, hence the African American's ongoing struggle for freedom. Evan Sr. and Evan Jr. walk side by side, the father's left wrist handcuffed to his son's right wrist per a court order punishing Evan Jr. for robbery, a crime the son later divulges to Mitch and Rodney inside the Memphis dive bar. As Evan Sr. and Evan Jr. struggle to synchronize their movement in the foreground, a white bus dominates the background. The entire length of the bus is painted with a red, black, and green border with "First AME Church 'The Oldest Black Church in Los Angeles' – 1872" stenciled in red between the red border and the black and green borders. Shortly thereafter, the handcuffed father and son prepare to board the charter that will take them to DC. Aghast at the site of two black men tethered to each other, George protests, "I would have hated to be on the same plantation with you. A runaway slave wouldn't have stood a chance." Lee thus recasts the generations-long struggle for freedom through two characters who embody both a literal and metaphorical legacy shared by all black men. The father and son's tethering, George's response to it, the date listed on the First AME Church bus, and the event to which the vessel prepares to embark parallel the history of the black freedom struggle, what Julie Armstrong describes as "a series of gains and losses extending beyond one short period of 'movement' during the mid-twentieth century."[17] Combined with the title sequence, this scene foregrounds the losses: slavery, including various fugitive slave legislation (1640s–Civil War); Jim Crow; and mass incarceration—commonly known as the "the new Jim Crow." In subsequent sequences, Lee signals this notion of the long civil rights movement more subtly, merging it with his central theme—legacy.

Viewers witness this merger soon after Evan Sr. and Evan Jr. get on the bus. As the action moves inside the charter, an enthusiastic Jeremiah (Ossie Davis) lurches down the aisle, brandishing his fist at every black man aboard with the greeting, "Black power!" As he (re)claims a seat in the back of the bus, Jeremiah introduces himself to Jamal (Gabriel Casseus), a young man who occupies the aisle seat in the adjacent row. Seemingly meaningless on the surface, their small talk underscores the historicity that Lee more clearly communicates in the opening title sequence, with Jamal interjecting an innocuous rhetorical question early in the conversation: "Not much leg room, is there?" The observation of the spatial configuration of the interior of a bus occupied only by black men, including the driver Craig (Albert Hall), enables Lee to reference a slave past that has profoundly influenced the present inherited by *all* of the riders—a present that necessitates activism such as the MMM. Using the makeup of the travelers, the nonviolent direct action in which they plan to participate, and the bus route—from the West in Los Angeles to the East in Washington, DC—Lee fashions the vessel into a chronotope for

FIGURE 9.1 The destination of the riders in *Get on the Bus* is the seat and symbol of (white) power in the US, and the Lincoln Memorial is perhaps the most potent site of memory for the black freedom struggle.

a slave ship, the director emphasizing this point through George, who frequently reminds the travelers that they are "gettin' ready to ride into history" (Figure 9.1).

Although George understands this history as the MMM, Jeremiah's presence aboard the bus references a more expansive civil rights history. During a scheduled stop at a Little Rock, Arkansas rest area, the men lament their lost road music. Jeremiah responds by retrieving a djembe from his bag and proclaiming, "We got music that goes way back yonder…back to the motherland." He then plays griot, keeping time on the djembe while sing-song narrating a tale of Africa:

> I see a ship/ It's a big ship/ Ain't no slave ship/ I don't see no chains/ I don't see no shackles/ It's a going-home ship. I cross the ocean/ Get off on the beaches/ I walk in the sand/ I step in the grass/ I say hello to the python/ In the baobab tree. I walk in the jungle/ I see the monkey/ I see the chimpanzee. I cross the river/ I see the crocodile. I come to my village/ I see the chief/ I see all the elders/ I see the warriors/ I see the women and children/ I see the fires/ I smell the cooking/ Hear the singing and drumming/ And dance all the dances. I cross the compound/ And there at the end/ In a little rise/ I see home. Jeremiah sees home!/ And they're glad to see me!

This (cultural) exchange brings us back to the film's title sequence and then back even further, full circle, to a time before blacks were confined in chains, thus confirming the charter chronotope. However, Jeremiah's relation of what can only be understood as an Edenic paradise foreshadows his death in a DC hospital as well as the collective transcendence the other riders achieve in the aftermath. At the steps of the Lincoln Memorial, the riders read the prayer Jeremiah had written over the course of their journey. Evan Sr. and Evan Jr. then leave behind their court-ordered tether at the foot of these same steps, thus bookending the title sequence. Like his biblical namesake, Jeremiah Washington does not physically live to witness the Promised Land; however, his spirit lives on in the remaining travelers, who affectionately call him "Pop," thus rendering the surname he shares with the "father of the United States of America" all the more significant.

Jeremiah's prayer at the Lincoln Memorial also functions as a bookend to an earlier prayer. Before the bus departs the First AME Church in South Central Los Angeles, Jeremiah suggests that the men have a word of prayer for the trip, which cussing, cocky, struggling actor Flip (Andre Braugher) interrupts after Jeremiah mentions by name others who did not make it to the Promised Land:

> Father God…we know that You was with Moses when he parted the Red Sea and freed the slaves from bondage. We know that You was with Noah when the rain came down forty days and forty nights. We know that You was with Malcolm when he went to Mecca, with Martin when he went to the mountaintop. And we're asking You, dear God, to be with us now on this historic journey to fellowship with one million black men.

By naming the two individuals most associated with the modern civil rights movement alongside Moses and Noah, Jeremiah elevates King and Malcolm to the pantheon of prophets, paralleling African Americans' 400-year struggle for freedom with the Biblical Israelites' seventy-year exile. Furthermore, by contriving many of the events Jeremiah includes in both of his prayers, Lee and Bythewood suggest that Jeremiah, as his given name attests, also belongs in the pantheon of prophets: he too did not get there with his fellow travelers, thus signaling *Bus* as a civil rights film that dramatizes the epic struggle of a people and a nation to fulfill its promise(s).

The film's focus on the MMM, an event that in retrospect carries minimal historical significance, signals Lee's intent to enter into conversation with a more distant (and highly memorialized) gathering on the National Mall—the 1963 March on Washington for Jobs and Freedom, the site where King delivered his iconic "I Have a Dream" speech. Although multiple characters reference the 1963 gathering in the film, none actually attended, including Jeremiah, the only pilgrim old enough to have marched on Washington. Xavier (Hill Harper), a college student who has been documenting the journey on a handheld camera to satisfy requirements for his film school thesis project, asks Jeremiah why he is going to the MMM, to which the elder man replies, "I got to go." The story preceding this proclamation explains why Jeremiah missed the 1963 march, implying that his presence at the 1995 gathering constitutes his atonement. Jeremiah decided against attending the March on Washington because he feared his participation might jeopardize his recently-acquired employment, a recollection that "provides useful moral instruction, offers an object lesson regarding the consequences of racism in the workplace, highlights difficulties associated with the misguided pursuit of material success, and challenges black men to maintain a meaningful involvement with their community."[18] Like the MMM, March on Washington, and the civil rights struggle as a whole, Lee argues for the necessity of active and positive participation by black men in the black community.

The most significant contribution of *Bus* is its insistence that participation, or "standing up," entails bringing others (up) along with you. Jeremiah takes this responsibility seriously, befriending and mentoring the young film student in the back of the bus. In addition to answering the central question of Xavier's documentary, Jeremiah teaches the young man how to properly play the djembe, which becomes a powerful symbol of the legacy the riders share. Having departed the hospital where Jeremiah succumbed to heart disease, the vessel prepares to leave the Lincoln Memorial, its final stop before heading back to Los Angeles. Before assuming his position in the driver's seat, George retrieves the djembe from Jeremiah's carry-on compartment, entrusting the instrument to Xavier with an encouraging word: "I hope you learned something from…Brother Jeremiah." Indeed, Xavier shows himself approved during the film's final image: the young filmmaker picks up where Jeremiah left off, carrying on the djembe's beat.

In *Bus*, Lee defines legacy as a verb—the act of passing it on. Jeremiah and Xavier (and Lee) are engaged in passing something on, and in so doing, they keep alive the history and culture that both enables and explains the black freedom struggle. The civil rights movement exists both pre- and post-modernity, despite what national mythology would have us believe. The Spike Lee Joint argues that the US motion picture industry assumes an active role in both affirming and perpetuating such myths, a difficult argument to ignore considering the 100 years of Hollywood (mis)representation of black folk and their lives. This is the front on which Xavier resumes the beat, which Lee dramatizes on the morning of the day that will end with the racial profiling of the travelers. As George drives in the direction of the rising sun, Xavier keeps him company and, having asked every other rider "Why are you going to the march?" and filming their responses, answers his own question by raising one of many videotapes containing his footage: "One day," he tells George, "I'm gonna let my kids see these tapes." His intention initiates a brief dialogue that indicts contemporary Hollywood for its typical approach to depicting black folk (black men in particular) and implies the necessity for black men to correct the record: When George states that "Hollywood thinks they got us all figured out. And the evening news," Xavier replies, "Yeah…they sum us up with the four R's—rap, rape, rob, and riot." Paula Massood notes that such critiques characterize the principle aim of the Spike Lee Joint, which "requires…audiences to question conventional structures of feeling, the normative approaches to life as lived in the United States, and to rethink national mythology."[19] Substituting "black folk" for "audiences," Lee appropriates the industry's own mechanism to construct countermythologies to wake up African Americans to history. In his impulse to turn the medium against itself for the preservation of the march for future generations, Xavier thus mirrors Lee, an award-winning filmmaker who has demonstrated a commitment to and development of a cinema that tells civil rights stories free of an intermediary white character. While Lee's work routinely runs afoul of the traditional Hollywood civil rights film, he appropriates the subgenre's cinematic shorthand to turn the subgenre against itself as a form of critique.

A Film about Civil Rights Movement Film

Incorporating the perspective of black characters enables Lee to both recall and challenge traditional misunderstandings of the modern civil rights movement. Armstrong defines these misunderstandings as "consensus memory…a story about the past [that]…continues to dominate popular culture…[and] leaves out stories of grassroots efforts, economic justice, self-defense, radicalism, and connections to other movements nationally and internationally."[20] One can argue that such memories achieve consensus in the popular imagination because of various "sites of memory…any space, object or practice (cemeteries, churches, rituals, sayings, monuments, symbols, texts, and so on) that stand at the crossroads of personal and collective meaning."[21] Lee routinely identifies Hollywood as the culprit of consensus memory, the director declaring mainstream US cinema to be an (a)historical tool devoted to the bottom line and which exploits sites of memory in order to at best, marginalize and at worst, erase members of traditionally underrepresented groups from the national past. The result is nothing less than the miseducation of generations of moviegoers about the social, economic, psychological, and political traumas resulting from US racism.

Such "historical" narratives continue to constitute what we think of as civil rights movement film. Sharon Monteith defines this subgenre as a domestic fiction set against the backdrop of the modern civil rights movement that marginalizes black folk, minimizes their active participation in the civil rights struggle, and moralizes about the struggle through white characters that become aware of institutionalized white supremacy through personal relationships with black domestic workers. To remind audiences of the "historicity" of their movies, both white and black filmmakers tend to distill the entire modern civil rights movement into something like history by intercutting montages of archival news footage depicting major moments in the movement, which often results in characters becoming stand-ins for political ideals and moral platitudes instead of fully-realized portraits. Monteith argues that audience (over)familiarity with this cinematic shorthand sparks a chain reaction to civil rights movement film: the movies themselves have become clichéd and leave audiences desensitized and misinformed about the movement, creating the perception that the struggle was settled in the 1960s.[22] Characterizing civil rights movement cinema as "racial conversion narratives," Monteith further argues that this formula results from standard practices in the US motion picture industry.[23] The aforementioned formula, like many Hollywood decisions, rises out of market research on national demographics.

A particularly erroneous assumption informs the US motion picture industry's interpretation of such research: because only blacks are interested in narratives about the civil rights struggle, and they comprise a small portion of the US population, civil rights stories are generally unprofitable. This assumption therefore dictates industry approaches to telling stories about the modern civil rights movement. The preferred approach, according to Monteith, involves getting white audiences to invest emotionally in the characters, hence civil rights films (such as 2011's *The Help*) with white protagonists.[24] Black filmmakers, perhaps even more than black audiences, bear the brunt of this Hollywood tradition because the foregrounding of white characters tends to result in film studios granting "white directors…the biggest budgets with which to tell civil rights stories."[25] Ultimately, black filmmakers often tell civil rights stories "in documentary forms, as deeply moving history lessons like Spike Lee's *Four Little Girls* (1997) and Charles Burnett's *The Murder of Emmett Till* (2003), or in biopics," such as *Malcolm X* (1992).[26] Lee is the only black director referenced multiple times in Monteith's essay, although she limits her attention to *X* and *Girls*—the director's most overt civil rights films. *Get on the Bus*, however, constitutes the director's most conscious civil rights film. Indeed, *Bus* should be seen as the second film in Lee's 1990s trilogy of civil rights retrospectives and not only because his characters copiously reference the civil rights struggle in dialogue. The director re-creates so many sites of memory in *Bus* that he fashions the fictional pilgrimage of black men from Los Angeles to DC for the MMM into a guided tour of watershed moments of the modern civil rights movement.

Lee exploits audience familiarity with generic signposts of Hollywood civil rights movement cinema from the outset, opening in long-shot on a steeple that the subsequent cut reveals belongs to First AME Church in South Central Los Angeles and therefore recalls houses of worship that doubled as organizational headquarters, rest stops, safe havens, trauma centers, and rallying posts for activists participating in the modern civil rights movement. Although worship centers remain some of the most segregated public spaces in the US, in *Bus* Lee reminds us of the most recognizable segregated spaces during the civil rights era, including and especially the setting for nearly the entire film—a bus. The Greyhound-like charter itself functions as the most obvious site of memory in *Bus*, referencing both the Montgomery bus boycott and the Freedom Rides. Largely organized by the Congress of Racial Equality (CORE), with some sponsorship from the Student Nonviolent Coordinating Committee (SNCC), the Freedom Rides protested the Jim Crow-enabled non-enforcement of 1946 and 1960 US Supreme Court decisions and a 1955 ruling from the Interstate Commerce Commission (ICC) that desegregated interstate travel. Comprised of blacks and whites, the Freedom Riders traveled to the Deep South from Washington, DC aboard Greyhound and Trailways buses, often under the threat of violence that necessitated the eventual formation of the Deacons for Defense and Justice. One such episode occurred in Anniston, Alabama on Mother's Day 1961: members of local Ku Klux Klan (KKK) chapters, working under police protection ordered by Birmingham Police Commissioner Eugene "Bull" Connor, slashed one of the Greyhound's tires as it departed the station, the bus making it only a few miles outside of town, where Klan members firebombed it with the driver and thirteen riders inside. Although none lost their lives, the activists were severely beaten, prompting ten students from Nashville to ride to Birmingham three days later, where they were arrested by Connor; before being transported to the Tennessee state line and released, the students sang freedom songs during their detainment. Having immediately returned to Birmingham, the travelers rode to Montgomery, where more than 1,500 supporters greeted them in First Baptist Church. Outside, however, a mob of over 3,000 whites gathered, defying the few US Marshals stationed to maintain order and defacing the church by throwing rocks and Molotov cocktails through its windows, setting off smoke bombs, and threatening to enter and assault the occupants therein.

Lee restages this historical moment in *Bus* through Craig, who drives the vessel into a ditch shortly after departing First AME Church in South Central Los Angeles. While lamenting his teenaged daughter's pregnancy to George, Craig's inattention results in the severing of the vehicle's axle, leaving the riders on the side of the road in the California desert waiting for a replacement bus. The men pass the time by singing impromptu songs about reaching their destination at the National Mall: these improvised, communal lyrics remix "Ain't Gonna Let Nobody Turn Me Around," a common cadence of the freedom rides, student sit-ins, marches, and meetings in real-life worship centers such as First Baptist Church in Montgomery. In the early 1960s, actual Greyhound drivers did let somebody turn them around, the threat of police-sanctioned mob violence prompting them to refuse Freedom Ride assignments. In his film, Lee recasts these drivers as Rick (Richard Belzer), who pilots the replacement bus and whom the director introduces to viewers by filming each rider from his position in the driver's seat. After piloting the travelers to the Memphis dive, Rick deserts his post, justifying his actions by making a faulty analogy of the MMM to a KKK rally based on Farrakhan's history of anti-Semitic rhetoric.

Through Rick, a Jewish bus driver whose parents participated in the modern civil rights movement, Lee takes viewers back to Mississippi Freedom Summer. The director fashions the desert location of the breakdown into a visual representation of the Mississippi Delta, filming the California desert segment in orange hue and capturing the visible ripple of humidity. In 1964, although blacks comprised over one-third of the population of Mississippi, the state boasted the nation's lowest percentage of registered black voters, thanks in large part to Jim Crow legislation that disenfranchised black citizens. This disenfranchisement prompted the Mississippi chapter of CORE to organize Freedom Summer, or "the Mississippi Summer Project," in order to register black voters. With help from state chapters of SNCC, the National Association for the Advancement of Colored People, and the Southern Christian Leadership Conference (SCLC), CORE brought in over 1,000 volunteers from across the country to join black Mississippians, most of whom were Northern whites and many of whom were Jewish. Rick's presence, as well as his dialogue, reminds the audience of the sacrifices Jews made during the civil rights struggle. The most well-known sacrifice involves Michael Schwerner and Andrew Goodman, both of whom were arrested, along with black Mississippian and CORE member James Chaney, by a Philadelphia sheriff's deputy with a KKK affiliation. The three civil rights workers were released after nightfall and then ambushed on the road by Klansmen who shot them before burying their bodies in an earthen dam.

Lee takes advantage of every instance when the riders get off the bus. At a rest area in Little Rock, hometown of then-President Bill Clinton, Jeremiah steals away to take heart medication in the men's room, a public space that in the not-so-distant past he would have been prohibited from entering. Lee also underscores Jim Crow history during the pit stop in the Memphis dive.

Gay buppie Randall (Harry Lennix) enters the men's room as Jamal freshens up in anticipation of a meal, prompting the former Crip who now follows the teachings of Islam to bumble, fumble, and stumble toward a hasty exit. Although Lee plays this scene for comedy by holding up Jamal's homophobia for ridicule, the former gangbanger's discomfort with sharing such a private space with Randall restages the equally erroneous, irrational, and xenophobic impulse underlying segregation of public restrooms in the South. Lee's clearest reference to this history, however, occurs before the awkward bathroom scene and recalls the black activism prompted in large part by segregation. At the bar, Evan Sr. and Evan Jr. join Mitch and Rodney, the pleasantries and small talk between the interracial patrons comprising an editorial placard reading, *things weren't always like this*. The configuration of the bar restages the lunch counter sit-ins staged by North Carolina A&T students inside a Greensboro Woolworth's, which inspired similar protests of publicly-segregated spaces throughout the South, including bathrooms, beaches, libraries, museums, parks, and swimming pools.

Lee also references more obscure occurrences of nonviolent direct action during the civil rights era. Organized by James Meredith, who in 1962 became the first black student to enroll at the University of Mississippi, The March Against Fear began on June 6, 1966. Intended as a march of one from Memphis to Jackson, Mississippi, Meredith sought to protest the state's non-enforcement of federal civil rights legislation such as the Civil Rights Act of 1964 and Voting Rights Act of 1965 and to inspire voter registration among blacks living in the Delta. Meredith invited only black men to join the march, the Deacons for Defense and Justice providing armed security for the activists who resumed the march after Meredith was shot by a white man on the second day of his journey. The first organized armed-security group during the modern civil rights movement, the Deacons originated in Jonesboro, Louisiana in November 1964 to protect black communities and civil rights workers from racist violence perpetrated by the KKK. Comprised primarily of World War II and Korean War combat veterans, the Deacons eventually organized twenty-one chapters throughout Louisiana, Mississippi, and Alabama, responding in affirmation to the call for "double victory" issued by influential black newspaper the *Pittsburgh Courier* in the 1940s. In *Bus*, Lee fashions the character Kyle (Isaiah Washington) into a composite of James Meredith and the Deacons, the maybe gay/maybe bisexual Desert Storm vet wounded in Iraq by the "friendly fire" of white, anti-black homophobes only to return stateside and face conditions that necessitate the MMM.

By dramatizing a fictional cross-country road trip in his script, Bythewood enables Lee to restage and revisit civil rights movement sites of memory. Departing from Los Angeles, the source of much Hollywood misinformation about the civil rights struggle, the journey begins where (too) many mark the struggle's conclusion. On June 5, 1968, after winning the California primary for the Democratic nomination for President, Robert F. Kennedy (RFK) was assassinated in Los Angeles' Ambassador Hotel. As US Attorney General during the presidency of his brother John F. Kennedy, RFK played a pivotal role in the freedom struggle. He dispatched Justice Department staff to Alabama during the Freedom Rides; pressured Greyhound to provide drivers for the Rides and the governor of Alabama to order the state highway patrol to escort those buses; petitioned the ICC to adhere to its 1955 ruling; and stationed US Marshals outside First Baptist Church in Montgomery before prompting his brother to threaten the Alabama governor with an order to deploy federal troops to the church, which resulted in the intervention of the Alabama National Guard. Likewise, prompted by activists on the ground in Mississippi in the aftermath of the disappearances of Chaney, Goodman, and Schwerner, RFK ordered a Federal Bureau of Investigation (FBI) inquiry and search. This search lasted seven weeks and had two noteworthy results: the recovery of Chaney's, Goodman's, and Schwerner's bodies (along with the remains of seven black men and one black boy, five of whom were never identified) and the opening of the FBI's first branch in the state of Mississippi.

The scheduled stops the bus makes once departing Los Angeles further signal civil rights movement sites of memory. The Little Rock rest stop recalls the integration of Central High School in 1957, when Governor Faubus ordered the Arkansas National Guard to prevent the "Little Rock Nine" from attending classes, and President Eisenhower countered by deploying the 101st Airborne Division of the US Army to protect the black high schoolers. Education figures into Lee's subsequent civil rights reference at the Little Rock rest stop, when Gary and Flip flirt with two coeds, one of whom wears a Spelman College sweatshirt. Presumably students enrolled at the all-female historically black college (HBCU), the young ladies hail from Dallas, where JFK lost his life to an assassin's bullet in 1963. The charter changes drivers for the second time when Rick deserts his post at a dive bar in Memphis, the site of Martin Luther King, Jr.'s assassination in 1968. By locating the second unplanned change of drivers in Memphis and having one of his characters insist (in the bar scene) that Farrakhan is but *one* of the black community's leaders, Lee challenges the consensus narrative that would have us believe that the civil rights movement—the various forms of active resistance as well as the conditions that necessitate such resistance—ended with King's death.

As the travelers depart Memphis, they are approached by native Memphian Wendell (Wendell Pierce), who desires to go to the MMM to acquire clients for his Lexus dealership, a motive the men discover only after allowing him on board. The subsequent vitriol he spews about and toward the black men on the bus mirrors 1990s news media narratives about the deficient, irresponsible, amoral, unethical, and inarticulate black man. Watkins astutely observes that the car salesman's condescending remarks about HBCUs like Tennessee State University (TSU) and Fisk University most illustrate that "African Americans, despite years of progress and struggle, continue to be victims of slavery, especially mental imprisonment, by succumbing to many of the racial myths and ideologies that have oppressed African Americans."[27] Wendell's self-hatred and the resistance displayed by the other riders' unified response to it—physically throwing the car salesman off the bus—constitute another of Lee's cinematic preoccupations, which Massood notes, "often ask African American audience members to consider the ways in which internalized racism can fragment—or unite—a community."[28] Lee also, however, uses Wendell to equate education with activism and civic-mindedness, *not* the individual pursuit of the kind of wealth that would enable the purchase of a Lexis, the car salesman's derision of TSU and Fisk in favor of his alma mater—fellow Nashville institution Vanderbilt University—recalling SNCC and Reverends James Lawson, Jr. and C.T. Vivian and their training of TSU and Fisk students such as Diane Nash in the philosophy and methods of nonviolent direct action. Most significantly, Wendell draws attention to the name of the charter company, Spotted Owl, proclaiming, "*we* [emphasis added] are an endangered species just like that owl on the side of the bus."

While critical appraisals of *Bus* confirm that Wendell's analogy thinly veils Lee's perspective on mid-1990s black manhood, it may be more productive to view the film as suggesting that *specific* black men, as well as other groups and actual sites of civil rights movement memory, comprise an endangered species. Riding into history constitutes action, and whether or not an individual chooses to act depends on his or her belief in a certain version of history. Because Wendell espouses "alternative facts," the budding activists aboard the Spotted Owl stand up by joining together to physically expel Wendell, just as they initially stood up by getting on the bus and hopefully will continue standing after the march and challenge others to stand up also, thereby affirming the call issued by the MMM/DOA Mission Statement. The fact that these men willingly stand alongside others of varying ages, sexualities, religions, classes, colors, and (in Gary's case) races suggests that the concept of solidarity itself is in need of conservation. The Little Rock rest stop sequence suggests as much, the coed in the Spelman sweatshirt (Paula Jai Parker) protesting the exclusion of black women from the MMM by proclaiming, "[W]e *need*... some solidarity. You cannot name *one* struggle in black America in which the sisters were not an active structure, an active force." Not only does this young lady recall Nash, but her use of *we* also implies the endangerment of individuals of all ages, sexes, sexualities, genders, religions, classes, colors, and races, who (unlike Wendell) learned their history and got woke. Ultimately, Hollywood lulls the majority of audiences asleep by obscuring this history in civil rights movement film, which endangers sites of memory by confining the struggle to the domestic realm. Therefore, as a means to an end, the Spotted Owl functions as the most endangered species in *Bus* as well as its most important site of memory. The group of disparate men must get on the bus in order to reach the MMM and stand up together (across all other kinds of difference) for justice, jobs, and freedom. The fact that this group of black men loses the first charter because of an error by one of their own represents Lee's actual view of 1990s black manhood. If we allow the means to break down, we cannot reach the end.

Bus represents Lee's means, and he reveals the end by riding into history therein. Pedagogy, not profit, constitutes the purpose for the director's cinema as a whole, this pedagogical impulse evident in each film's means of reacting to the past. Massood suggests that conversing with history is the primary concern of the Spike Lee Joint, which she characterizes as

> a polyphonic system of cultural and political references engaged in diegetic and extradiegetic dialogues...[that] explore[s] the shared trauma of racism and its continuing social, economic, and political effects...to introduce a distinct, historicized, African American point of view into a medium that is often solely associated with entertainment.[29]

The early Spike Lee Joint articulates this polyphony. The protagonist of his debut film, *She's Gotta Have It* (1986), decorates her apartment with portraits of MLK and Malcolm X. In *School Daze* (1988) and *Do the Right Thing* (1989), as in the epigraph to this chapter, Lee directs our attention to his slumbering people with the characters Dap (Larry Fishburne) and Mister Senor Love Daddy (Samuel L. Jackson), Dap closing *School Daze* and Daddy opening *Right Thing* with the proclamation "WAKE UP!" Although Dap and Daddy issue this call within separate dieges, the extradiegetic subtext remains the same: *Know your history, otherwise you are destined to repeat it.* In both films, Lee shows rather than tells: Dap organizes nonviolent student protests against the administration of fictional Mission College, an HBCU Lee models on his undergraduate alma mater Morehouse College, thus recalling the sit-ins staged by North Carolina A&T students in 1960. Set twenty years after King's death, *Right Thing* features a major plot point focusing on the only known photograph of King and Malcolm together, which in part instigates a climactic uprising that references both the Birmingham Children's Campaign (1963) and the Watts Rebellion (1965). The only two imperative titles in Lee's thirty-year career, *Do the Right Thing* and *Get on the Bus*, encapsulate the Spike Lee Joint, which aims to educate African American audience members in order to prompt activism—to get them ready to ride into history.

Spike Lee: Filmmaker of the Freedom Struggle

Lee incorporates copious references to the long civil rights movement throughout his early cinema, films such as *Mo' Better Blues* (1990), *Jungle Fever* (1991), *Malcolm X* (1992), *Crooklyn* (1994), *Clockers* (1995), and *Girl 6* (1996) all signaling the civil rights struggle as an under-examined framework for reading the Spike Lee Joint. Lee telegraphs this framework in the opening scene of *Get on the Bus* as Evan Sr. and Evan Jr. pass the First AME Church on their way to the Spotted Owl, the son protesting their destination. Gesturing to the handcuffs, Evan Jr. gripes, "Look how stupid we look!" Evan Sr.'s last word recalls the Montgomery bus boycott: "Walk." Moments later, Jeremiah departs a city bus near the church, snatching off his hospital ID bracelet before boarding the Spotted Owl. Lee recasts Rosa Parks by introducing Jeremiah as he exits a city bus with a confined wrist and claims a seat in the back. The secretary for the Montgomery chapter of the National Association for the Advancement of Colored People (NAACP), Parks is often credited with initiating the boycott by refusing to relinquish her seat on a city bus to a white man and move to the "colored section" in the back. On her stance, Parks often describes the joy she felt upon her arrest: "it was the very last time that I would ever ride in humiliation of this kind."[30] Jeremiah rephrases these sentiments in Lee's film when he greets the bus driver with a proclamation that the younger man promptly affirms:

JEREMIAH: Never felt better in my life!
GEORGE: Well, then, you got to give me some of what you got.

In this brief exchange, Lee both foreshadows Jeremiah's fate and states his film's central theme: in order to progress, we must go back, while we still can, and study at the feet of those who struggled before us. All of the riders, especially Xavier (the young filmmaker and inheritor of Jeremiah's drum), will learn about their "ancestral roots" from Jeremiah, their elder.

Get on the Bus commands all of us to join the struggle, to *get ready* for battle by first learning history. When Evan Sr. and Evan Jr. stop at a line forming outside the Spotted Owl, they hear George shouting, "It's time to get on the bus!" For Lee, the time to get angry, get going, get together, and get on board is *always* now—a belief he makes clear through Craig, who must stay behind after driving the first Spotted Owl into a ditch. As the men resume their journey on a new bus, Craig shouts his farewell: "Freedom now!" His cry recalls the 1965 painting by Reginald Gammon that constitutes the cover of the *Cambridge Companion to American Civil Rights Literature* (2015), a visual representation of both the desire and imperative to speak and act. Lee has spent his life as a filmmaker doing just that, and in *Get on the Bus*, his most ambitious and expansive civil rights film, he affirms the power of art to move people, to wake them up, to get them to stand up and to raise up—not only a storm of protest but also the next generation of freedom fighters.

Approaches to Teaching Spike Lee's *Get on the Bus*

Discussion Questions

1. Who is the intended audience for *Get on the Bus*, and what does the makeup of this audience suggest about Lee's purpose? In what way(s) does Lee appeal to his intended audience, and how does he make his cinematic vision accessible in ways that might expand his audience?
2. At the time of the film's release, mainstream movie critics read *Get on the Bus* as a road picture. What road pictures have you seen? In what way(s) does Lee appropriate the conventions of these road movies? Consider whether Lee grounds his film as a road picture only to disrupt audience expectations later, thereby suggesting a different genre altogether.
3. On February 2, 2016, in commemoration of the twentieth anniversary of the verdict in the OJ Simpson case, the FX cable network began broadcasting the anthology series *The People v. OJ Simpson: American Crime Story*. On June 11, 2016, ABC began broadcasting the five-part ESPN Films documentary *OJ: Made in America*. Although these two television series largely make use of hindsight, *Get on the Bus*—released a year after the verdict—makes multiple references to the Simpson verdict within its diegesis, which suggests *immediate* responses to the verdict. What can viewers learn from *Bus* about the cultural impact of the Simpson verdict in terms of perception: in other words, do the characters view the verdict differently based on age, race, political ideology, class, or sexual orientation? Draw parallels

between the multiple perspectives the characters in *Bus* voice about the Simpson verdict and perspectives on other, perhaps equally controversial, current events.

4 Obviously, the MMM functions as Lee's catalyst for making *Get on the Bus*. A largely forgotten Spike Lee Joint, one could argue that the film has faded from memory because the MMM itself has been forgotten. The passage of time might account for such cultural amnesia; however, the March on Washington took place thirty-two years *before* the MMM and, by and large, remains a vivid national memory. To what might we attribute US culture's forgetting of the MMM? What are the potential consequences of such active forgetting? And although largely forgotten, do you think the *spirit* of the MMM has endured and if so, how has it manifest in twenty-first-century US culture?

Research and Writing Projects

1 In "Buck Passing: The Media, Black Men, OJ, and the Million Man March," Ishmael Reed argues that "[b]lack men have been designated by the culture as the sacrificial lambs for male evil…an ongoing vindictive attack on black men by…neoconservative ideologues, who believe that black male behavior is the root of all social pathologies." Reed indicts mainstream newspapers and magazines—*New York Observer, New York Times, Village Voice, New Yorker, New Republic, Ms., Atlantic Monthly,* and *Vanity Fair*—for participating in what he perceives as a smear campaign. Write an op-ed that responds to Reed's argument by contrasting Lee's vision of black masculinity in *Get on the Bus* with the pathological view of black masculinity in mid-1990s news/opinion pieces.

2 Read Sharon Monteith's essay "Civil Rights Movement Film" in the *Cambridge Companion to American Civil Rights Literature* and identify the standard themes and tropes that define this film subgenre. Write an essay in which you trace one of these themes or tropes through at least four civil rights films. Examples: *The Help, The Butler, Selma, Mississippi Burning, Ghosts of Mississippi,* and *Get on the Bus*.

3 After viewing *Malcolm X, Get on the Bus,* and *4 Little Girls*, write a biographical essay of Lee that highlights his participation in civil rights activism—as a human being, a public figure, and a filmmaker—and also defines the Spike Lee Joint as its own film genre.

4 Research any of the geographic sites of memory referenced in *Get on the Bus*—Little Rock, Dallas, Memphis, Birmingham, Nashville, and Washington, DC. Prepare a presentation that features the civil rights history particular to that location. Include in your presentation the ways in which that history is (or is not) remembered.

Notes

1 Kaleem Aftab, *Spike Lee: That's My Story and I'm Sticking to It as Told to Kaleem Aftab* (New York: Norton, 2005), 2.
2 MMM/DOA Executive Committee, "Declaration," in *Million Man March/Day of Absence: A Commemorative Anthology*, ed. Haki R. Madhubuti and Maulana Karenga (Chicago: Third World, 1996), xiv.
3 Maulana Karenga, "The Million Man March/Day of Absence Mission Statement," in *Million Man March/Day of Absence: A Commemorative Anthology*, ed. Haki R. Madhubuti and Maulana Karenga (Chicago: Third World, 1996), 142.
4 Ibid.
5 Craig S. Watkins, "Reel Men: *Get on the Bus* and the Shifting Terrain of Black Masculinities," in *The Spike Lee Reader*, ed. Paula J. Massood (Philadelphia: Temple University Press, 2008), 143.
6 Haki R. Madhubuti, "Took Back Our Tears, Laughter, Love, and Left a Big Dent in the Earth," in *Million Man March/Day of Absence: A Commemorative Anthology*, ed. Haki R. Madhubuti and Maulana Karenga (Chicago: Third World, 1996), 2.
7 Ibid.

8. Karenga, "The Million Man March/Day of Absence Mission Statement," 140.
9. Watkins, "Reel Men," 144, 151.
10. Elvin Holt and William H. Jackson, "Reconstructing Black Manhood: Message and Meaning in Spike Lee's *Get on the Bus*," *CLA Journal* 47.4 (2004), 411.
11. Ishmael Reed, "Buck Passing: The Media, Black Men, OJ, and the Million Man March," in *Million Man March/Day of Absence: A Commemorative Anthology*, ed. Haki R. Madhubuti and Maulana Karenga (Chicago: Third World, 1996), 129.
12. Ibid., 130–131.
13. Richard Muhammad, "The Truth, the Media, and the Million Man March," in *Million Man March/Day of Absence: A Commemorative Anthology*, ed. Haki R. Madhubuti and Maulana Karenga (Chicago: Third World, 1996), 135.
14. Karenga, "The Million Man March/Day of Absence Mission Statement," 148.
15. Madhubuti, "Took Back Our Tears," 2.
16. Holt and Jackson, "Reconstructing Black Manhood," 420–421.
17. Julie Buckner Armstrong, "Introduction," in *The Cambridge Companion to American Civil Rights Literature*, ed. Julie Buckner Armstrong (New York: Cambridge University Press, 2015), 2.
18. Holt and Jackson, "Reconstructing Black Manhood," 419–420.
19. Paula J. Massood, "Introduction: We've Gotta Have It—Spike Lee, African American Film, and Cinema Studies," in *The Spike Lee Reader*, ed. Paula J. Massood (Philadelphia: Temple University Press, 2008), xvi.
20. Armstrong, "Introduction," 6.
21. Ibid., 5.
22. Sharon Monteith, "Civil Rights Movement Film," in *The Cambridge Companion to American Civil Rights Literature*, ed. Julie Buckner Armstrong (New York: Cambridge University Press, 2015), 124–125.
23. Ibid., 126.
24. Ibid., 128–131.
25. Ibid., 136.
26. Ibid., 137.
27. Watkins, "Reel Men," 153.
28. Massood, "Introduction," xvi.
29. Ibid., xxii–xxiii.
30. "Civil Rights Icon Rosa Parks Dies at 92: Long Known as the 'Mother of the Civil Rights Movement," *CNN.com*, last modified October 25, 2005.

10

"MY CHILDHOOD IS RUINED!"

Harper Lee and Racial Innocence

Katherine Henninger

> I did not tell you that it would be okay, because I have never believed it would be okay. What I told you is what your grandparents tried to tell me: that this is your country, that this is your world, that this is your body, and you must find some way to live within the all of it.
>
> Ta-Nehisi Coates, "Letter to My Son," 2015

> What had she done that she must spend the rest of her years reaching out with yearning for them, making secret trips to long ago, making no journey to the present?
>
> Harper Lee, *Go Set a Watchman*, 2015

The news in February 2015 that a "lost" 1957 novel by Harper Lee—a sequel of sorts to her 1960 classic *To Kill a Mockingbird*—would be published that July was greeted with the type of enthusiasm one imagines of nineteenth-century readers awaiting the next installment of *Great Expectations*. The prospect of finding out "what comes next" for Lee's beloved child characters, Scout and Jem Finch, and their lawyer father, Atticus Finch, thrilled news outlets and social media alike. Predictably, anxieties weren't far behind. What if the "newly discovered" manuscript wasn't very good? Did the notoriously reclusive eighty-nine-year-old Lee actually authorize its publication? Was releasing the novel greedy publisher exploitation or even elder abuse? But these concerns did not stop advance orders from rocketing *Go Set a Watchman* to the top of amazon's best-seller list, where it remained, off and on, for many months. When early reviews of *Watchman* appeared shortly before its July 14 release date, however, excitement and anxiety gave way to anguish from a source that almost no one had anticipated: Atticus, generally considered the paragon of American legal practice and the world's best father, was in the new novel revealed to be a full-fledged Citizens' Council-leading racist. Perhaps inevitably given *Mockingbird*'s status as one of the most-read and best-loved novels in American literature, professional critics read the two novels in conjunction and found a clash of affect not only between the books but also for readers. *New York Times* critic Michiko Kakutani, for example, described *Watchman* as "disturbing reading" that leaves readers "baffled and distressed."[1] For Dianne Williamson of the *Worcester Telegram*, learning that Atticus is a racist is like discovering Holden Caulfield was a pedophile.[2] Social media pronouncements by *Mockingbird* fans were more personal, if not more dramatic, ranging from preemptive self-protection ("I won't be reading this book. I need to remember Atticus my own way") to profound disillusionment ("My childhood is ruined!")[3]

While such hyperbole is amusing (if not distressing), this chapter proposes to take the notion of ruined childhood seriously, as it is indeed one of the major themes put forward by Lee in *Watchman*. Set in contemporary (mid-1950s) Alabama in the aftermath of the Supreme Court's *Brown v. Board* decision, *Watchman* chronicles twenty-six-year-old Jean Louise ("Scout") Finch's return to Maycomb, Alabama from her new home in New York City to visit her ailing father. Through a series of flashbacks to her Southern childhood intertwined with her present-day experiences, she reflects upon family, class, race, religion, sex, and gender roles in the changing South, and her own simultaneous embodiment of, and resistance to, those changes. In the figure of her idealized father, Jean Louise incarnates the fondest of her memories, personal and regional: Atticus is Scout's, and her South's, moral compass and best hope on matters of justice, truth, and the American way. When Jean Louise discovers mid-visit that Atticus not only is participating but also playing a leadership role in white supremacist resistance to the movement for African American civil rights—a role that appears to contradict everything he has raised her to believe—it represents the crisis of her life and of the novel. In the series of verbal confrontations that she initiates afterward, which might well be summarized as versions of "My childhood is ruined!", Lee meditates on the dangers, and ambivalent power, of maintaining a childish innocence into adulthood, particularly regarding race.

These meditations are not always coherent, ideologically or artistically. As many reviewers have pointed out, *Watchman* often reads as underdeveloped both in style and in content. But as Mason Stokes has argued regarding white supremacist fictions, books do not have to be "great" to be valuable for understanding the workings of race in US culture and literary history.[4] Marred by unpolished prose as they sometimes are, Jean Louise's frank attempts to grapple with her cultural and personal "enlightenment" constitute both the extraordinary promise and the failure of *Watchman*. My intention here is to read Lee's evocations of ruined childhood and white rage in *Watchman* in dialogue with the dramatic (albeit preliminary) reader response upon its publication. Doing so will necessitate a brief review of Lee's constructions of childhood in *Mockingbird* as it is that beloved text—paradoxically an expanded and radically truncated exploration of the ideological environment that shapes Jean Louise in *Watchman*—that stands in for childhood itself in contemporary readers' comments. For if, as James A. Crank has asserted, *Watchman* has come along right "when we really needed it," *Mockingbird* is clearly the novel that was and is still *wanted*.[5] Read on its own terms, and especially in the context of *Mockingbird*'s continued popularity, Lee's "latest" novel affords an unprecedented opportunity to see the literary deployment of childhood in action, both for a writer and for her readers.[6] The extent and manner in which childhood racial innocence is allowed to be ruined in each text, and the extent and manner of the rage this ruination occasions, offer an important lens into the desires, and the perceived needs, of contemporary readers, both in 1960 and in 2015.

The precise origins and status of the manuscript now published as *Watchman* continue to be a source of ongoing controversy.[7] The following facts are generally agreed upon: composed early in 1957 after friends Christmas-gifted Lee a year's financial support to focus on her writing, a manuscript titled *Go Set a Watchman* was initially submitted to JB Lippincott Publishing in May 1957. A prominent editor there, Tay Hohoff, recommended that Lee revise the manuscript to focus on the sections that dealt with children's point of view. This Lee did over a period of two more years, reconfiguring *Watchman*'s primary characters, physical setting, and some descriptions of both into the vastly different novel that is *Mockingbird*. After a series of experiments, Lee transformed *Watchman*'s omniscient third-person narration to a complex first-person account dually focalized by a child between ages six and eight, and the adult that she becomes. The action of the novel was removed from the mid-1950s (with flashbacks to the 1930s) and limited to three years in the Great Depression beginning in 1933, with the occasional flash-forward perspective of an adult Scout presumably speaking in the 1950s.[8] Despite an unmistakable commonality of authorial voice and vision, the two novels share almost nothing in terms of plot: the adult struggles (or struggles for adulthood) that constitute the core of *Watchman* occur nowhere in *Mockingbird*, and neither of *Mockingbird*'s central plot-driving characters, Tom Robinson or Boo Radley, exists in *Watchman*.[9] As Hohoff advised, childhood remains at all times the frame and focus of *Mockingbird*, and when that novel was published to near-universal popular and critical acclaim in 1960, winning the Pulitzer Prize for fiction in 1961, Hohoff's editorial instincts were vindicated. Fifty-five years of continuous printing, more than forty language translations, and upward of forty million copies later, his "ingenuity" in guiding Lee is receiving renewed praise for rescuing the gem of the most beloved classic of American literature from the "lumpy," "distressing" alluvium that is *Watchman*.

While by all accounts Lee was elated by the success of *Mockingbird*, at least initially, her only public statement on the composition of *Watchman* and *Mockingbird* since 1964 alludes to the power dynamic between writer and publisher with perhaps a hint of regret: "I was a first-time writer, so I did as I was told."[10] Without discounting *Mockingbird*'s extraordinary achievements, I contend that "doing as she was told" amounted to a dramatic curtailment, and eventually a complete betrayal, of Lee's evident project in *Watchman*. A white female coming of age story in which maturity is utterly contingent on recognizing and confronting whiteness as the source of racial injustice—not just individual whites but *whiteness* itself—was transformed into nearly its opposite: a story in which the maturing "loss of innocence" locates racist injustice in individual "backward" whites while powerfully *preserving* the innocence of whiteness for (and as) the future. Given *Watchman* as the source material that Lee (and Hohoff) would have had in mind, the work of repression accomplished in *Mockingbird* seems astonishing. Fortunately, the new novel could rely on a singularly effective device with a long tradition of simultaneously revealing and concealing the workings of whiteness in American literature: childhood.

To Kill a Mockingbird and US (White) Racial Anxiety

Key to childhood's manifold power in US history and cultural expression, as recent scholarship has shown, is a complex and fraught relationship with the notion of innocence. Springing from the central insights of Philippe Ariès,[11] the field of childhood studies has been devoted to exploring "the child" as ideological field and figure, "not only a biological fact but a cultural construct that encodes the complex, ever-shifting logic of a given group and therefore reveals much about its inner workings."[12] In the US context, Anna Mae Duane, Caroline Levander, and Karen Sánchez-Eppler, among others, have documented the crucial role of childhood as metaphor in the founding and growth of the new nation, establishing the child as a figure that both naturalizes and troubles American hegemonies of race and citizenship. Interested more in limning the borders of American exceptionalism than in enforcing them, this work nevertheless outlines a persistent and outwardly paradoxical association of childhood both with the purity and potentiality of American independence, and with those (e.g. slaves, Native Americans, white women) subjugated—rendered radically *dependent*—within that freedom. In the tension between these states, the poetics of childhood, asserted by Roni Natov as fundamentally addressed to the "persistent longing for childhood in adulthood and those states of mind we connect with childhood"[13]—a liminal space of return and reconnection with lost innocence, linguistic and physical immediacy, personal and historical memory, creativity, timeless nature, and pastoral simplicity—works hand in hand with hegemonic white anxiety: a racialized fear of the dangerous malleability, fundamental dependence, and "innocent" recklessness of the child, who must thus be disciplined and protected. Registering and covering over such anxiety,

Robin Bernstein has recently argued that figures of childhood in the long nineteenth century provided the "perfect alibi": childhood innocence, always raced white, naturalized a performed "holy ignorance," or "not-noticing," of social hierarchies that effected "the production of racial memory through the performance of forgetting."[14] In theories of national formation, the "persistent longing" for, and literary recovery of, childhood innocence so central to Natov's poetics represent the mechanisms of a national racial innocence that inscribes racial boundaries, even as it appears to transcend them, enabling whiteness and its power never to have to speak its own name.[15]

While criticism rarely fails to note child focalization in *Mockingbird*, curiously little has been said about the role of this focalizing with regard to formations of race and nation. This is all the more surprising since in most respects, *Mockingbird* could be considered a textbook example of the sort of racial erasure-by-inscription analyzed by Bernstein and others, and its success is a clear heir to the *Uncle Tom's Cabin* childhood-industrial complex. As in Harriet Beecher Stowe's novel, Lee uses an innocent white girl's perspective on an innocent black man's fatal mistreatment not only to raise awareness of racial injustice but also to encourage readers to "feel right" about it through sympathetic identification *with the child*. *Mockingbird*'s two-pronged meditations on "innocence," emphasizing first white childhood and then black victimization—themes one early critic found to be "enemies of each other"[16]—in fact work together in ways familiar to readers of nineteenth-century literature (which seem especially retrograde when read next to *Watchman*). The extraordinary success of the novel testifies to the strength of its affective strategies, and the subsequent Oscar-winning film adaptation, stage and courtroom reenactments, *Mockingbird*-themed restaurants and young adult novels, and children named Atticus mirror the cultural phenomenon that was *Uncle Tom's Cabin*. Clearly, like Stowe's novel, *Mockingbird* satisfied a national (and international) narrative hunger and continues to do so to the extent that the announcement of a second novel forthcoming from Lee was characterized as a "national event." The critical and popular disappointment expressed when that event actually came to pass indicates the depth of national investment in the particular form of childhood that *Mockingbird* offers. Often discussed as a novel about childhood's inevitable "loss of innocence," *Mockingbird*, in fact, demonstrates the ways that childhood, standing in for the nation, *comes into* a racialized innocence designed specifically to register the ever-present anxiety of whiteness while averting ruin with the promise of futurity.

In this respect, *Mockingbird* tells a very old story. As Holly Blackford has ably demonstrated, Lee, in *Mockingbird*, draws from nineteenth-century US generic traditions as varied as Emersonian philosophy, Stowian melodrama, Jamesian modernist experimentation, and Southern regionalism. Blackford traces how, like those of her literary child predecessors—Stowe's Eva, Henry James's Maisie, and Mark Twain's Huck—Scout's consciousness is wholly conditional, formed through her passive internalization of the voices and environments that surround her. Like Twain, Lee exploits the gap between situation and the naïve "innocence" of a child's analogical perception to create extreme ironies that not only satirize human egocentricity and fallibility but also "can indicate gaps between national ideology and practice, which is to indicate, in fact, American double consciousness."[17] Unlike Twain, who leaves the work of ironic interpretation entirely to Huck's readers, Lee selectively incorporates the guiding voice of the adult Scout's narration to provide distance and to render the ironies, Blackford argues, "more accessible" to readers.[18]

Double consciousness, the split between an acting self and an observing self, was, as Blackford notes, a modernist preoccupation. However, *American* double-consciousness hinges particularly on race and class, as DuBois famously articulated it, and is a profoundly alienating state. How does Lee, in *Mockingbird*, move readers from painful double consciousness to a readerly experience so pleasurable as to provoke a veritable frenzy at its "ruin"? Several critics have approached this question as a factor of the text's accessibility, enabled through familiarizing and soothing structures of genre focalized by a child. For Claudia Durst Johnson,[19] the predominant genre is the gothic, a mode "obsessed with transgressing boundaries" that, as Teresa Goddu has illustrated, lies at the center of American literature's negotiations of race and national identity.[20] Strikingly, in Johnson's reading, the whiteness of the novel's "enthralling" childhood and its implications for forming self- or national identity are untheorized and thus remain unmarked. Joining Levander's and Bernstein's scholarly projects of re-marking this "innocence," Blackford asserts that the key to *Mockingbird*'s pleasurable accessibility is the soothingly familiar way in which the novel mythologizes race relations in the mode of Uncle Tom stage show melodrama.[21] Lee updates the Tom show, moving it to the courtroom drama popular in the 1930s and offering Scout as a "feral," queerly "integrated Eva-Topsy."[22] Yet by preserving the essence of the racial melodrama, Lee "taps into a thriving American literary tradition to which readers have been conditioned to react: they must not only think about but also *feel* the outrage of persecuting innocence."[23] Thus, passions are awakened and paradoxically soothed by the familiar pleasures of ritualized racial melodrama, encouraging a simultaneous yearning for progress and nostalgia for the past that Blackford identifies as "foundational to the mythos of American literature."[24]

As her Aunt Alexandra constantly admonishes, the child Scout repeatedly fails to perform her assigned role in this melodrama in ways befitting her gender, class, or race. Parroting the prejudices of her Alabama environment, Scout, unlike Little Eva, shows no natural propensity for performing a "holy ignorance" or not-noticing of racial hierarchies. Scout's "integration," which several other critics have labeled her "queerness," threatens her ability to embody innocence as well, particularly the type of racial innocence assigned to white girls, as illuminated by Bernstein. And yet, by the end of the novel (and in the lasting memory of its readers), Scout embodies white racial innocence just as surely as does Little Eva. In part, this is again a function of melodrama, which, as Blackford argues, "ironically reinforce[s] popular culture's resistance to complexity and, by extension, miscegenation and integration."[25] But equally important, I would argue, is that Scout *comes* to embody racial innocence in a process that engages some highly traditional, and pleasurable, dynamics of region. By limiting the action of *Mockingbird* to the early 1930s South, the period of the adult Scout's childhood, Lee uses a familiar technique of addressing contemporary racial anxieties in a setting safely past. As well, she liberally deploys "charming" regionalist literary conventions—pastoral setting, amusing common folk, "colorful" eccentrics, exotic clime (the novel's endless summer)—elements that Theodore Hovet and Grace-Ann Hovet criticize for "combin[ing] to create a yearning for a seemingly lost age of innocence that diverts readers from looking too closely at the dark side of southern life embedded in the narration."[26] But the greater regional pleasure of the novel derives precisely from the "dark side of southern life," against which Lee can position the racial innocence of the child. Scout must accomplish racial innocence in the South, a region that Lee's novel and, as Jennifer Rae Greeson and Leigh Anne Duck document, the American nation have (lovingly) rendered as backward, stagnant, and immature, even childlike.[27] Over the course of the novel, Scout and her readers are schooled in proper class and race "obliviousness," which, as a white child, she can then perform and naturalize for those readers. That she succeeds in doing so, despite and within "southern darkness," heightens the value of that innocence and is a major source of *Mockingbird*'s "life-changing" affects.

With her lawyer father as her guiding light, Scout learns to reject her regional knowledge of social hierarchies in favor of an unmarked rhetoric of equality. Atticus's rationalist view of human nature and equal rights under the law echoes Cicero through to the founding documents of the US. Yet what Atticus models for his children and neighbors is less a national vision than the technology that has been so effective in supporting that vision: racial innocence—the precise performance of innocence that, Bernstein argues, has worked to render whiteness, and the nation, racially unmarked. As his frequently barbed comments show, Atticus is acutely aware of the racist hypocrisies and failures of Southern whiteness, although he disclaims any personal understanding of them.[28] Yet, whether in private or in public, he performs "not-noticing" these qualities in his fellow citizens. Mr. Cunningham, who has confronted Atticus and his children as part of a lynch mob, is, in Atticus's explication to Scout, "basically a good man...he just has his blind spots along with the rest of us"; to Scout's query if he is indeed a "nigger-lover," Atticus responds, "I certainly am. I do my best to love everybody."[29] For the many critics who consider *Mockingbird* as bildungsroman, Scout's journey is toward recognizing that Atticus is her, and her South's, proper role model: she must move from disdaining her father for not doing "anything that could possibly arouse the admiration of anyone" to respecting and ultimately emulating his form of heroism.[30]

That heroism is concretized in *Mockingbird* in two related ways: Atticus's constancy—his "there"-ness—for his children and his committed, and unsuccessful, defense of a black man accused of raping a white woman. Even before the publication of *Watchman*, Atticus was occasionally criticized for his failures (to challenge structures of racism, to more aggressively defend his client) and for his success (as a classic racial paternalist and "white savior" figure), though such criticisms often received strong protest from other readers.[31] While Lee undeniably substitutes Atticus's white paternalist gallantry for black activism as the primary force in the fight for civil rights, the only thing that he actually "saves" in *Mockingbird* is whiteness. By deploying the time-honored "white trash scenario" at court, Atticus at once quarantines racist evil to "trash" poor whites and claims the moral high ground for his own class (himself and the "many" Maycomb whites who secretly support his efforts). Even in the midst of the trial scene, Lee inserts biting commentary on the class prejudice behind this strategy,[32] but these moments are overshadowed by and even incorporated into the text's hagiographic emphasis on Atticus's probity. Indeed, the most trenchantly voiced critique of Maycomb's mores comes from Atticus's mouth, as further evidence and teaching of his iconoclastic Southern justness. The limitations of Atticus's performance of racial innocence in the racially corrupt "real world" of Maycomb County, however, are painfully clear at the end of *Mockingbird*. In nearly every respect, and especially after the trial, the South of *Mockingbird* remains a racial and class dystopia: its racist discourse encroaches even into the Finch home when Aunt Alexandra hosts the missionary society ladies' tea, and class antagonism in the form of Bob Ewell attacks the very bodies of the Finch children. Arguably, Atticus's resolute performance of racial and class "not-noticing" enables both of these violations. Certainly, his embodiment of "innocence" saves no one.

That task falls to Scout. Scout's struggle and success in the novel is to become more like Atticus, but in important ways, she plays *against* Atticus to reinstate childhood as the primary vehicle and savior of racial innocence in the novel. Only *Mockingbird*'s children are surprised or especially devastated by the trial verdict: this is their moment of coming into American double consciousness, ruination often described as their "loss of innocence." Older brother Jem is especially affected, his rage lasting several weeks before he can regain the equilibrium of "forgetting." For Scout, though, this moment is just one of many in the process of learning to perform racial innocence. When her friend Dill weeps at the injustice of the trial, Scout attempts to console him by saying, "after all he's just a Negro"[33]; she does not reach the cathartic release of "sudden tears" herself until she recognizes the othered Boo as the man who has saved her and Jem's lives, and notes the parallels between Radley and Robinson as "mockingbirds."[34] In Scout, Lee tweaks American literary conventions of childhood racial innocence, presenting such innocence as much acquired as it is natural. Even so, Scout's status as a child ultimately preserves and retroactively naturalizes a modern performance of racial innocence. Constraining the diegesis entirely to the nostalgic past—while Scout's double-voiced narration gestures to a narrative present of not-forgetting, the practical shape of that present is strictly veiled—enables a fantasy vision of racial justice deeply rooted in Atticus's Southern past and endlessly deferred to an American future. In this, *Mockingbird* depends upon the historical naturalizing function of childhood to re-create racial innocence in its own image, simultaneously registering and soothing the (white) anxieties of a nation (again) in the midst of extraordinary racial upheaval. In her newly innocent embrace of Boo, Scout trades Southern ignorance for "holy ignorance" and thus assumes a particular form of whiteness that has been, and remains, crucial for a pleasurable experience of US national identity. Bewildered and displaced by Bob's successful assault on his own "innocence," Atticus is recuperated by perpetual parenthood as he tucks his children into bed to remain by their sides: "He would be there all night, and he would be there when Jem waked up in the morning."[35] Lee skillfully uses her white child protagonist and Southern setting to bring readers to a state of American double-consciousness and then to bring them back to the safety of whiteness. In the process, she creates a new iteration of childhood that preserves US "racial innocence" and the South in the past *and* for the future, at a time when both were threatened with ruin.

Overarching the conventions of romantic individualism, melodrama, Gothicism, and regionalism, Lee re-activates tropes of American childhood in her Southern setting to transform the novel's many tragedies into a promise of national triumph. What *Mockingbird* preserves—*creates* in order to preserve—is white Southern childhood as American childhood, a salvational space-time of awakening white double-consciousness and coming into a childlike racial innocence that can put it safely back to bed. This is a racial innocence that knows better and is all the stronger for forgetting. Locked in the warm, comfortable past, it projects change into the future and puts the present off-limits. The adult Scout's gently ironic gaze backward is through a one-way mirror, reflecting in Atticus a desired past and in the child Scout a fantasized future of white redemption. Its South is a chromotope of pleasure and danger, the very worst and the very best of whiteness (and martyred blackness). It is a child South fully capable of redeeming itself and the nation: who "we" really are and want to be. As Adam Gopnik opined upon the release of *Watchman*, Lee's writing "makes one feel nostalgic for one's Southern childhood even if one never had a Southern childhood."[36] Judging from their passionate comments, it would seem that for a great many readers, *To Kill a Mockingbird* is their Southern childhood. And as these readers learn to look with Scout beyond Southern racism, toward Atticus and his ideal American justice, and past Atticus to their own futures, the book becomes their American childhood, inviolate.

Go Set a Watchman and a Holy Ignorance of Whiteness

This American childhood is precisely the childhood *Watchman* sets out to ruin. Where *Mockingbird*, following American literary tradition, offers childlike racial innocence as a solution, *Watchman* excoriates it as *the* problem. *Mockingbird*'s child Scout must come into an Atticus-like racial innocence after a hard awakening to the injustices of Southern society; she passes through a period of double consciousness in which she learns to respect and emulate her father's performative not-noticing. *Watchman*'s adult Jean Louise arrives on the page fully formed by Atticus's performance, though apparently without the slightest consciousness of its performativity. She is twenty-six years old, a resident of New York City, where, as she explains to a shocked Alabama acquaintance, "I don't know that a great big fat Negro man's been sitting beside me on a bus until I get up to leave. You just don't notice it."[37] Over the course of the novel, however, Jean Louise's self-diagnosed "color blindness" is revealed to be much less a factor of not-noticing blackness than a "holy ignorance" of whiteness and its power structures. While clearly conscious of contemporary racial discrimination and African American resistance, Jean Louise appears almost willfully oblivious of the role of "her kind"—a race and class status apotheosized by Atticus—in perpetuating injustice. Although technically an adult, Jean Louise retains a childlike belief in her father's essential goodness, to the extent that an unthinking, unthought "love of her father" is "the most potent moral force in her life."[38] As in *Mockingbird*, Lee uses episodes from Jean Louise's childhood to chart how Scout comes to respect and even "worship" Atticus, but where *Mockingbird* encourages readers to accept Scout's faith in the Southern past as their own, *Watchman* explores the implications of maintaining such "innocence" into adulthood, in and for the region and nation. Deliberately and forcefully violating Jean Louise's childhood trust in Atticus's dispassionate paternalism, Lee invites readers into what for many of her contemporaries, and ours, is uncharted territory: confronting racial injustice not as a black body in pain or a despised and easily dismissed white Other but as a system of white power embodied in the self.

Doing so constitutes, ultimately, a rejection of the rhetorical and affective strategies that are the foundation of *Mockingbird*'s appeal. But just as Jean Louise has been lulled into "complacen[cy] in her snug world,"[39] Lee first engages traditional literary pleasures of regionalism and childhood in order better to ruin them. *Watchman* introduces Jean Louise Finch rolling homeward on a train to Maycomb, taking in the Southern scenery passing by "with a delight almost physical,"[40] but the source of Jean Louise's joy is ambiguous: is it the unpainted Negro houses she sees or the TV antennas on top, which in 1957 would have been a sign of modernization? Despite Jean Louise's frequent nostalgic glances to the past, she and *Watchman* are firmly located in a national present of racial and economic change. The action of the novel takes place entirely within the 1950s of its composition and is centrally concerned with the South's new realities. These include not only organized black protest and white backlash—National Association for the Advancement of Colored People (NAACP) activism, the Supreme Court's *Brown v. Board* ruling, the Emmett Till trial, Citizens' Councils—but also economic development and its threat to traditional Southern class structures. Passages describing Maycomb's eccentric "off-the-books" past that also appear verbatim in *Mockingbird*, are in *Watchman* prelude for an extended description of how the town has changed post-World War II. New prosperity has brought old political regimes to the brink of defeat, some African Americans are able to buy used cars, and former tenant farmers have flocked to Maycomb to establish families and businesses. The third-person narrative voice, which often slides into free indirect discourse from Jean Louise's point of view, asserts that these new residents with their "matchbox" houses and "comic" neon business signs have "ruined the old town's looks" but also that "[a]lthough Maycomb's appearance had changed, the same hearts beat in new houses, over Mixmasters, in front of television sets."[41] However, even if, according to the narrator, "the rest of the town" refuses to acknowledge the newcomers' existence, evidence of ongoing change is everywhere: Maycomb is clearly not the "tired old town" Scout remembers in *Mockingbird*.[42]

Jean Louise, like the narrative voice, exhibits conflicting feelings about this change. The complex temporality of the novel, which flows between present and past tenses (sometimes within the same sentence), with flashbacks to Jean Louise's childhood and Maycomb's history evoked by present events, which they in turn illuminate, reflects Jean Louise's dual orientation toward nostalgia and modernity. The security she feels in Maycomb—her fluency with its traditions and unwritten history, her conviction that her hometown beau, Henry, is her "own kind," and her utter faith in her father as the embodiment of competence and (wryly expressed) honesty—enables Jean Louise to express her own iconoclasm, particularly with regard to Southern gender roles. Having an Aunt Alexandra who wears whalebone corsets and is a "last of her kind" Southern lady adds the thrill of provocation to Jean Louise's insistence on wearing pants and talking about menstruation in mixed company. It also, as she well understands, allows Jean Louise to shirk her "daughter's duty" and pursue painting in New York. Having a respected lawyer from an Old Family for a father empowers her to declare ("primly") to Henry that she will have an affair with but not marry him and later, to laugh off community rumors that the two have gone skinny-dipping.[43]

These actions establish Jean Louise as a modern girl, just as her nostalgia for the South of her childhood reveals a deep conflict in her understanding of both its past and its present. Returned for her annual visit home, Jean Louise continually expresses distaste and surprise at the changes she encounters. A late night visit with Henry to the Finch ancestral lands epitomizes the lure of the past and shock of new realities for Jean Louise. The approach to Finch's Landing is described in near-Gothic terms: on a high bluff, a two-rut road vanishes among dark trees, leading to an antebellum two-story white house surrounded by porches. Nodding to the clichés of Southern literature that would have this house "in an advanced state of decay," the narrator posits as twin surprises that the Finch House is in excellent condition (it has been purchased by a hunting club) and that Jean Louise does not mourn its loss.[44] But when Henry surprises her with news that the last of the surrounding Finch lands have also been sold, Jean Louise's voice betrays enough dismay that Henry accuses her of "Going Southern on us," like *Gone with the Wind*'s Gerald O'Hara: "I believe you are the worst of the lot. Mr. Finch is seventy-two years young and you're a hundred years old when it comes to something like this."[45] Atticus is, in fact, renowned for his ability to "move on." Similar to the way he returns to his "impassive self" immediately after the trial in *Mockingbird*, Atticus sells Jean Louise's childhood home soon after Jem dies of a heart attack—to one of those former country folk, who razes it and builds an ice cream shop. Intellectually, Jean Louise can dismiss her own nostalgia—"Conservative resistance to change, that's all"[46]—but the tension between her modern and nostalgic desires appears to increase each hour of her visit. To Henry, Jean Louise explains her reaction to the land sale in a way that invokes both the South's clichéd "authenticity"—Maycomb, not New York, is "the world"[47]—and the nostalgia behind that designation. Jean Louise declares (though only to herself) that she would marry Henry and return South to Finch's Landing but not to modern Maycomb. Jean Louise's recalcitrant relation to Southern modernity even has a physical manifestation: she repeatedly rams her head against the doorframe when trying to enter Henry's new car.

Indeed, Lee's structural gambit in *Watchman* might best be described as armchair Freudianism. Jean Louise readily admits to Henry that she wants to marry her own father, repressed Aunt Alexandra is inspired to marry her husband when he "drive[s] a pole through a ring," and Jean Louise's eventual confrontation of Atticus is figured (by Atticus and his brother, Jack) as a delayed but necessary step in her individual ego formation.[48] As the tension between Jean Louise's notion of "the world" and Maycomb's new realities mounts, Jean Louise increasingly experiences flashbacks to her childhood that amount to a return of the repressed. Where *Mockingbird* uses childhood to re-create and preserve childhood racial innocence by way of gesturing toward a hopeful future, *Watchman* returns to childhood in a search for the origins of a strange "innocence" Jean Louise has apparently carried forward into adulthood. Over the course of the first chapters, Jean Louise is called a "damn child"[49] by Henry (for refusing to commit to marriage), "innocent as a new-laid egg"[50] by Alexandra (for refusing to acknowledge Henry's "white trash" background), and scolded as "Scout," her childhood nickname, by Atticus (in disapprobation for her shocking mention of "The Curse"). At first, such infantilizations are directly tied to Jean Louise's refusal to conform to Southern feminine gender and class expectations. Indeed, *Watchman* is notable in mid-century Southern literature for its frank and non-pathologized treatment of female bodily maturation, with childhood flashbacks to Scout's first menses, a false pregnancy scare, breast "falsies," and unfeminine adolescence treated with humor and a remarkable lack of trauma. Jean Louise's indisposition to perform traditional

Southern femininity is treated as inherent, not as a subject of shame.[51] Gradually, however, the true subject of these flashbacks is revealed to be less the child Scout's extraordinary ignorance about her maturing female body but a parallel development she has repressed: the development of her own privileged "innocence" regarding race and class.

None of the five major flashbacks to Jean Louise's childhood focus on racial interaction *per se*, although all either feature or are bookended by such interactions. Appearing in roughly chronological order, the first two episodes feature Scout in full tomboy mode, a young, spirited, and mischievous child; in the later three, she has entered puberty, no less spirited but more bewildered about the gendered and sexed world she is obliged to enter. In each case, Atticus is "there," a figure of calm strength, good humor, and essential justness—a safety net cushioning Jean Louise from the worst effects of her natural, exuberant irreverence. Indeed, the primary purpose of the first two flashbacks, which occur in the novel *before* the "revelations" regarding Atticus's Citizens' Council activities, is to establish Atticus's constancy, the basis of Jean Louise's "worship." As in *Mockingbird*, the pastoral freedom and playful logic of the children, alongside Atticus's amused tolerance, is the affective glue of the novel and the basis of Jean Louise's (and readers such as Adam Gopnik's) nostalgic fantasy of Southern childhood. Long summer days of unstructured play are interrupted only by Calpurnia calling the children in for lemonade. One such day, related in the second flashback, Scout, Jem, and Dill reenact a revival sermon, replete with the preacher's speech defect and the added innovation of Dill donning a sheet to represent the Holy Ghost. Mid-"baptism," they are discovered by Atticus and the preacher and his wife, who have come to dinner. What appears to be evidence of Atticus's shame (excusing himself from table with two tears running down his cheeks following the preacher's condemnatory dinner blessing) is actually a sign of his own (mild) iconoclasm. When Scout discreetly asks Calpurnia whether Atticus is very upset, Cal answers to the whole table: "Mr. Finch? Nawm, Miss Scout. He on the back porch laughin'!"[52]

In the classic American tradition of *Huckleberry Finn*, the antics of childhood are used here to satirize adult cultural foibles, and this scene appears to cement Atticus's fundamental sympathy with his children's "innocent" burlesque of Maycomb's cherished pieties. But alongside establishing "[i]ntegrity, humor, and patience" as "the three words for Atticus Finch,"[53] this scene and the other flashbacks offer equally important, but to Jean Louise unrecognized, lessons about race. As the scene transitions back to present action, the narrator reiterates, "*Mr. Finch? He laughin'*," an encapsulation both of Atticus's conduct and of Calpurnia's speech.[54] Provider of lemonade, love and discipline alike, Calpurnia serves "behind the scenes" at the Finch's house and in Jean Louise's consciousness. While Jean Louise readily acknowledges Calpurnia's centrality in her upbringing, the racial *systems* that Calpurnia daily embodies constitute Jean Louise's "unseen everyday," illuminating the "'obscene' species of racial blindness" that Patricia Yaeger has called the "unthought known" of Southern white literature.[55] As Calpurnia scrubs Jean Louise "viciously" after the revival, "thrust[ing]" her into a pink dress and throwing patent leather shoes at her feet, Jean Louise observes and erects the fetish of Cal's strength: "She watched big scarecrow fingers perform the intricate business of pushing pearl buttons through holes too small for them, and she marveled at the power in Calpurnia's hands."[56] In nostalgic memory, Jean Louise again observes, but does not examine, Calpurnia's racial performance at the preacher dinner: "With company came Calpurnia's company manners: although she could speak Jeff Davis's English as well as anybody, she dropped her verbs in the presence of guests; she haughtily passed dishes of vegetables; she seemed to inhale steadily."[57] Calpurnia's bold declaration of Atticus's laughter may indeed signal her own proud allegiance to the Finch children (as Jean Louise's nostalgic memory would seem to have it); the scene of childhood presents a fantasized wholeness—Atticus, Calpurnia, Scout, and Jem, united within and against a Southern hypocrisy. This, in a nutshell, is the structural and affective mode of *Mockingbird*.

In *Watchman*, Lee employs this mode in order to shatter it. As in *Mockingbird*, images of Jean Louise's somnolence and unconsciousness pervade *Watchman*: the flashbacks to childhood often occur while Jean Louise is dozing; her first response to feelings of security is usually sleepiness; and in church, Jean Louise sleeps "with her eyes open through the lesson, as was her custom."[58] But these episodes of somnolence are accompanied by increasingly urgent calls to wake. The section (Part III) where Jean Louise becomes aware of her father's Citizens' Council activities begins with Aunt Alexandra's cry, "Jean Louise, Jean Louise, wake up!"[59] While Jean Louise and Atticus easily laugh off Alexandra's manufactured scandal (the false accusation of skinny-dipping), the injunction is clearly indicated by later events to apply to Jean Louise's "innocent" unconsciousness more generally. The prolonged scene of her discovery of Atticus's and Henry's participation in the Maycomb Citizens' Council is a temporal kaleidoscope of the courthouse Council meeting observed and flashbacks through Jean Louise's memories of Maycomb's politicos, Atticus's successful acquittal of a black man accused of raping a white woman, the deaths of Mrs. Finch and Jem from heart attacks, Atticus's childrearing practices, and Jean Louise's lonely femininity-challenged adolescence. Reduced to numb illness, Jean Louise leaves the courthouse and returns to her childhood home, now a "square, squat, modern ice cream shop," buys a scoop of vanilla and promptly vomits.[60]

The source of Jean Louise's nausea is her coming into American double consciousness, a new awareness of the duplicitous disconnect between the words and meanings of "respectable men" such as her father, coupled with a new sense of being observed and "not wanted" by the Maycomb folks she has previously considered "her kind." Though it is not immediately apparent to Jean Louise, this is the ruin of her own racial innocence, which she at first experiences as Atticus's betrayal of her childhood trust. Struggling to reconcile Atticus's voice from the "warm comfortable past" ("*Gentleman, if there's one slogan in this world I believe, it is this: equal rights for all, special privileges for none*") with the visual evidence refuting her belief in the "white trash scenario" of Southern racism ("Below her, on rough benches, sat not only most of the trash in Maycomb County, but the county's most respectable men"), Jean Louise embarks on a mental search for the source of her former blindness.[61] Her current anguish takes her to previous moments of anguish, primarily through flashbacks to other childhood awakenings. As with the pre-revelation flashbacks, these are generally humorous, charmingly naïve episodes of childhood "innocence" that feature Atticus's constancy (if not always competency) and Calpurnia's practical wisdom. And like all returns, these dreaming glances backward contain images and phrases that "bubble up" into present events, hinting at the repressed roots and future outcomes of Jean Louise's present conflicts. For example, at the onset of her first menstrual period—an occasion that causes puberty-ignorant Scout to scream, Atticus to become helpless, and Calpurnia to "t[ake] her in hand"—the child Jean Louise "consider[s] that a cruel practical joke had been played upon her: she must now go into a world of femininity, a world she despised, could not comprehend nor defend herself against, a world that did not want her."[62] In addition to the imagery of rude awakening, the language of this memory prefigures Jean Louise's feelings upon discovering "respectable" Maycomb's active role in white domination. Leaving the courthouse, "She looked at Maycomb, and her throat tightened: Maycomb was looking back at her. Go away, the old buildings said. There is no place for you here. You are not wanted."[63] Similarly, post-revelation, Jean Louise finds brief peace in the moments between sleep and full consciousness, a state she recalls cherishing at a past time of extraordinary childhood anxiety, when, still ignorant of biology, she believed that she had been impregnated by an "Old Sarum" boy's French kiss. Begging Calpurnia to let her give birth in secret at her home in the "Quarters," Jean Louise receives instead from Cal the facts of sex. Upon this "awakening," the adolescent Jean Louise experiences the return of security and immediately falls asleep.

But not before realizing that Calpurnia has called her "Miss Scout" for the first time outside of a "high company" context. Typically, Lee buries the significance of this realization under the humor of the episode. Scout's analysis of Calpurnia's speech—"I must be getting old"[64]—perfectly illustrates not only her continued childlike myopia but the process by which racial knowledge becomes "unthought." If readers notice or question the racial "etiquette" Calpurnia performs in this scene (as Lee, through Jean Louise's comment, signals them to do), Jean Louise herself refuses to do so, slipping happily into the comfort of unconsciousness. To the character Jean Louise, these adolescent flashbacks represent childhood episodes of extreme-to-the-point-of-humorous ignorance, thanks to a combination of the sheltering "snug world" Atticus provides and her own gullibility; she can readily see parallels between these earlier states and the painful "enlightenment" she currently experiences and even laugh at her former "innocence." What she cannot see, even though Lee includes abundant evidence in each flashback, is that the gender role (and attendant "proper" female embodiment) to which Jean Louise has struggled her whole life to adapt goes hand in hand with a specific race and class performance. Indeed, as the "Miss Scout" episode illustrates, Jean Louise's sexual ignorance is explicitly replaced by a "holy ignorance" of race. Her frantic search of Atticus's (to her mind) previously unblemished record as a "gentleman" reveals the extent to which racial and class innocence is central to Jean Louise's image of Atticus and thus to her image of herself. Reading the newspapers in New York, Jean Louise barely scans stories about the Southern Citizens' Councils:

> one glance down a column of print was enough to tell her a familiar story: same people who were the Invisible Empire, who hated Catholics; ignorant, fear-ridden, red-faced, boorish, law-abiding, one hundred per cent red-blooded Anglo-Saxons, her fellow Americans—trash.[65]

Despite the sarcastic reference to "fellow Americans," in Jean Louise's mind, these people have no relation to her personal identity; they are not "her kind." Confronted with Atticus's prominent place at the Citizens' Council table, Jean Louise is forced to revise this view of her father's and her Maycomb's racial innocence—Atticus has "betrayed her, publicly, grossly, and shamelessly."[66] As abject as she feels leaving the courthouse, still, Jean Louise does not yet question her own racial innocence.

A visit to Calpurnia's home inspires such self-examination, resulting in the most dramatic awakening in the novel. Jean Louise feels momentary relief upon hearing Atticus insist upon defending Calpurnia's grandson against charges of manslaughter, only to experience a second betrayal as it becomes clear his motive for doing so is to prevent NAACP lawyers from mounting a more effective, and segregation-challenging, defense. Once again bumping her head against the car doorframe, Jean Louise drives on a dirt road "until she could go no farther," to reach Calpurnia's house in the Quarters.[67] In *Mockingbird*, when Scout and Jem accompany Calpurnia to her church, its African American members become "a solid mass of colored people" to defend the children against one woman's challenging of their presence.[68] As *Watchman*'s Jean Louise approaches Calpurnia's house, the black community and family members who have gathered there in support perform the rituals of racial etiquette, removing hats, standing straight, and "becoming as one" to let her pass.[69] Unlike the church scene in *Mockingbird*, however, which ends in Calpurnia's reassuring welcome to Scout to visit her at home "any time,"[70] Calpurnia, using her "company manners," repudiates Jean Louise's gambit to continue performing childhood racial innocence and pointedly *marks* her whiteness: to Jean

Louise's anguished cry, "What's the matter? I'm your baby, have you forgotten me? Why are you shutting me out? What are you doing to me?" Calpurnia replies, "What are you all doing to us?"[71] Although when pressed, Calpurnia denies having hated the Finches, Jean Louise's first feeling is again one that her entire childhood is ruined. But reflecting on this, she has a mature revelation: her relation to Calpurnia has been structured around an unthought but deeply known racism as entrenched in Jean Louise's continuing appeals to Cal's mammy-care as it is in the childhood rhyme that percolates from her unconscious as the chapter ends. "*Eeny, meeny, miny, moe. Catch a nigger by his toe. When he hollers let him go…*," Jean Louise reflects, "God help me."[72]

Jean Louise here becomes conscious, if only briefly, that her "color blindness" has not been an inability to think of people in terms of race (as her Uncle Jack diagnoses) but an inability to see her own whiteness at work. This new awakening informs—though to wildly fluctuating extents—Jean Louise's subsequent glosses on her childhood memories as well as her confrontations with Aunt Alexandra; Uncle Jack; Henry; and, finally, Atticus. Through these interactions, wherein Jean Louise expresses both her rage and her love, Lee meditates on both the dangers of American racial innocence and the potential power of the idealism it is meant to embody. The egalitarian ideals Atticus instills (along with, crucially as the novel makes clear, his privileged class and race position) make it possible for Jean Louise to live by her own lights, to wear what she wants to wear, and to be outspoken in the face of racial injustice, even, and especially, to her own father.[73] And yet Atticus's performance of racial innocence, and Jean Louise's blind belief in that performance, is exposed as the most insidious source of racial oppression in the novel. Unlike in *Mockingbird*, Atticus's articulations of America's highest ideals cannot save white innocence, separating the good white from the bad—rather, they mask the *whiteness* that ensures the ideal cannot ever be attained. In *Watchman*, in ways so direct they are jarring even to modern readers, Lee appears dedicated to a white confrontation of that whiteness.

Deprived of the comforts of racial innocence, however, both Jean Louise and the novel flounder for a response. The series of statically written arguments that Lee stages between Jean Louise and her closest relations that dominate the second half of *Watchman* reflect not only the unedited roughness of a draft novel but also the discomfiting frankness with which Lee explores Jean Louise's predicament as an allegory of American regional and national relationship.[74] With its zinger-style retorts and furious denunciations, Jean Louise's confrontation of Atticus reads like a neoabolitionist fantasy of a white liberal response to "old-style" Southern racism.[75] Unlike Jem's disillusioned rage in *Mockingbird*, which seethes internally until he can "forget," Jean Louise's anger erupts and escalates, attacking everything from Atticus's self-serving reading of American history, to his parenting choices (he should have married "some nice dim-witted Southern lady who would have raised [Jean Louise] right").[76] Despite *many* instances of unexamined racism in her own argument, Jean Louise vehemently (and often very effectively) counters Atticus's increasingly grotesque defense of white supremacy by insisting that his brand of "respectable" whiteness is responsible for racial injustice. Atticus the Father aligns himself with America's Founding Fathers, and it is no stretch to construe, as does Jean Louise, that Atticus's newly visible performance of "racial innocence" is the hypocritical foundation of both region and nation. Jean Louise's rage and despair spring from this "betrayal" of her own sense of innocence and the deracinating double-consciousness that is her new condition:

> I'll never forgive you for what you did to me. You cheated me, you've driven me out of my home and now I'm in no-man's-land but good—there's no place for me any more in Maycomb, and I'll never be entirely at home anywhere else.[77]

When Atticus parries with a characteristic, dispassionate retreat to the neutrality of love, again offering himself as Father/land, Jean Louise explodes, calling him a "double-dealing, ring-tailed old son of a bitch" and vowing to go "so far away from Maycomb County it'll take me a hundred years to get back."[78]

But as Lee quickly makes clear, Jean Louise's fiery resolve to flee the betrayers (human and regional) of her lost innocence is actually a desperate attempt to retain the comfort of that innocence for herself. More than one early reviewer of *Watchman* commented upon the "uncanny" similarity of Jean Louise's feelings and those experienced by *Mockingbird* fans upon learning of Atticus's activities. Shock, dismay, queasiness, outrage, denial (this isn't the "real" Atticus), conspiracy-theory (lawyer and publisher lying), denunciation (the book should never have been published), and outright rejection (refusal to read) are the most common, in-common reactions. Just as Jean Louise initially determines to "sponge out what she had seen and heard, creep back to New York, and make [Atticus] a memory,"[79] many readers have shunned *Watchman* altogether in order to "stick with my beloved *To Kill a Mockingbird*" and "remember Atticus my own way." And as Jean Louise quickly extrapolates from personal to national alienation, many readers immediately made a connection between losing *Mockingbird*'s childhood innocence and "national disillusionment," and ruin ("Why do they always spoil things…should have left well enough alone…"). Arguments for rejecting *Watchman* in favor of *Mockingbird* range from personal nostalgia and vague claims (on a sports site) that "what's important" is to "see the best versions of ourselves"[80] to more concrete arguments (from a civil rights attorney) that the "ugly truth" of a racist Atticus Finch "merely dampens the call to justice of all those who thought that, just maybe, another world was possible."[81]

Ultimately, Lee in *Watchman* dismisses any moral argument for a nostalgic preservation of racial innocence as *immorally* childlike. Crucially concerned with the present time of racial change, Lee evokes the nostalgic pleasures of Scout's Southern childhood in *Watchman* not (only) to preserve them but to explore their implications for the South and the nation. For *Mockingbird*'s Scout, as for many readers of that text, memories of her childhood South are a source of security, a founding fantasy of racial innocence and authenticity at the core of her Southern—and our, American—identity. Awakened by Atticus's "betrayal," and schooled by Calpurnia, *Watchman*'s Jean Louise learns to read her childhood not for what she had thought it secured but for what it has rendered unthought. "Shattering" the images of Atticus and Henry in her final childhood flashback, Jean Louise recognizes that her (modern) desire for a nostalgic Southern past severs her relation to, and relationships in, modernity. Maintaining the "holy ignorance" that has been so core to her identity means that Jean Louise has had to, and must continue to, freeze the living South into a phantasmic past of her own invention, leading to a lament that could apply equally to Lee's post-*Mockingbird* fate: "What had she done that she must spend the rest of her years reaching out with yearning for them, making secret trips to long ago, making no journey to the present?"[82] The great promise of *Watchman* is that both Jean Louise and Lee clearly recognize this as a tragic and untenable state, with implications not only for Jean Louise's maturity but, more importantly, for perpetuating systemic racism in the South and the nation.

The (White) Resistance to Whiteness

The failure of *Watchman* is that neither author nor protagonist can figure an effective way forward.[83] Lee raises, and clearly rejects, whiteness's strongest strategies for keeping itself "unmarked": self-protective nostalgia for childhood racial innocence, "reluctant" accommodation of racism (ex-fiancé Henry's approach), and quarantining "bad whites" to the South, to be self-righteously shunned. But from there, she reaches an impasse; in one of the novel's many clichés, Jean Louise says that she can neither beat her Maycomb relations nor join them. It is in her ironic condemnation of Atticus's bad parenting (failure to "raise her right" for living with white hypocrisy) that Lee reaches the crux of the matter: Jean Louise can no more evade the heritage and implications of her whiteness than she can erase her parentage. She must, as Natasha Trethewey has so compellingly done in her recent poetry, confront that the whiteness her father so shockingly represents is part of *her*—indeed, it has made her who she is—and must be acknowledged and grappled with as such.[84] Shockingly (depressingly), rather than allow "Scout" to chart a way through her struggle, Lee has her literally beaten into an alcoholic stupor by her Uncle Jack, in which state she apparently instantly finds comfort, forgetfulness, and forgiveness for her father. Worse, Jean Louise's break/breakdown is revealed to have been fully anticipated, even fervently wished for, by Atticus, a final sign of his self-effacing wisdom. Then, the book ends.

And yet, the damage has been done. In taking Atticus off his pedestal, well before she could have anticipated how high it would become, Lee has successfully, as Jon Smith has advocated for Southern studies generally, "disrupted everyone's enjoyment" of American racial innocence. The news—which, as Ta-Nehisi Coates has recently reiterated, is certainly not news to generations of African Americans—that whiteness *depends* upon the oppression of black bodies to maintain its dream, has been delivered.[85] And as several early reviewers noted, and some *Mockingbird* fans determined to avoid, after reading *Watchman*, there is no being tucked sweetly back into unconsciousness.[86] Alongside Jean Louise, readers receive some version of Coates's message to his son that opens this chapter: all is not okay, it is far from clear how it will ever be okay, but the necessity of finding "some way to live within the all of it" demands engagement and resistance—to whiteness from "whites." When Jean Louise reflects that "I did not want my world disturbed, but I wanted to crush the man who's trying to preserve it for me,"[87] it is not to absolve Atticus but to acknowledge her own complicity and responsibility moving forward. In 2015, when racial innocence has assumed an "adult" guise of post-racialism, and the sad necessity of "I AM A MAN" placards is mirrored by the sad necessity for a "Black Lives Matter" hashtag, it is hard not to be struck by the uncanny (and, yes, sad) timeliness of Jean Louise's "revelations" and *Watchman*'s publication—what Andy Crank has called the "fearful symmetry of Lee's renewed relevance."[88]

Though my reading is charitable, it is not my intention to idealize Lee's achievement in *Go Set a Watchman*. Its literary quality is uneven, it features one of the most annoying "characters" in Southern literature (Uncle Jack), and it appears to pose physical abuse and alcohol as a reasonable solution to women's rage. Most egregiously, the casual, unthought racism that haunts *Mockingbird* also pervades *Watchman,* even and especially in the passages meant directly to confront that racism.[89] Nonetheless, in *Watchman,* Lee made an important, and to this day radical, effort to reveal the role of racial innocence in sustaining white supremacy from the perspective of an (adult) child who has not only participated in but embodied that innocence. For all the good *Mockingbird* has inspired, it encourages readers, as Atticus so offensively says of "Negroes" in *Watchman*, to remain in their "childhood as a people."[90] Indeed, it suggests childhood as our nation's best hope. Had her editor, Tay Hohoff, devoted her considerable talents to helping Lee refine the novel she was *trying* to write in *Watchman*, rather than shaping it into another story altogether, mid-century American literature might have received something far more disturbing and significant: an effective literary model for confronting national hegemonies of whiteness from the inside. Instead of a ruined childhood, we might be contemplating a prototype for American maturity.

Approaches to Teaching Harper Lee's *To Kill a Mockingbird* and *Go Set a Watchman*

Discussion Questions

1. Were you one of the millions of schoolchildren assigned Lee's *To Kill a Mockingbird* since it was first published in 1960? If so, reflect on your own experience of reading the novel. How old were you when it was assigned, and what do you most remember about the way it was taught? If you never read the novel, what (if anything) had you heard about it? Were there any other novels, or other forms of literature, that addressed race and civil rights that you were assigned? How were these themes and histories taught in your school?
2. Many fans recall reading *To Kill a Mockingbird* as a transformative experience for their understanding of racism in the US and in their own lives. While she admits that Atticus's racism in *Go Set a Watchman* reflects an "ugly truth" in American culture, civil rights attorney Anne Richardson defends *Mockingbird* as an inspiring story and worries that *Watchman*'s story "merely dampens the call to justice of all those who thought that, just maybe, another world was possible." Do you agree? Why or why not? Do you believe this argument applies equally to both white and black audiences?
3. Harper Lee's focus on 1930s childhood in *To Kill a Mockingbird* left plenty of room to imagine the future lives of Scout and Jem and the US as a nation. The publication of *Go Set a Watchman* was one of the most highly anticipated literary events of 2015, in part because readers were eager to treat the novel as a sequel and find out "what ever happened." What sort of possibilities for imagining the future does Lee leave open in *Go Set a Watchman*, and why do you think so many readers found its ending so disheartening? What are the different effects of setting tales of racism and civil rights activism in the past as opposed to the present?
4. In both of Lee's novels, Scout's growing awareness of race is integrally tied to her growing awareness of herself as female. Compare the treatment of gender and race in *To Kill a Mockingbird* and/or *Go Set a Watchman*. How does Scout react to her place as a girl/woman in Southern culture? Is this similar to or different from her reaction to racial prejudice? How do class and race affect gender expectations?

Research and Writing Projects

1. Research President Barack Obama's major speeches on race, particularly his Philadelphia "A More Perfect Union" speech (2008), his 2015 eulogy for the victims of the Charleston church massacre, and his "farewell address" in January 2017. Compare his rhetoric on race to that of Atticus Finch. Where are their arguments and words especially similar, and where do they differ? While it is highly likely that Obama and his speechwriters were aware of the Atticus of *Go Set a Watchman*, Obama chose to invoke only the Atticus of *Mockingbird*. Analyze what this choice says about Obama's strategies for moving the nation forward in the quest for civil rights in the twenty-first century. What are the strengths and possible drawbacks of this approach?
2. Many critics have argued that Americans' understandings and fond memories of *To Kill a Mockingbird* and Atticus Finch spring more from the 1962 film version starring Gregory Peck than from the novel itself. View the film in comparison to the novel. How does the film (deliberately shot in black and white) visualize Lee's characters, settings, and themes of racial innocence and guilt? Put *To Kill a Mockingbird*'s film imagery in dialogue with documentary film and photographs of civil rights activism made in the same period.

How do these images compare or contrast? What larger narratives of civil rights and American identity do they present?

3   Research the role of Citizens' Councils in the South during the civil rights movement and find examples of their public rhetoric. To what extent did their words contradict and/or incorporate the "justice for all" rhetoric espoused by Atticus in *Mockingbird*? What happened to the Citizens' Councils? What vestiges of their rhetoric do you find in contemporary US debates over civil rights and "law and order"? What strategies of resistance have been most effective against anti-civil rights groups, then and now?

4   Lee's different strategies for critiquing American racism in *To Kill a Mockingbird* and *Go Set a Watchman* might be roughly described as romantic (providing a model for being our best selves in a corrupt society) versus realist (exposing the racist underpinnings of an idealized "color blind" America). As a group, cite examples from the novels and debate the strengths and weaknesses of each approach. Can you find examples of these competing strategies in contemporary civil rights activism or literature?

5   Education is a central theme in both of Lee's novels as it was in major civil rights court cases such as *Brown v. Board of Education*. Research some of the ways that children learn and internalize racism within and outside of school. What are some approaches that are, or could be, used to teach children anti-racist values?

6   In a *New York Times* editorial ("Let Black Kids Just Be Kids" July 26, 2017), Robin Bernstein argues that the "disturbing racial history" of childhood innocence continues to affect contemporary civil rights. Citing studies showing that black children are regularly perceived as older and less in need of protection and nurturing than white children, Bernstein says such perceptions help explain why African American children are disproportionately caught up in the criminal justice system. Choosing your own example from recent events or popular culture, prepare a presentation that analyzes how ideas of childhood interact with race in contemporary society.

Notes

1   Michiko Kakutani, "Harper Lee's Go Set a Watchman Gives Atticus Finch a Dark Side," *New York Times*, July 10, 2015.
2   Diane Williamson, "'Watchman' Makes Mockery of Beloved Character," *Telegram* (Worcester, MA), July 14, 2015.
3   The selection of reader comments in this chapter is taken from various blogs, tweets, tumblr, and comment sections regarding *Watchman* and will not receive individual citation.
4   Mason Stokes, *The Color of Sex* (Durham, NC: Duke University Press, 2001).
5   Qtd. in William Thornton, "Will 'Go Set a Watchman' change how 'To Kill a Mockingbird' is taught?" *AL.com*, August 6, 2015.
6   Discussing *Watchman* in relation to *Mockingbird* invites a confusion of chronology and terminology. The precursor novel was penned three years earlier but set twenty years later and published fifty-five years later than *Mockingbird* and is thus tempting to read as a sequel. On the other hand, since it was written second, *Mockingbird* could be read as a prequel to *Watchman*. With several descriptive passages reused verbatim, *Watchman* has been labeled a mere draft of *Mockingbird*, with the latter novel the "real" story. Several critics have questioned whether *Watchman* in its own right deserves consideration as a novel at all.
7   Lee's attorney claims to have discovered the manuscript in Lee's safety deposit box in summer 2014. In his unauthorized biography of Lee, Charles Shields describes Lee writing (and delivering in sections to her agent Marvin Crains) a manuscript titled *Go Set a Watchman* over a period of two months in January and February 1957. With Crains's guidance, Lee then revised that manuscript until May 1957, when he deemed it ready to submit to Lippincott under his preferred title, *Atticus*. Whether the "newly discovered" *Watchman* manuscript is the one originally submitted to Crains in February, the May 1957 version submitted to Lippincott (sans the title change), or something different altogether is unclear. To date, neither Lee (before her death), her lawyer, or her publisher has offered further clarification.

8. Exactly when and from where the adult Scout offers her adult perspective is not specified in *Mockingbird*, although she would necessarily be speaking no earlier than the late 1940s and no later than 1960.
9. A few lines referring to Atticus *winning* acquittal, by proving consent, for an unnamed one-armed black man accused of raping a white woman in *Watchman* prefigure the pivotal trial section of *Mockingbird*, in which Atticus heroically *fails* to prove Tom Robinson's innocence. The narrative function of such a case in each novel is diametrically opposed.
10. As quoted in a February 3, 2015, HarperCollins press release.
11. His groundbreaking *Centuries of Childhood* was originally published in French the same year as *To Kill a Mockingbird*.
12. Caroline Levander and Carol J. Singley, *The American Child* (New Brunswick, NJ: Rutgers University Press, 2003), 4.
13. Roni Natov, *The Poetics of Childhood* (New York: Routledge, 2006), 6.
14. Robin Bernstein, *Racial Innocence: Performing American Childhood from Slavery to Civil Rights* (New York: New York University Press, 2011), 8.
15. Ibid., 6–8.
16. Harding Lemay, "Children Play; Adults Betray," *New York Herald Tribune*, July 10, 1960.
17. Holly Blackford, *Mockingbird Passing: Closeted Traditions and Sexual Curiosities in Harper Lee's Novel* (Knoxville: University of Tennessee Press, 2011), 154.
18. Ibid., 20.
19. Claudia Durst Johnson, *To Kill a Mockingbird: Threatening Boundaries* (New York: Twayne, 1994).
20. Teresa Goddu, *Gothic America* (New York: Columbia University Press, 1997), 5.
21. Blackford, *Mockingbird Passing*, 89.
22. Ibid., 96.
23. Ibid., 90. Paradoxically, *Mockingbird*'s success in updating this affective structure also enables it to mask the various "alternative canons lurking in the subtexts"—particularly narratives of sexual queerness—that structure the overall tale (Blackford 2011, 10).
24. Ibid., 95.
25. Ibid., 91.
26. Theodore R. Hovet and Grace-Ann Hovet, "'Fine Fancy Gentlemen' and 'Yappy Folk': Contending Voices in *To Kill a Mockingbird*," *Southern Quarterly* 40.1 (2001), 69.
27. See Jennifer Rae Greeson, *Our South* (Cambridge, MA: Harvard University Press, 2010) and Leigh Anne Duck, *The Nation's Region* (Athens: University of Georgia Press, 2006).
28. Atticus declares, "Why reasonable people go stark raving mad when anything involving a Negro comes up, is something I don't pretend to understand" (117).
29. Harper Lee, *To Kill a Mockingbird* (New York: Hachette, 1960), 210, 144.
30. Ibid., 118.
31. For example, legal ethicist Monroe Freedman's 1992 critique in *Legal Times*, "Atticus Finch, Esq., R.I.P.," generated years of protest and counter-protest in that legal journal and others. Toni Morrison's is perhaps the most famous voice labeling *Mockingbird* a "white savior" narrative.
32. The adult Scout narrator attributes Maycomb's tolerance of Dolphus Raymond's interracial relationship versus its vilification of Mayella Ewell to the fact that Raymond comes from "a fine old family" and owns a riverbank.
33. Lee, *Mockingbird*, 266.
34. Ibid., 362.
35. Ibid., 376.
36. Adam Gopnik, "Sweet Home Alabama: Harper Lee's *Go Set a Watchman*," *The New Yorker*, July 27, 2015.
37. Harper Lee, *Go Set a Watchman* (New York: HarperCollins, 2015), 181.
38. Ibid., 117.
39. Ibid., 118.
40. Ibid., 3.
41. Ibid., 45–46.
42. Lee, *Mockingbird*, 6.
43. Lee, *Watchman*, 14, 85–86.
44. Ibid., 71.
45. Ibid., 74–75.
46. Ibid., 46.
47. Ibid., 75.
48. Ibid., 72.
49. Ibid., 14.

50 Ibid., 36.
51 Nor does the novel suggest latent lesbianism: Jean Louise expresses frank admiration for Henry's body and clearly enjoys his physical advances. Nevertheless, *Watchman*'s frank depictions of Jean Louise's female bodily maturation and "liberated" sexual desire, her ambivalent gender performance and the pointed lack of a viable model of heterosexual relationship provide ample material for feminist and/or queer readings that are beyond the scope of this chapter.
52 Lee, *Watchman*, 70.
53 Ibid., 114.
54 Ibid., 70.
55 Patricia Yaeger, *Dirt and Desire* (Chicago, IL: University of Chicago Press, 2000), xii.
56 Lee, *Watchman*, 69.
57 Ibid., 70.
58 Ibid., 91.
59 Ibid., 85.
60 Ibid., 112.
61 Ibid., 105, 108.
62 Ibid., 116.
63 Ibid., 111.
64 Ibid., 139.
65 Ibid., 104.
66 Ibid., 113.
67 Ibid., 155.
68 "Lula" is the only African American in *Mockingbird* that voices open disaffection with the racial status quo. She appears in this one scene, is silenced, and disappears.
69 Lee, *Watchman*, 156.
70 Lee, *Mockingbird*, 168.
71 Lee, *Watchman*, 159–160.
72 Ibid., 162.
73 Henry's defense of his own political expediency is delivered with a crucial statement of Jean Louise's (and by more damning extension, Atticus') class privilege: because she is a Finch, she is allowed to flout Maycomb gender and race mores in ways that as a child of poverty he cannot.
74 From its opening moments, conversation between Atticus and Jean Louise centers around the way the South is depicted in Northern newspapers, and subsequent arguments between Jean Louise and her relations regularly feature the relation of region to nation.
75 Among Jean Louise's best "zingers": "They're people aren't they? We were quite willing to import them when they made money for us" (246). Revising the meaning of her childhood memories, Jean Louise delivers a scathing indictment of Atticus's legal priorities some twenty years before Monroe Freedman: "I remember that rape case you defended, but I missed the point. You love justice, all right. Abstract justice written down item by item on a brief—nothing to do with that black boy, you just like a neat brief. His cause interfered with your orderly mind, and you had to work order out of disorder. It's a compulsion with you, and now it's coming home to you—" (248). Nevertheless, for Gopnik, *Watchman*'s fantasy does not go far enough: the novel, he believes, would be stronger had Calpurnia shook her head "yes."
76 Lee, *Watchman*, 249.
77 Ibid., 248.
78 Ibid., 253, 258.
79 Ibid., 241.
80 Hemal Jhaveri, "'Go Set a Watchman' Shouldn't Change Your Opinion of Atticus Finch," *For the Win/USA Today Sports*, July 15, 2015.
81 Anne Richardson, "What Can 'Go Set a Watchman' Teach Us That 'To Kill a Mockingbird' Cannot?" *Los Angeles Review of Books*, August 14, 2015.
82 Lee, *Watchman*, 225.
83 To be fair, few white-centered novels in the fifty-five years between *Mockingbird* and *Watchman* have even tried.
84 See Natasha Trethewey, *Native Guard: Poems* (New York: Mariner, 2007).
85 See Ta-Nehisi Coates, *Between the World and Me* (New York: Spiegel & Grau, 2015).
86 Some readers have tried using a strategy of regional containment: while the outcry over Atticus's racism is over a betrayal of an *American* (and thus apparently timeless) icon, these readers now take comfort that Atticus is "merely" Southern, from the now-distant past. A more nuanced historical analysis of *Watchman*'s Atticus as representative of Southern and national politics is offered by Crespino. The February 2016 announcement that screenwriter Aaron Sorkin would adapt *Mockingbird* for Broadway

using *only* the 1960 novel to inform Atticus's character suggests how persistent is the national desire for salving narratives of racial innocence.
87 Lee, *Watchman*, 277.
88 Andy Crank, "Unkillable Mockingbird," *Los Angeles Review of Books*, September 2, 2015.
89 Often Jean Louise's critique of institutional racism is itself grounded on racial paternalism and its slurs: "I heard you on the subject of Zeebo's boy this morning…nothing to do with our Calpurnia and what she's meant to us, how faithful she's been to us—you saw nigger, you saw NAACP, you balanced the equities, didn't you?" (247–248). Here, Jean Louise simultaneously demonstrates both her new ability to read her childhood memories for their racial meaning (revising the "innocent" flashback of Atticus "balancing the equities" to get Scout and Henry out of a high-school scrape) and the still-unthought depth of racialist belief that grounds her character and perhaps Lee's.
90 Lee, *Watchman*, 246.

APPENDIX OF ADDITIONAL TEACHING SOURCES

Matthew Spencer

An interdisciplinary seminar in civil rights literature would draw from a wide range of source material to contextualize and enhance the required reading. The following list of organizations, documentaries, and podcasts suggests such a context, either broadly or with reference to a specific author or literary text.

Organizations

The National Association for the Advancement of Colored People (NAACP) provides a large number of materials at their website (*naacp.org*). While many of these are related to membership and administration within individual chapters, there are also several tools for wider use, including manuals for training and advising as well as the "I Matter" tool kit, which is designed to help young people organize in response to police violence.

The Southern Poverty Law Center provides a wealth of information about teaching tolerance in the classroom, much of which is related to the civil rights movement. These include *Teaching Tolerance Magazine*, *tolerance.org*, and a series of film kits that are free for use in K-12 schools, schools of education, public libraries, houses of worship, and youth-serving non-profit organizations. Film kits particularly relevant to our purposes are *Selma: The Bridge to the Ballot*, *Mighty Times: The Children's March*, and *America's Civil Rights Movement: A Time for Justice*.

The American Civil Liberties Union (ACLU) offers information about civil rights through their website (*aclu.org*). A wide range of topics are covered, and news stories are constantly added as new issues emerge. The organization also offers a number of multimedia sources and publications, including reports on civil issues that are available for download.

Documentaries

4 Little Girls. Directed by Spike Lee. 1997. Burbank, CA: HBO Home Entertainment, 2010. DVD. Director Spike Lee directs this heartbreaking documentary about the 1963 Sixteenth Street Baptist Church bombing in Birmingham, Alabama.

13th. Directed by Ava DuVernay. 2016. Los Gatos, CA: Netflix, 2016. Video on Demand. DuVernay's documentary includes commentary from civil rights activists and law experts regarding the 13th Amendment to the US Constitution and how its ambiguity and interpretation have led to the current mass incarceration crisis in the African American community.

The African Americans: Many Rivers to Cross. Directed by Phil Bertelsen, Sabin Streeter, Jamila Wignot, and Leslie Asako Gladsjo. DVD. 2013. Arlington, VA: PBS, 2014. DVD. This documentary miniseries is hosted and narrated by Henry Louis Gates, Jr. and is sweeping in scope. The six episodes cover the African American experience from the middle passage to the inauguration of Barack Obama as the first black president of the US.

American Experience: Reconstruction: The Second Civil War. Directed by Llewellyn M. Smith. 2004. Arlington, VA: PBS, 2009. DVD. This miniseries covers the years from 1863 to 1877 when the US was recovering from the trauma of the Civil War. Focusing both on prominent political figures and on the common citizen, it provides vital context for the post-war oppression that would eventually culminate in the upheavals of the civil rights movement.

The Black Power Mixtape 1967–1975. Directed by Göran Hugo Olsson. 2011. New York, NY: MPI Home Video, 2011. DVD. Made up of footage shot by Swedish journalists between 1967 and 1975, this documentary presents the Black Power movement of the era in a renewed light. Major figures such as Angela Davis, Huey P. Newton, and Eldridge Cleaver appear, alongside other influential leaders. The recovered footage presents the transition from the civil rights era to the Black Power era in a way that makes it tangible and gives it a face.

Brother Outsider: The Life of Bayard Rustin. Directed by Nancy Kates and Bennett Singer. 2003. Warren, NJ: Passion River Films, 2010. DVD. Brings to light the life of Bayard Rustin, recovering his influence in the civil rights movement from the margins of history. As an openly gay black man, Rustin faced intense prejudice and racism in his work but was unflinching in his pursuit of equality. Reclaiming the legacies of people like Rustin in the civil rights era opens it to new understandings and honors their memory.

Colored Frames. Directed by Lerone D. Wilson. 2007. San Francisco, CA: Microcinema International, 2011. DVD. This documentary takes an illuminating look at African Art beginning with the civil rights era and leading to the present day. In doing so, it reclaims artists that may have otherwise fallen through the cracks of popular history.

Eyes on The Prize: America's Civil Rights Years 1954–1965. Directed by James. A DeVinney, Orlando Bagwell, Callie Crossley, Judith Vecchione, Sheila Curran Bernard, Madison D. Lacy, Louis J. Massiah, et al. 1987. Arlington, VA: PBS, 2010. DVD. Beginning with the murder of Emmett Till and concluding with the 1963 march to Selma, this multipart series covers the major figures and events of the civil rights era and serves as a touchstone for documentary efforts that came after it.

Freedom on My Mind. Directed by Connie Field and Marilyn Mulford. 1994. San Francisco, CA: California Newsreel, 2004. DVD. This acclaimed documentary was the first to explore the Freedom Summer struggles to register voters in Mississippi between 1961 and 1964. Greater social aspects of the movement are covered, but the film really shines in its presentation of its individual emotional impact.

Freedom Riders. Directed by Stanley Nelson. 2010. Arlington, VA: PBS, 2011. DVD. Based on Raymond Arsenault's book *Freedom Riders: 1961 and the Struggle for Racial Justice*, this documentary uses testimony from a wide range of participants (riders and politicians) as well as chroniclers (journalists) to bring a six-month period of American history to life.

Hey, Boo: Harper Lee & To Kill a Mockingbird. Directed by Mary McDonagh Murphy. 2010. New York, NY: First Run Features, 2011. DVD. Covering the life and success of writer Harper Lee, this documentary also delves into the social impact of *To Kill a Mockingbird* on both her era and subsequent generations of readers.

I Am Not Your Negro. Directed by Raoul Peck. 2017. New York, NY: Kino Lorber, 2017. DVD. Narrated by Samuel L. Jackson, this impactful documentary focuses on the life and work of writer James Baldwin, including a novel he left unfinished at the time of his death. Jackson's dramatic readings of Baldwin's prose and archival footage of Baldwin help punctuate the legacy of his life and work.

The March. Directed by John Akomfrah. 2013. Arlington, VA: PBS, 2013. Narrated by Denzel Washington, this documentary commemorates the fiftieth anniversary of the 1963 March on Washington for Jobs and Freedom. Especially illuminating are the interviews with key figures who worked with organizing committees and experienced the march firsthand.

Slavery by Another Name. Directed by Samuel D. Pollard. 2012. Arlington, VA: PBS, 2012. DVD. This thoughtful documentary challenges the widely held belief that slavery was completely banished with the issuing of the Emancipation Proclamation. The installation of sharecropping and other forms of oppressing African Americans through labor are illuminated as legal continuations of slavery.

Soundtrack for a Revolution. Directed by Bill Guttentag and Dan Sturman. 2009. Sydney, NSW: Australian Broadcasting Corporation, 2013. DVD. Taking a fresh angle on the civil rights era, this documentary focuses on its powerful music. Freedom songs are traced from their beginnings on picket lines and in marches, and contemporary artists perform many in a new light.

Podcasts

Code Switch. An extension of the larger Code Switch division of National Public Radio, this podcast covers issues of race and identity in contemporary society, with a focus on developing events and debates. Their coverage of the events in Charlottesville, Virginia, in summer 2017 reflects this mission and includes a podcast as well as other multimedia coverage.

Our National Conversation about Conversations about Race. Anna Holmes, Baratunde Thurston, Raquel Cepeda, and Tanner Colby host this multiracial, interracial conversation podcast in which issues around race in America are approached from multiple viewpoints. While no longer in production, an episode archive is available.

Race Matters. Hosted by Merleyn Bell and produced by the University of Oklahoma's literary publication, *World Literature Today*, this podcast includes interviews with experts and activists on the topic of race in the US. Topics range from the philosophy of whiteness to the future of black history month.

This American Life. Hosted by Ira Glass and covering the diversity of the American experience, it is not unusual for this podcast to touch on issues of race and civil rights. The episode "The Problem We All Live With" is worthy of special attention. *New York Times Magazine* reporter Nikole Hannah-Jones takes the reins from host Ira Glass in an exploration of school desegregation and how, in many ways, the practice never ended. The show's focus is the Normandy School District in Normandy, Missouri, which borders Ferguson, Missouri. Hannah-Jones takes the listeners through the public debate around the school system and the aftermath on the students caught in the middle.

INDEX

4 Little Girls (Lee) 70, 77, 143, 165

Abernathy, Ralph D. 20, 24–5, 34, 36, 121, 128n57
Across That Bridge: Life Lessons and a Vision for Change (Lewis) 3, 69, 78n3
Albany, Georgia 8, 47, 50; Albany Movement 74
AME Church shooting (Charleston, SC) 69; motivation for 78n4; *see also* Pinckney
"American History" (Harper) 10–1; analysis of 71–3; approaches to teaching civil rights movement poetry 78; and modality 71–2; sites of memory in 72
Antifa 51
apartheid: in America 77; anti-apartheid movement 26; in South Africa 17, 19
archival memory 12, 100–1
Armstrong, Julie 8, 15n16, 16n44, 29n7, 69, 81, 133; *see also* Cambridge Companion to Civil Rights Literature
Aydin, Andrew 4, 10, 15n14, 19, 29n6, 30n19, 31n51; *see also* March: Book One

Baker, Ella Jo 2, 91, 93
Baldwin, James 9, 11, 14, 54, 66–7, 67n20, 167; Hamitic theory 57–8; Nation of Islam and unification 58; *see also* "Down at the Cross"
Baltimore 90, 125
Barber, Reverend William 13, 110, 126
beloved community 2, 14n8, 91–2
Birmingham, Alabama *3*; 1963 children's campaign 41, 119, 132, 141; America's Armageddon 73; church bombing in literary memory 11, 69–78, 83; City of Perpetual Promise 71, 77; and Martin Luther King 60–2; iconic photographs of 112, 116–17, 126; as setting for *Bombingham* 6–8; as site of memory in *Get on the Bus* 138, 143 in *Song of Solomon* 12, 83–5; unforgettable day 76–7; *see also* Sixteenth Street Church; *see also* "Letter from Birmingham Jail"

"Birmingham Sunday" (Hughes) 11; analysis of 73–4; approaches to teaching civil rights movement poetry 78; references to China 74; and song 74
Black Lives Matter 29, 51, 106, 159
Black Power Movement 41, 166
Boehner, John (House Speaker) 95, 97
Bombingham (Grooms) 70; and storytelling 6–8
Bond, Julian 2, *3*, 8, 15n16
Bourbon at the Border (Cleage) 12, 95–105; approaches to teaching 105–6; and archival memory (Holloway) 12, 100–1; as challenge to rhetoric of US exceptionalism 98, 105; embodied trauma in 97, 99–106; post-traumatic stress disorder in 102; *see also* Freedom Summer (Mississippi Project)
Browder v. Gayle 33, 35
Brown v. Board of Education 9, 15n16, 22, 28, 41, 49, 118, 132, 146, 152, 161; as beginning of classical phase of the civil rights movement 5, 27
Browning, Joan C. 44, 51
Bunch, Lonnie G. III 9, 109
Burke, Solomon 12; as inspiration for *Song of Solomon* 80–2, 86, 88, 92–3

The Cambridge Companion to Civil Rights Literature (Armstrong) 8–9, 15n16, 16n44, 69–70, 142–3
Carry Me Home: Birmingham, Alabama: The Climactic Battle of the Civil Rights Revolution (McWhorter) 73
"Caught in the Middle" (Cade) 47, 51
Central High School 25, 27, 41, 140; *see also* Little Rock, Arkansas
Chaney, James 98–9, 138–9
Charleston, South Carolina 69, 72, 76–7, 160; *see also* AME Church shooting
Charlottesville, Virginia 9, 76–7, 167
Civil Rights Act 27, 41, 73, 109, 139
Civil Rights Film 135–7, 142–3

Civil Rights Literature: affective power of 8, 70; as challenge to dominant narrative of the civil rights movement 6–10, 41, 88, 91, 109–10, 113, 118, 136; rich tradition of 4, 6, 8–9, 15n16; scholarship of 16n44; seminar in 2, 165; teaching resources for 166–7

Civil Rights Movement: in art 166; collective autobiography as the narrative form of 40–3; consensus narrative of 28, 38, 40–1, 54, 76–7, 136; and drama 106; history and memory of 92, 96–7, 100 102–4, 136; and Hollywood myth-making 136–7, 141; *Martin Luther King and The Montgomery Story* comic as origin story for 21–7; oversimplification of 28–9, 81, 132; in poetry 67, 70, 131; as process 2, 4, 7, 47, 50, 69, 77, 113; references to in *Song of Solomon* 81–5, 88–91; sites of memory in *Get on the Bus* 130, 139–40; and storytelling 1–14; testimonial accounts of 32, 37–8; visual legacies of 109–12, 120–5; *see also* "The Long Civil Rights Movement"

civil rights music 16n47; in *Get on the Bus* 134, 138; and healing 93; Joan Baez's rendition of "Birmingham Sunday" 70; John Coltrane's "Alabama" 70; and Poor People's Campaign 122, 125; recollections of the movement in 97; singing as a movement activity 8, 12, 43; in *Song of Solomon* 80–1, 90–1; *Soundtrack for a Revolution* 167

Civil Rights Reader: American Literature from Jim Crow to Reconstruction (Armstrong and Schmidt) 81

Civil War 14, 73, 133, 166; and Reconstruction 14, 32; *see also* Confederacy

Claudette Colvin: Twice Toward Justice (Hoose) 10–1, 33–4, 37–8; approaches to teaching 37–8; Montgomery bus boycott 33–4; retrieving lost history 34

Cleage, Pearl 12, 95–101; *see also Bourbon at the Border*

Coates, Ta-Nehisi 9, 14, 145, 159

Coleman, Jeffrey 70, 74, 78

collective memory 12, 72, 95

Collins, Addie Mae 69, 70

Collins Rudolph, Sarah 12, 71

Confederacy: removal of flag 76–7; removal of monuments 14, 76; reference to Robert E. Lee in George Wallace's inaugural 59

Congress of Racial Equality (CORE) 19, 85, 98, 137

Connor, Eugene "Bull" 69, 77, 83, 138

consensus narrative 6, 8, 11, 38, 42, 49, 76, 109, 140; concise version of dominant narrative 40–1; as "the King years" 28; *see also* Civil Rights Movement

Critical Race Theory (CRT) 54

Dallas, Texas 11, 64, 83, 125; as site of memory in *Get on the Bus* 13, 140, 143; *see also* "Undelivered Remarks"

Deacons for Defense and Justice 137, 139

Declaration of Independence 56, 62–3

Deep in Our Hearts: Nine White Women in the Freedom Movement 11, 42–4, 51–2; approaches to teaching collective autobiography 51–2; as critical revision of civil rights narrative 42; white women's subjectivity 44

Dehn Kubitschek, Missy 1

destiny: as rhetorical device in nonfiction texts 54–68

Detroit, Michigan 88; as setting for *Bourbon at the Border* 12, 99, 104–6; as setting for *Song of Solomon* 82, 85, 93

double consciousness: in *To Kill a Mockingbird* and *Go Set a Watchman* 148, 150–1, 155, 157

Double V Campaign (WWII) 41, 139

Dowd Hall, Jacquelyn 4, 8–9, 15n16, 27, 30n35, 40; *see also* "The Long Civil Rights Movement"

"Down at the Cross: Letter from a Region of My Mind" (Baldwin) 54; analysis of 57–8; approaches to teaching selected nonfiction texts 66–7

Dubek, Laura 1–16, 29n6, 69–79, 80–94

Du Bois, W.E.B. 2, 85, 100, 125, 148

DuVernay, Ava 40 79n15, 165

Emancipation Proclamation 82, 106, 167

Emmett Till in Literary Memory and Imagination (Metress and Pollack) 8

emplottedness 30n35, 42

Eyes on the Prize: America's Civil Rights Years 1954–1965 3, 17, 166

Facebook: social movements 10, 17, 28

Fackler, Katharina 12–13, 109–28

Faubus, Governor Orval 83, 140

Fellowship of Reconciliation (FOR), 10, 14n8, 18, 30n22: *see also Martin Luther King and The Montgomery Story*

Ferguson, Missouri 9, 69, 77, 125, 167

The Fire Next Time (Baldwin) 9, 11, 57; *see also* "Down at the Cross"

first-person plural: in women's autobiography 43, 50, 62, 66: in Jill Freedman's *Old News: Resurrection City* 113

Fleming Jr., Julius B. 12, 95–108

"Four Spirits" (MacQueen) 71, 77

Freedman, Jill 10, 13, 109–28; *see also Old News: Resurrection City*

"Freedom-Faith" (Hall) 48

Freedom Rides 13, 41, 52; as site of memory in *Get on the Bus* 137–9; *Freedom Riders* 166

Freedom Summer (Mississippi Summer Project) 12; and *Bourbon at the Border* 96, 98–106; in *Get on the Bus* 138, 166; *Freedom on My Mind* 166

"From Little Memphis Girl to Mississippi Amazon" (Simmons) 44, 46, 51

Gandhi: portrayed in *Martin Luther King and The Montgomery Story* 19–20, 22, 24–5

Gates, Henry Louis 166

Get on the Bus (Lee) 13, 129–43; approaches to teaching 142–3; as call to action 142; and civil rights film 136–7; history and legacy 129, 132–6, 140; MMM/DOA mission statement 129–30;

screenplay of 129–30, 135, 139; sites of memory in 137–40; see also Million Man March
"Getting Out the News" (Mary E. King) 43, 49–51
Go Set a Watchman (Lee) 9, 13–14, 145–61; approaches to teaching 160–1; promise and failure of 158–9; reception of 145–6; and ruined childhood 151–8
Goodman, Andrew 98–9, 138–9
Greensboro, North Carolina: lunch counter sit-ins 17–18, 126, 139
Grooms, Anthony 6–7, 70; see also *Bombingham*

Hamer, Fannie Lou 93, 100, 103, 105
Hands on the Freedom Plow: Personal Accounts by Women in SNCC 10–11, 42–51; approaches to teaching collective autobiography 51–2; as historiographic intervention 42–3; revising generational autobiography 45–7
Harper, Michael 10–1, 71–3; see also "American History"
Hassler, Alfred 20–2, 24–7
Hazlett, John: generational autobiography 45
Henninger, Katherine 13, 145–64
Hinton, Corrine 11, 54–68
Hollywood 13, 126, 129; and civil rights film 136–7, 139, 141
Hoose, Phillip 33–5, 38; see also *Claudette Colvin: Twice Toward Justice*
Hughes, Langston 10–11, 70, 73–4, 76; see also "Birmingham Sunday"
Hurston, Zora Neale 1–2, 10, 13; see also *Their Eyes Were Watching God*

"I Have a Dream" (King) 11, 84, 135; analysis of 60–3; approaches to teaching selected nonfiction texts 66–7; in dominant narrative of the civil rights movement 27, 41; destiny as rhetorical device in 54, 62–3
"I Wish I Knew (How It Would Feel to be Free)" (Burke) 80–2, 88

Jeter Naslund, Sena 23, 71, 77
Jim Crow 54, 70, 81, 138; Jim Crowism in *Bourbon at the Border* 102, 105; laws 17, 28; legacy of 14; the new Jim Crow 133; protest of 19, 22, 115, 137
Johnson Reagon, Bernice 8, 43
Jonesboro, Louisiana 139; see also Deacons for Defense and Justice

Kelly Ingram Park 3, 71, 77
Kennedy, John F. 11, 54, 61, 63–7, 140; role in black freedom struggle 63–4; see also "Undelivered Remarks for Dallas Citizens Council"
Kennedy, Robert F. 83, 123, 139
Kennedy, Ted (Senator) 4
King, Jr. Martin Luther 2, 14n8; and Christian destiny 60–2; as hero of *Martin Luther King and The Montgomery Story* comic 21–4; influence of Langston Hughes's poetry on 73; and socio-economic justice 73, 109; see also "Letter from Birmingham Jail"; see also "I Have a Dream"
Ku Klux Klan 24, 69, 79n33, 137

Lee, Harper 9; relationship to editor Tay Hohoff 146, 159; see also *Go Set a Watchman*; see also *To Kill a Mockingbird*
Lee, Spike 13, 70, 129–44, 65; see also *Get on the Bus*
legacy 6, 46, 50, 80, 82, 90, 97, 105; political uses of 95–6, 107n12; Poor People's Campaign 110; visual legacies 13, 112, 118, 120, 123–5, as verb in *Get on the Bus* 133, 135–6
"Letter from Birmingham Jail" (King) 54, 78; analysis of 60–2; teaching approaches to selected nonfiction texts 66–7
"Letter to My Adolescent Son" (Wiley) 50
Lewis, John 2, 15n13; and *March* 3–4, 6, 8–10, 60, 119; and *Martin Luther King and The Montgomery Story* comic 19, 26
Lincoln Memorial 13, *134*, 135
Little Rock, Arkansas 2, 13, 25, 27, 41; as site of memory in *Get on the Bus* 134, 138, 140, 143
"The Long Civil Rights Movement and the Political Uses of the Past" (Dowd Hall) 4, 40
Lortie, StarShield 11–12, 69–78
Los Angeles, California: as setting in *Get on the Bus* 13, 129, 131–5, 137–40
Lyons, J. Michael 10, 14n8, 17–31

MacQueen, Elizabeth 71, 77
Malcolm X 12, 82, 85, 87, 89, 91, 141; Spike Lee's *Malcolm X* 137, 143
March Against Fear 139
March: Book One (Lewis) 3, 10, 29
March: Book Three (Lewis) 3–4
March on Washington for Jobs and Freedom 11, 41, 69, 77, 80, 126; compared to Poor People's Campaign 110, 114–15, 119, 125–6; and "I Have a Dream Speech" 63; Obama's reference to 96; as site of memory in *Get on the Bus* 135, 143
Marching for Freedom: Walk Together, Children, and Don't You Grow Weary (Partridge) 11; analysis of 33, 35–7; approaches to teaching 37–8; bearing witness 37
Martin Luther King and The Montgomery Story 10, 14n8; analysis of 17–28; approaches to teaching 28–9; Christian orientation and universalism of 20–2, 25, 28; Fellowship of Reconciliation (FOR) 18, 30n22; global reach of 10, 17, 27–8; "The Montgomery Method" explained in 25; as nodal text 19, 28; as origin story for the civil rights movement 10, 19 21–2, 24, 27, 29
mass incarceration 13–14, 50, 133, 166; in *13th* (DuVernay) 79n15, 165
Maull McKinstry, Carolyn 75–7
Memphis, Tennessee 2, 13; as site of memory in *Get on the Bus* 130, 133, 138–40, 143
Metress, Christopher 6, 8–9, 30n35, 41
Middle Passage 7, 13, 86, 166; in Michael Harper's "American History" 72

Million Man March 13, 129–32, 143; MMM/DOA Mission Statement 130, 132, 140; role of Louis Farrakhan in 130; *see also Get on the Bus*
Mississippi *see* Freedom Summer (Mississippi Summer Project)
Monteith, Sharon 41, 136–7, 143
Montgomery, Alabama 17, 21, 33; bus boycott 21, 24–5, 27–9, 34, 41, 83, 118; as site of memory in *Get on the Bus* 137, 141
Morrison, Toni 10, 80–94, 97, 103–4, 162n37; *see also Song of Solomon*
"My Real Vocation" (Zellner) 50

Nash, Diane 10, 93, 140–1
Nation of Islam (NOI) 57–8, 85, 89, 130
National Association for the Advancement of Colored People (NAACP) 18, 98, 110, 138, 142, 152, 166; Wichita Youth Council 18
National Conference of Christians and Jews 26
National Museum of African American History and Culture (NMAAHC) 9–10, *18*
National Welfare Rights Association 123
"Neither Black Nor White" (Martinez) 45
Newton, Huey 123, 166
nonviolent direct action 41, 57; and *Get on the Bus* 129, 133, 139–40; philosophy of nonviolence 4, 14n8, 63; as advocated in *Martin Luther King and the Montgomery Story* comic 19, 21–2, 24, 26

Obama, Barack 12, 92, 166; commemorations of Rosa Parks and King memorials 95–7; 106n6; eulogy for Reverend Clementa Pinckney 70, 76–7; inauguration of as frame story for *March* (Lewis) 4, 8; reference to Atticus Finch in farewell address 14; remarks at opening ceremony for the National Museum of African American History and Culture 9–10; speeches of 160
Old News: Resurrection City 10, 12; analysis of 109–25; approaches to teaching 126; as challenge to consensus narrative 109; photographs in *114, 116, 117, 118, 120, 123*, 124; and politics of respectability 119; press coverage of 110, 115; protest as performance 110–12, 115; countering riot iconography 12, 110, 116, 118

Parks, Rosa 23, 33–5, 83, 93, 95–8, 106n6, 114, 132, 142
Partridge, Elizabeth 35–6, 38; *see also Marching for Freedom*
Plessy v. Ferguson 17, 82–3
Poor People's Campaign 12–13; visual representations of in *Old News: Resurrection City* 109–26
Powell, Nate 4, 19
"Put Your Heart on the Line" (Jackson and Edmonds) 132

Reed, Ishmael 131, 143
"Resistance U" (Holsaert) 48
Resnik, Benton 20–1, 30n13, 30n22
Resurrection City 109–10, 113, 120–2, 125; *see also Old News: Resurrection City*; *see also* Poor People's Campaign
Robertson, Carole 69, 70, 73
Rodrigues, Elizabeth 11, 15n20, 30n35, 40–53
Royce, Josiah *see* beloved community
Rustin, Bayard 27, 31n61; *Brother Outsider: The Life of Bayard Rustin* 166

Schwerner, Michel 98–9, 138–9
Scott Hill, Tonya M. 11, 54–68
Scott King, Coretta 22, 36
Seale, Bobby 123
segregation 24, 33–4, 41, 56–7, 70, 73, 96; challenges to 41, 83–4, 115–16, 139, 156; desegregation 22, 24, 27, 41, 61, 167; in the inaugural speech of George Wallace 11, 58–60
Selma, Alabama 35, 37; Selma to Montgomery March 41, 119, 126, 166; in *March: Book Three* 4; *Selma* (DuVernay) 40, 143; *see also Marching for Freedom*
"Shiloh Witness" (Browning) 44, 48, 51
sites of memory 13, 72; Spike Lee's use of in *Get on the Bus* 129–30, 136–7, 139–41, 143
Sixteenth Street Church (Birmingham) 11, *71*, 83, 165; bombing of in civil rights movement poetry 69–79; in consensus narrative of the civil rights movement 76; *see also 4 Little Girls*
slavery: in "American History" 72; and generational autobiography 46–7; in George Wallace's inaugural speech 59; in *Get on the Bus* 104, 133, 140; legacy of 14, 32, 56; and racial inequality in *Bourbon at the Border* 104; as risky historical text 32; slave narrative tradition 7; *Slavery by Another Name* 167; in *Song of Solomon* 81–2
Song of Solomon (Morrison) 10, 12–13, 16n47; analysis of 80–94; approaches to teaching 92–3; as challenge to dominant narrative of the civil rights movement 82–3, 88–9; and legacy 82, 90, 92
Southern Christian Leadership Conference (SCLC) 13, 22, 25, 41, 57, 80, 91; strategy for Poor People's Campaign 109–10, 112, 115, 120, 122–5, 138
Southern Poverty Law Center (SPLC) 165
Stride Toward Freedom (King) 30n32, 61
Student Nonviolent Coordinating Committee (SNCC) 42, 81, 98, 137; *see also Hands on the Freedom Plow: Personal Accounts of Women in SNCC*

Take Your Choice: Separation or Mongrelization (Bilbo) 60
Teaching the Civil Rights Movement: Freedom's Bittersweet Song 9
"They Sent Us This White Girl" (DeLott) 49
"This is the Last Time" (Western Caravan) 125
Till, Emmett 11, 83, 118, 152, 166; rap homage to 97; documentary *The Murder of Emmett Till* (Burnett) 137

Their Eyes Were Watching God (Hurston) 1–4, 13
To Kill a Mockingbird (Harper) 13, 145–59, 161n6, 167; approaches to teaching 160–1; childhood and racial innocence 146–51, 53–61; Scout and American double consciousness 151, 155, 157; US (white) racial anxiety 147–51
"The Transformation of Silence into Language and Action" (Lorde) 69

Uncle Tom's Cabin (Stowe) 13, 148
"Undelivered Remarks for Dallas Citizens Council" (Kennedy) 11, 54; and American leadership 64–5; analysis of 63–5; approaches to teaching selected nonfiction texts 66–7
US Capitol: commemoration of Rosa Parks 95, 97; visual representations of in *Old News: Resurrection City* 113, 115, 119–20

Vietnam: the influence of *Martin Luther King and The Montgomery Story* comic in 17, 26; as setting for *Bombingham* 6, 70; as site of memory in *Bourbon at the Border* 101; war in 109, 121
Voting Rights Act 5, 109–10, 139; and consensus narrative of the civil rights movement 13, 27, 41, 43, 49, 112

Walker, Alice 12, 70, 74–6; *see also* "Winking at a Funeral"
Walking with the Wind: A Memoir of the Movement (Lewis) 3, 27
Wallace, George 4, 10–11, 35–6, 54, 57, 77; analysis of inaugural speech 58–60; approaches to teaching selected nonfiction texts 66–7
Ware, Virgil 15n32, 70
Washington, DC 9, 12, *18*; as destination in *Get on the Bus* 13, 129–30, 133, 137, 143; and Poor People's Campaign 110, 113; *see also Old News: Resurrection City*
The Watsons Go to Birmingham—1963 (Curtis) 70, 77
"We Shall Overcome" 43, 69, 121
"We Turned This Upside-Down Country Right Side Up" (Mants) 50
Wesley, Cynthia 69–70, 73, 75
While the World Watched: A Birmingham Bombing Survivor Comes of Age During the Civil Rights Movement (Maull McKinstry) 75–7
White Citizens' Councils: in *Go Set a Watchman* 14, 143, 152, 154–6, 161; *see also* Ku Klux Klan
whiteness: challenges to white power *23*, 83, 92, 115, *134*; and racial anxiety in *To Kill a Mockingbird* 147–51; source of racial injustice in *Go Set a Watchman* 13, 147–51, 156–9; white women's racial identity in *Deep in Our Hearts* 44, 49
Why We Can't Wait (King) 6, 77
"Wild Geese to the Past" (Curry) 44
Williams Jr., Jesse 13, 129–44
"Winking at a Funeral" (Walker) 12; analysis of 74–6; approaches to teaching civil rights movement poetry 78; the personal as political 76
Words of Protest, Words of Freedom: Poetry of the Civil Rights Movement and Era (Coleman) 70, 78
Wright, Richard 1–2
Wright/Hurston Foundation 2

Zarnowski, Myra 11, 32–9
Ziada, Dalia (American Islamic Congress) 26–7
Zoharah Simmons, Gwendolyn 44, 46–7, 51, 52n24

For Product Safety Concerns and Information please contact our EU representative GPSR@taylorandfrancis.com
Taylor & Francis Verlag GmbH, Kaufingerstraße 24, 80331 München, Germany

www.ingramcontent.com/pod-product-compliance
Lightning Source LLC
Chambersburg PA
CBHW080937300426
44115CB00017B/2858